Transport and Communication
in Early Medieval Europe
AD500-1100

Transport and Communication in Early Medieval Europe AD500-1100

Albert C. Leighton

David & Charles : Newton Abbot

ISBN 0 7153 5439 6

Uniform with this book
Medieval Regions and their Cities
by Josiah Cox Russell

Set in Times New Roman
and printed in Great Britain
by Bristol Typesetting Company Limited
for David & Charles (Publishers) Limited
South Devon House Newton Abbot Devon

Contents

List of Illustrations

*Unless otherwise stated, all photographs are reproduced
by permission of Bildarchiv Foto Marburg*

Introduction

LITTLE HAS BEEN written on the history of transport and communication in western Europe between AD 500 and AD 1100. The reasons for this become apparent rapidly to anyone who tries to remedy the situation. There is relatively complete information concerning such matters in the late Roman Empire: there are frequent mentions of Roman methods of transport and communication in the surviving literature. The use of comparatively permanent materials such as the metals and various types of stone has allowed many examples illustrative of Roman practice to survive. Roman road-building is described in the literary sources but, what is more important, the roads themselves exist. They can be traced not only by ground reconnaissance but by aeroplane and satellite survey and their methods of construction can be studied by excavation. Proud emperors commemorating their achievements and pious descendants honouring their ancestors resulted in the erection of columns, arches, and monuments complete with inscriptions and, often, bas-reliefs providing invaluable insights not only into their careers but also into Roman methods and techniques of communication and transport. Archaeology and, more recently, submarine archaeology, has revealed much, but the fortuitous preservation of Pompeii and Herculaneum as a result of the eruption of Vesuvius in AD 79 has perhaps told us more with its works of art, graffiti, plaster-casts of actual Romans, and even wall paintings and mosaics showing vehicles and ships.

The decline of Roman influence and the coming of less advanced peoples to western Europe meant not only a deterioration in the organisation and quality of transport and communication but a reduction in the quality of material available for the study of such matters. The period from AD 500 to AD 1100 provides little grist for the scholar's mill. In comparison with both late Roman and late medieval times, very little was written. Of what was recorded, little has survived, and of what has survived, little contains information relating to transport and communication. The decline in artistic capabilities has resulted in few survivals, and their crudity makes them difficult to interpret. The nature of early medieval road construction means that their roads have left few traces. Wood was a material peculiarly suited to the capabilities of early medieval man but lacking the potential for survival of metals or stone. Wood was the common construction material for houses, bridges, ships, and vehicles but fire, flood, wreck, and hard usage have meant the disappearance of practically all early medieval woodwork.

To attempt to bridge the gap between 500 and 1100 in our knowledge of transport and communication is to try to discover whether that history is primarily one of continuity and, eventually, progress stemming from the situation existing in the late Roman Empire, or whether it is largely a matter of the development and adoption of innovations and improvements without reference to classical precedent. To determine what was original and what was derived from the Romans, it is necessary to glean, sift, and winnow all available information from the existing sources, whether they be written, archaeological, or artistic. To achieve as complete a picture as possible the evidence must be examined from many viewpoints. What was transported and how was it conveyed? How was communication achieved? Consideration must be given to such things as the vehicles, the roads, the draught animals and their harness; the ships and their methods of propulsion; the limita-tions and obstructions interposed by man and nature; the effects of changing technology and of custom and habit; and even to the comparison of costs necessary to accomplish the functions of transport and communication in late Roman and early medieval times.

1

Initial considerations - the people, materials, and concepts transported

INDIVIDUALS AND SMALL GROUPS

THE INDIVIDUAL TRAVELLER in early medieval times left few records for posterity. Unknown pilgrims traversed undetermined routes towards well-known shrines while using unspecified means of transport. Only rarely do the few sources give us the specific information we would like to have. In the usual situation an individual's presence at successive locations is given, but with no indication of the time consumed in travel, or the means of transport utilised for the stages of the journey. The individual one met on the road might be a pilgrim, messenger, merchant, migrant, or vagabond. Often he might unite in himself several such callings.

The individual pilgrim should be given credit as one of the few means by which any semblance of international contact was maintained. In his wanderings he was often the unwitting carrier of ideas, techniques, and even germs. After his return he was a man apart. He had seen and could describe holy sights and scenes of great interest to his untravelled neighbours. He had communicated, often with surprising efficiency, despite many language barriers, with the natives in the lands he had traversed. He had learned different ways of accomplishing some of the necessary tasks of daily living and in the process might very well have brought back a useful foreign tool, in addition to the relics which were probably his main concern.

Often he owed his return to the fact that he was a helpless but unprofitable object to the predatory lords with their warbands through whose territory he had to pass.

A pilgrim whose travels furnish many illustrative incidents is the Englishman, St Willibald, who later became bishop of Eichstätt in Germany.[1] About 721 he prevailed upon his father (later St Richard) and his brother Wynnebald (also later to be St) to accompany him on a pilgrimage to Rome. It was a carefully prepared journey. They carried the necessary money. A band of friends and relatives came to take ship with them. The captain collected their fares and off they went over the Channel in a ship propelled by more than one sail as well as oars. After disembarking they pitched their tents near Rouen which had a market where they could obtain food and necessary supplies. A leisurely journey on foot with frequent digressions to pray at the shrines of saints on the way brought them eventually to Lucca where Willibald's father died. The company continued and passed 'safely through the ambushes of fierce and arrogant soldiery' until they came to Rome.

Despite having reached the object of his pilgrimage, Willibald was not satisfied. He wanted to live a more severe life and go on pilgrimage to a more remote location. Consequently, he persuaded two others to accompany him and set out to become the first Anglo-Saxon pilgrim to Jerusalem. At Naples they encountered a ship from Egypt which took them to Ephesus by way of the strait of Messina, Catania, Syracuse, and Monemvasia in the south-eastern Peloponnesus, where Slavs were already located in strength. This is important evidence for the extent of Slavic penetration to the south in the early eighth century. On land, Willibald and his companions had to beg for bread, but they seem always to have afforded ship travel when it was available or necessary. This pattern was repeated frequently as they travelled alternately by foot and ship from Ephesus along the coast of Asia Minor, over to Cyprus, and then to Tortosa on the Syrian coast. It was near here at Homs (Emesa) that Willibald had his first encounter with Moslem officialdom. They were arrested by the

Saracens, not for religious reasons, but because they had no identifying documents and came from a nation unknown to the Saracens. As suspect spies they were imprisoned. Even here they made out surprisingly well. A rich merchant sent dinner and supper in to them daily, and twice a week they were escorted to the bath, while on Sundays they were taken to church through the market-place where the merchant bought them whatever they wished. Their release was finally achieved when the Caliph, Emir-al-Mummenin, decided they were harmless.

Released from their not very onerous captivity, Willibald and his companions continued on foot to the Holy Land. Besides the religious sites where they stayed to pray they also made note of strange and exotic sights such as herds of water buffalo observed at the sources of the Jordan covering themselves up to the neck in water. Willibald, of course, was more interested in the holy places he had come to visit and gives the only detailed and accurate account of the major shrines of Christendom to survive from the eighth century. Another of the rarities encountered by Willibald—and one which he did not expect to live to tell about—was a lion he met in an olive grove in Samaria.

We cannot think too harshly of Willibald for becoming one of the earlier medieval customs evaders, but his method may have been instructive to less pious individuals. He wished to pass the control point at Tyre with some balsam he had purchased at Jerusalem. This had aromatic as well as medicinal and theological properties. Physical concealment was not enough. He would still have been detected by olfactory evidence. With considerable ingenuity he set a reed filled with petroleum in the neck of his calabash of balsam. Guards unsealing the calabash only saw and smelled the petroleum which quite overpowered the balsamic odour. Having passed customs, Willibald was ready to take ship to Constantinople, but no ship was ready to take him. After a long wait his party embarked and sailed throughout the winter from 30 November until the week before Easter—a most unusual procedure, since it was not customary to sail in the Mediterranean at that season.

After two years at Constantinople Willibald 'hitched' a ride to the West with returning papal envoys by way of Syracuse, Reggio, and the Lipari islands where he encountered another phenomenon to add to his repertoire of strange and unusual sights—the volcano or Hell of Theodoric into which the Ostrogothic king was supposed to have been thrown. Willibald attempted to climb the mountain and look into the crater. On his return to Italy seven years after his departure from Rome, he settled down at Monte Cassino, where he served one year as *cubicularius* (sexton or janitor), the second year as *decanus* (dean or deacon, one of the highest positions in the monastery), and the following eight years as *portarius* (doorkeeper). This does not seem a very successful career, but can perhaps be explained by saying that in these very disturbed times it was necessary to have at the monastery gate a man of experience, with a knowledge of mankind, able to make decisions. His wandering days were apparently over, when on a trip to Rome he told of his travels to Pope Gregory III. The Pope relieved him of his duties at the request of St Boniface, the apostle to the Germans (and probably a relative), and sent him to the north where he became first bishop of Eichstätt in Bavaria.

In his later years Willibald dictated his memoirs to a nun whose name remained unknown until 1931 when Bernhard Bischoff interpreted a cryptogram found with an early manuscript of the biography which gave her name as Hugeburc.[2] This provides not only an early example of female literacy but also shows that the Anglo-Saxons had attained such a level of literary skill that they were no longer satisfied with mere communication but were now showing off by producing cryptograms to conceal meaning from unintended recipients. This word-play is characteristic of the Celtic peoples and perhaps tells us something about Anglo-Saxon education and relations with the Irish. St Willibald, then, typifies the early pilgrim. He had seen the Holy Land with its shrines; he had witnessed awesome phenomena and strange beasts and had brought back strange products. The picture that remains to us is of a world amazingly well organised. This is not a Dark Age but a time when ships, more advanced than we should expect from the archaeological finds, cross the English Channel regularly, captains collect fares, travellers are equipped with tents, and customs and toll barriers impede the way.

Later pilgrims were motivated not so much by simple piety and curiosity as St Willibald had been but by more practical motives such as seeking forgiveness for their sins by undertaking pilgrimages for penance. Noblemen like the Counts of Anjou and the Dukes of Normandy frequently found themselves on pilgrimage for such reasons. Pilgrimages could no longer be casual. Organisation was now required and instructions were prepared telling how pilgrimages should be conducted. An example of this type of literature is found in the Canons of King Edgar the Peaceful who ruled England (under the guidance and supervision of St Dunstan from 959 to 975.[3] The pilgrim was urged to leave his weapons at home. In the conditions of the time this made him neutral. He could not protect himself but neither was he a danger to those whom he encountered. This impression was heightened by the injunction to make his journey barefoot. His poverty and piety were apparent and he was not an attractive object for plunder. Several instructions operated to conserve limited lodgings and food supplies. He was urged to fast, abstain from meat, and never spend a second night in any location. His social attractiveness was lessened by the avoidance of iron utensils to care for his hair and fingernails, and the avoidance of warm baths made it easier for him to keep out of soft beds and escape entangling alliances with the other sex. Even the release of drunkenness was forbidden him. He was to concentrate on the object of his journey—pray fervently, implore divine intercession, and constantly repent of his sins. Faithful adherence to the rules would bring him to successful atonement.

Later pilgrims could benefit from hospices set up and administered by the Church along the pilgrim routes. Eventu-

B

ally a traditional uniform for pilgrims developed, consisting of a beard, a staff, a broad-brimmed hat, a grey mantle, and appropriate badges such as the shell from Compostella.

As a convenience to those who provided them with food and lodging, some pilgrims bore messages, but there were others to whom the carrying of letters was a compulsory duty or a means of livelihood. These were often primitive and barbaric successors to the admirably organised public postal system of the Roman Empire—the *cursus publicus*. The imperial public post survived as an effective institution in the eastern (Byzantine) empire at least until the time of Emperor Justinian (527-65) who was accused by the historian Procopius. (*Anecdota* [*Secret History*] xxx) of ruining it. In the name of economy Justinian closed down the posting stations on the north shore of the Gulf of Nicomedia and forced the couriers —all proud picked men accustomed to riding the swiftest of horses—to sail from Byzantium to Helenopolis on the south shore of the gulf in the little boats normally used to cross the Bosporus. While the best of horsemen, they were probably inept sailors and were in frequent danger since they had to set out regardless of the weather and might be wrecked by storms and tossed about by contrary winds, making it difficult to maintain any sort of regular schedule. Before Justinian's reforms they had been accustomed—by frequent change of mounts— to cover as much as ten normal days' journey—perhaps 250 miles—in a single day.[4]

Justinian also initiated additional economies by closing down most of the posting stations—except on the road to Persia where considerations of national security still necessitated rapid communication. Formerly, it had been customary for each of the stations to have a herd of forty carefully selected horses available for the couriers. Since the stations were only a few miles apart, it had been possible to gallop between stations change to fresh horses, and achieve surprising distances. Now, the messengers were forced to use the same mount all day and had to conserve its energy. Justinian made this simpler for them by substituting mules—traditionally averse to unnecessary

galloping—for the spirited horses hitherto available.[5] Loss of
morale and efficiency was severe. In addition, the local economy
was adversely affected. Landowners had had a ready market
for their products in the posting stations with their horses and
numerous staffs of grooms and veterinarians.

As reflected in the Theodosian Code (particularly in section
viii), the organised system of the *cursus publicus* declined in
the West as the Roman Empire lost control of the provinces,
but there were occasional curious survivals. Apollinaris Sidonius was still able to use its facilities in 467 (*Epistolae* I. v.) on
a journey from Gaul to Rome. Theodoric, the Ostrogothic king
in Italy, tried to preserve as much as possible of the Roman
administrative system and still maintained a system of messenger relays to Spain in the early sixth century (Cassiodorus,
Variae Epistolae v. 39). Another of the barbarian kingdoms,
that of the Visigoths in Spain and southern France, still attempted to maintain a public post in the seventh century (Lex
Visigoth. V.4.19).

Despite the fact that in Merovingian Gaul it was still possible to obtain services for transport in the king's name as
late as 589,[6] this was the area in which the greatest confusion
and insecurity for messengers was found. Clergymen were
often couriers. If there was any advantage in literacy in a
messenger, it was more likely to be found among the clergy
where many members of the old Gallo-Roman aristocracy
had taken leading positions. The pattern had been established
in the late fifth century with the switchover of many important
lay nobles like Apollinarius Sidonius to bishoprics in the
church, where they could work more effectively for their people
in the chaos resulting from the breakdown of Roman administrative machinery with the coming of the barbarians. The direct
conversion of the Franks to Catholic Christianity gave this
Gallo-Roman 'clerical' nobility an opportunity to continue not
only as spiritual leaders but also as royal advisers. Gregory
of Tours, with his relatives and ancestors, provides an example.

Messengers were frequently seen in pairs. Perhaps this was
an attempt to obtain security by sending duplicate letters. If

this was the intention, it frequently miscarried. The Count of Limoges intercepted two men carrying letters for a bishop and sent them under guard to the king. The bishop denied writing the letters and the overzealous count received his retribution two months later by dying of a stroke.[7] In another case, the pretender, Gundovald, sent out two clergymen as messengers, one of whom, the Abbot of Cahors, was carrying a letter hidden under the wax of a wooden tablet.[8] The discovery of the letter bespeaks a thorough investigation and the abbot was beaten and imprisoned. In an attempt to deter secret communication, King Guntram ordered all roads to be watched and all travellers searched, even to their clothes, shoes, and 'other things.[9] Sometimes attempts were made to pass information without a messenger. A Jewish sentinel at the siege of Arles in 508 tied a letter to a stone and tried to fling it to the Frankish lines (Vit Caes I, 28). All these methods and more were known to classical antiquity and it is a question whether such ruses were believed to be original by their perpetrators or whether they had read such accounts as those in Herodotus 1.123, 5.35, and 7.239 or Book 31 of Aeneas Tacticus, and were attempting to put them to use.[10]

It is certainly apparent that there was little respect for the clergy in Merovingian Gaul. Even high-ranking churchmen were subjected to seizure, search, and torture when they were carrying letters. The practice of concealment was sometimes extended even to the person. Fredegar (III, 72) says that a royal prince was concealed in a bag, handed through a window, and taken away by a mounted servant. If messengers were in danger, it is also true that they were sometimes dangerous themselves. The wicked queen Fredegund sent assassins in the guise of messengers (Gregory of Tours, *History* VIII, 44).

As late as 650 the Merovingians still spoke as if a public postal system was in existence, and rights to requisition post horses, packhorses and necessary supplies are included in the Formulae (Marculf, lib 1, no 11), but it is doubtful, in the chaotic conditions of the time, whether the requested services were always forthcoming. It is more likely that the decline in lay literacy which occurred during this period was accompanied by an increase in the use of couriers carrying oral messages. Such a retrogression in method also meant a lowering in status of the messenger. No longer was it necessary to use literate or high-ranking clergy. Any poor freeman or serf could pass over the roads on foot carrying a message in his head and attracting little attention from road guards or marauding bands. Such a service could have little speed, regularity, or dependability but, in any case, the messenger was probably considered expendable.[11]

A different type of messenger appeared in the time of Charlemagne. The *missi dominici* not only carried information but were empowered to act for the monarch as they made their rounds inspecting conditions and hearing cases. They travelled comfortably and luxuriously, fending off bribes occasionally from anxious litigants, and providing a supplement to, as well as a supervision over, the activities of the count in nominal authority over a district. The *missi* were nobles themselves, clerical as well as lay, and normally travelled in pairs, a bishop and a count. The combination was necessary. Not only could they watch each other's conduct, but, given the state of education at the time, this was probably the only method by which physical authority and literacy could be achieved in a single embassy.[12]

The institution of the *missi* was only an expedient and without the prodding of a strong ruler could not be effective. The successors of Charlemagne were not strong men and did not use their *missi* efficiently. They appointed counts to be *missi* over their own territories and while this may have cut down on travelling, it negated the inspection and supervisory aspects of the system. Such a *missus* could not be expected to report adversely on himself.[13] Under such conditions of declining central authority there was a tendency to use individuals of lower social status as messengers and to include the service as one of the manorial dues. In the middle and late ninth century a variety of names are used for individuals who perform messenger or transport service. Sometimes the words are indicative of the status of the individual or the way in which he carried out the service. *Caballarii* were serfs who carried messages or transported light articles on horseback. *Paraveredarii* were also horsed serfs who performed similarly. *Sindmanni* were dependents doing carrying or messenger service. *Scaremanni* and *scararii* were armed retainers who performed such services on horseback, on foot, or even in boats.[14] The use of foot messengers reflected not only a lowering of status but also a continuing scarcity of good horses and a reluctance to have them used by the lower classes. There were of course certain geographical situations in which foot messengers were more effective than horsemen. Charles the Bald in 877 established a system of horse and foot couriers through the Alps between France and Italy.[15]

Anglo-Saxon England witnessed a similar change in the status of messengers, but at a later date, the usual culture-lag between England and the Continent being evident. Bishop Oswald of Worcester in about 970 granted leasehold of church lands to certain men of the noble class (*thegns*) who were expected, in return, to perform specific services, including riding to deliver the bishop's messages.[16] Within a hundred years, shortly before the Norman Conquest, mounted men (*geneats*) who did not belong to the aristocracy were found carrying messages. The *geneat* at this time, although not noble, was a superior peasant. Many of his duties were concerned with horses and riding service. He acted as a guard, took care of horses, and carried messages far and near wherever he was ordered. The development of this class of non-noble mounted messengers is probably indicative of an increase in the numbers and availability of horses at this period. This is confirmed because even the next lower class of peasant, the *gebur*, sometimes had a horse to help with his work.[17]

The predominance of merchants of Eastern Mediterranean origin in the late centuries of the western empire and in Merovingian Gaul has often been noted. Syrians are often spoken of as being particularly active and widespread. St Jerome says they have a passion for trade and spread throughout the whole world. They came from Tyre, Beirut, and Heliopolis to settle in Italy and elsewhere in the west. Procopius speaks of a Syrian sea trader living in Naples. They loaned money at usury in Ravenna. Gregory of Tours mentions a rich Syrian at Bordeaux, Eufronius, who had made his house into a church (Hist VII, 31), and Eusebius, a Syrian merchant at Paris, who bribed his way to the bishopric there (Hist X, 26). Jewish merchants, money-lenders, and physicians were also active in Merovingian Gaul. The first of the western peoples to acquire trading talent were the heathen Friesian sea-merchants.[18]

Such merchants did not have peculiar requirements for transport. Their goods, such as silks, furs, and spices, were often of great value but little weight or volume. The condition of the roads was of little importance to them. Goods could be carried, even concealed, on the person or strapped on the backs of a few pack-animals and even the most difficult terrain could be negotiated. Such a merchant was more concerned with the danger of robbery and the expense of tolls than with natural obstacles. With the spread of Islam, eastern merchants found their connections becoming more tenuous and difficult and, in any case, western Christians were bound to be attracted to trade and eventually to learn its techniques. Anglo-Saxon merchants were found along with the Friesians at the fair of St Denis in 753.[19] Christian merchants soon perceived the advantages to be derived from passing as pilgrims and so evading customs charges. The prevention of this deception was the subject of correspondence between Charlemagne and King Offa of Mercia. If traders were discovered mingling with the pilgrims at the toll gates they were to pay the established tolls. This indicates that these traders operated on a very small scale, perhaps concealed their wares, and so differed little in appearance from the genuine pilgrims. Since no fines were to be levied or goods confiscated there was no desire to discourage or eliminate the trade, but only to ensure that some traders did not obtain an unfair advantage over the others. The trade, while small in scale, was advantageous and judged worthy of preservation by the rulers.[20]

Another category of person likely to be encountered trudging the roads was the landless class—the vagabonds, beggars, and ruffians who had no place in society. Their origin is a matter of dispute. Doubtless a contributing cause was an increase in population. One son could inherit the father's position or status, a daughter or two could be disposed of in marriage, and an occasional child could be absorbed into the religious community. Once these positions were filled there was no place in the system for additional people. Those who were in excess of the needs of society had to be supported either by their own ingenuity or by the public bounty. Their condition was a matter of frequent concern to the monarchs. Charlemagne was perturbed by the unlawful disinheritance by the magnates of the heirs of freemen, who were forced by poverty to become thieves.[21] His bishops and abbots deprived both the rich and the poor of their possessions by promising them the bliss of the heavenly kingdom. Their resulting poverty led them to crime.[22] The resources and administrative organisation of the early medieval state were insufficient to provide for the maintenance of such a non-productive class and consequently their survival was largely due to their own initiative. Perhaps an evolutionary principle was involved and only the fitter survived, with their wits sharpened and their bodies toughened. Henri Pirenne sees in them the genesis of the new merchants of the tenth century and eventually of the middle class.[23]

LARGE GROUPS OF PEOPLE

On land in the early Middle Ages, the individual, even if a member of a group, normally provides his own transport, going either by foot or on horseback. Although the Romans had been able to provide mass transport of people in vehicles, this method had become very uncommon. The nature of water transport, however, is such that an individual moving by water will normally be a member of a unit, or group, adapted to the size of the vessel.

The type of group which had the most direct effect on human affairs was the army. The low state of discipline found among lᴏᴛᴠᴏᴅ ᴡᴡᴏ́ ᴍᴜᴜ ᴠᴜ ᴜᴜ ᴜ ᴜ ᴜ ᴜ ᴜ ᴜ ᴛᴏ ᴠ ᴏᴏᴠᴏᴏᴅ them to be dangerous to friend as well as to foe. To the peasants along the route the passage of an army was similar in effect to a plague of locusts. Charlemagne attempted to alleviate the effects of a moving army by requiring that the troops bring supplies of food for three months with them on carts.[24] The time for the assembly of the army was changed from March to May. This was probably done in order that the horses should have some grass to feed on along the roads. This would lessen the possibility that the horsemen would raid the stores of the inhabitants through whose lands they passed on their way to the muster.

In an area of such difficult communications rulers had to be constantly on the move in order to preserve any semblance of order. In addition to this there was also the necessity for constant movement caused by the court and its adherents consuming all the food provided by any one location. It is likely that the Frankish royal dwellings were placed systematically at definite intervals along the military roads in order to provide supplies for moving courts or marching men.[25] Occasionally it may have been possible to proceed towards the north at such a speed as to meet the harvests along the way. Unfortunately the pressure of external events, such as the need to protect and advance the frontiers and to evangelise and convert the newly-conquered heathen, prevented any such regularity and standardisation in the use of royal resources. Estates which were not visited by the king had to transport some of their products to his location.[26]

When an early medieval ruler settled down in one place it was generally a sign of old age or ill health. Charlemagne spent his last few years at the curative hot springs at Aachen, which developed some of the characteristics of a fixed capital. A similar change took place in what became the Holy Roman Empire. The early German emperors were great travellers who wore themselves out proceeding from one royal villa to another throughout the realm. As the economy developed the emperors found the newly developed towns more attractive than their estates and better located for administration. By the twelfth century their peregrinations tended to be from city to city rather than between their own villas.[27]

The frequent movement of courts must have resulted in relatively efficient and rapid travel. Frequent practice in preparation for movement must have resulted in the establishment of a standardised routine for the packing and loading of the necessary paraphernalia. According to Walter Map, Henry I of England ordered the customs governing his household and its movements to be written down. Arrangements for its transport and schedules for its stopping places were made well ahead of time and were well publicised.[28] Each item to be moved undoubtedly had its proper place in a particular load on a certain pack-animal or, later, in a specific vehicle. *The Constitution of the King's Household,* in the time of King Stephen, is like the instructions of Henry I noted by Walter Map and describes how the royal chapel with its relics was carried about on two packhorses, for each of which a penny a month was allowed for shoeing.[29] The arrangement must have worked satisfactorily, for the chapel was still maintained in the same way by King John in the next century.[30] The routine for unpacking and setting up in the new location must likewise have become very efficient through constant practice. Such movements of armies and courts necessitated the development of a form of staff planning. Despite the example of Henry I it is unlikely that written memoranda commonly played a part in the dissemination of instructions for movement. Verbal instructions and customs were sufficient to initiate and carry out most such operations.

Another group which soon saw the value of collective action was the merchants. The Eastern merchants (Jews, Byzantines, and Syrians) may have enjoyed the favour and even the protection of the Frankish kings, but even they found it advisable to combine their resources and travel in caravans.[31] This was necessary even if they possessed fiscal and judicial privileges and performed commissions for royalty and the clergy. There was always danger from lawless elements, so it was necessary for them to band together for their own defence and to carry lances and swords.[32] When travelling beyond the Rhine they were furnished with armed escorts by the princes.[33]

If such precautions were needed by protected merchants, how much more urgent must have been the need of the native merchants slowly developing out of the class of landless men. Their goods were likely to be bulkier and less valuable and so more easily detected and appropriated. With no place in society and no protection from the authorities their only recourse was to convince the lords that they provided a worthwhile service and to band together for mutual protection. They had to make their own arrangements for the furtherance of their aims and activities. That they were often able to do this is a tribute to their ingenuity and a further indication that they were eliminating their unfit members and developing a class of extremely capable individuals. Some local lords, particularly the Counts of Flanders, early recognised the potentialities and the benefits to be derived from fostering their activities.

The greatest group movements of the early medieval period were the migrations of whole peoples in the fifth century. It is doubtful if they added much to the development of transport. They came in any way they could, using whatever means of transport was at hand. If the Roman roads lay in the desired direction, they used them. The movement was essentially unplanned. They pressed ahead where resistance was least. Their search for sustenance was continuous and difficult. If they were not given supplies they took what they could. While they wanted to benefit from the material advantages possessed by the higher civilisation, they only succeeded in ruining the economy. The barely functioning economic machine which the Romans had only been able to maintain by endless tinkering was broken down by the unskilled hands of the barbarian invaders.[34]

The Crusades, which began at the end of the eleventh

century, were more an example of mass hysteria than a group movement, particularly in their popular manifestation. The ignorant peasants whose enthusiasm had been roused had Jerusalem as a goal but little knowledge of its distance or direction. They made few plans but merely started moving. Some even followed a goose as a guide. As no arrangements had been made for their provisioning they took from the peoples through whose territory they passed, expecting Jerusalem to materialise around the next corner or over the nearest hill. The wonder is that some of them managed to travel as far as Constantinople. The Emperor Alexius delivered himself of them by transporting them across the Bosporus where they were abandoned to the Turks.[35]

The nobility who led the Princes' Crusade took more time and made some preparations for the journey. Godfrey of Bouillon pawned his lands to the Church to outfit his men. Duke Robert delivered Normandy to his brother, William Rufus. They arranged to have markets provided along the route where supplies could be replenished. Of the several routes followed only that taken by Count Raymond of Toulouse down the eastern shore of the Adriatic offered extreme difficulties. The forces of the princes arived at Constantinople in relatively good condition.[36]

There is great variation in the transport of groups by water, ranging from a few on a ferry boat or raft to whole hosts on fleets of sizable ships. Gaul was particularly suited to inland water navigation by the fortunate location and the gentle course of its rivers (Strabo, *Geography*, 4.1.2 and 4.1.14). Sidonius, in his journey by *cursus publicus* referred to above (p 19), travelled down the Po in a passenger boat (*cursoria*) propelled not only by the current but by oars and barge-poles (*Epistolae*, I.v). Sometimes disasters were invited by overloading boats. Gregory of Tours (*History*, VIII, 14) was followed on a ferry-boat by uninvited rabble. The boat filled with water as well as people, but did not sink, owing to the presence of St Martin's relics. St Martin was effective for merchants as well as clergy. A salt trader at Metz took aboard a group of passengers, commended them to the protection of St Martin, and went to sleep. The boat made its way down the rocky Moselle through the night and the party awoke to find themselves safely at Trier (Gregory of Tours, *Miracles of St Martin,* IV, 29). We have already seen groups of pilgrims with St Willibald negotiating passage with the captain on cross-channel and Mediterranean shipping (above, p 14). Sea transport ranged from single raiding companies like those of Hengist and Horsa and the early Vikings to fleets of many hundreds of ships transporting whole armies like those of the later Vikings and William the Conqueror. Once an area was secured, wholesale migrations could take place, and women, children, relatives, household goods, and customs could be brought in with resulting change to the ecology of the area.

ANIMALS

Draught animals were normally expected not only to transport themselves but to earn their keep by dragging or supporting the additional weight of goods or riders. Only when an uncongenial element such as water was encountered could the draught animal expect to be transported.

    The transport of animals was undertaken frequently and efficiently by the Romans. The rare and exotic beasts used for exhibitions and contests in the arena had to be hunted, captured, and then transported over land and sea to make a Roman holiday spectacular and successful. The dangers of capture and the difficulties of transport often seem insuperable. How could the Romans move giant pythons, bring rare rhinoceroses all the way from India, and transport hippopotamuses from Central Africa? Zoologists can attest to the problems involved. The hippopotamus, for example, would have to travel in a tank of water.[37] The sources not only tell us, but even show us the Roman techniques of animal transport. A mosaic pavement 190 feet long in the Piazza Armerina in central Sicily, dating from about AD 300, gives a most detailed picture of the hunting and moving of such animals.[38]

The consequence of such activity over the centuries was the disappearance of certain species and the increasing rarity of others. This undoubtedly disturbed the ecological balance of areas even beyond the bounds of the empire but it also favoured the extension of agriculture and made safer life and work in the fields in frontier districts. The capture of bears and lions for the circus was beneficial to the frontier farmers.

While it would be unwise to blame the downfall of the western empire on the increasing scarcity of rare beasts for the arena, this could have contributed to the discontent of the urban proletariat and perhaps have facilitated the acceptance of Christianity among them. There are indications in the letters of Symmachus of the increasing difficulties of procuring satisfactory attractions and the growing problems of transporting them safely. In 401, at a time when the empire was in serious difficulties, it seems odd that the services of high officials and the *cursus publicus* should be utilised to such a large extent for the procurement and transport of unique beasts and other attractions for the games at Rome. The problems of Symmachus mounted terrifyingly. Of sixteen exceptional chariot horses (four teams) imported from Spain, only one team survived the voyage in good enough condition to race.[39] Weak and starving bear cubs from Dalmatia were no help.[40] Crocodiles had been secured with great difficulty but had to be killed because they refused to eat.[41] Even Saxon gladiators, intended as a special attraction, committed suicide by strangling each other before the performance rather than cooperate to achieve the same result in the arena for the amusement of the mob.[42] It is doubtful whether Symmachus was able to present much of a show.

Some attempts were made to continue games even after the fall of the western empire, but with the decay of public institutions it is questionable whether exotic animals could have been brought to them (Cassiodorus, *Variae* III, 51). In 541, when the Franks acquired Provence, their kings presided over the circus at Arles (Procopius, *De Bello Gothica* I. 13), and in 577 King Chilperic had amphitheatres built at Soissons and

Paris to present circuses (Gregory of Tours, *Hist* V. 17). It is not likely that these games appealed particularly to the Franks, since they were notorious 'do it yourselfers' and preferred to participate in blood sports like hunting and fighting.

The Romans had been able to move elephants by ship[43] but it is doubtful whether this was often done in the west after the breakdown of the public post. In the Byzantine empire in 578, twenty elephants were captured from the Persians and brought to Constantinople. (Gregory of Tours, *Hist* V. 30. Dalton in his edition of the History, Vol II, 545, says Gregory copied this chapter from Paul the Deacon!) It was probably one of these elephants that was presented to the Khakhan of the Avars by the Emperor Maurice.[44]

Fig 1   Roman elephant transport as shown in the Piazza Armerina mosaic, *c* AD 300

This fashion of presenting an elephant as a curiosity rather than as a war animal or work animal was followed by Harun al-Rashid in presenting his only elephant to Charlemagne, but the difficulties of transport were much greater than for the Romans in moving this unaccustomed burden. It was four years before the Jew, Isaac, the sole survivor of a mission to Harun, returned in October 801 with the elephant. He had probably travelled by ship from the eastern Mediterranean to North Africa. From there he took ship again to Porto Venere near La Spezia. Charlemagne had ordered the preparation of a fleet to receive and forward the elephant, but apparently difficulties were encountered because plans were changed and from Porto Venere the elephant had to make his own way under the guidance of Isaac by land. Having arrived in October, too late to cross the Alps under his own power because of the snow, he spent the winter in Vercelli, surmounted the Alps when they became passable and arrived in Aachen on 20 July in 802 to become the Emperor's special pet.[45]

Probably no elephant had crossed the Alps since the time of Hannibal and it is not likely that any had been seen in western Europe since the days of Diocletian.[46] Charlemagne's elephant had no successors in western Europe until that indefatigable collector, the Emperor Frederick II, brought one back to Italy from the Holy Land in 1229. A few years later, St Louis of France imported another which was given to Henry III of England.[47]

It was often necessary to transport horses over water, but it took some time for western Europe to regain the capability it had held under the Romans—and for hundreds of years earlier. (Perhaps the earliest example of the transport of horses by ship is furnished by a Late Minoan II gem (1450-1400 BC) which shows a horse being transported in a galley and perhaps marks the introduction of the horse to the island of Crete.)[48]

The evolution of the sea transport of horses in the early Middle Ages can be traced. When the Vikings first began serious operations in England, they seized horses after landing and used them to increase their mobility on land.[49] Less than thirty years later their ships were transporting not only the warriors and their families but also their horses from the Continent to England.[50] This was probably not so large an operation as that undertaken by Duke William for the conquest of England in 1066. His method of horse transport is plainly shown in the Bayeux Tapestry. No special modifications seem to have been made in the ships in order to accommodate the horses. The transports differ from the other ships only in not being ringed with shields. As many as ten horses are seen in a ship, many with their riders on their backs, which is not likely to have been the case. No special handling gear is apparent in the disembarking of the horses. They merely step over the low gunwales into the shallow water.[51] There was probably little improvement in method between the Vikings in 892 and Duke William in 1066. In both cases, ships developed primarily for carrying people were used without modification to carry horses. Ships of such small size and low freeboard could easily have been swamped by any simultaneous movement of the horses to either side. It was fortunate that the voyage was short.

By the end of the eleventh century ships of larger capacity were available, at least in the Mediterranean. When Robert of Normandy's detachment of the First Crusade crossed from Brindisi in April 1097, one ship fell apart and at least 400 people as well as many horses and mules and much money were lost.[52] The Byzantine Empire was well equipped with ships for specialised purposes. William of Tyre (*History of Deeds done beyond the Seas,* Book 20, 13) describes a Byzantine fleet as having 150 galleys with beaks and double tiers of oars, 60 larger, well-armoured horse transports with openings in the stern to load and unload the animals, also with bridges to embark and land men and horses, and 10 or 20 *dromones,* huge ships with supplies, arms, engines, and machines of war. By the Fourth Crusade, at least, Venice was able to build such specialised ships. The Venetians built ships for the knights and foot sergeants and transports (*vuissiers*) for the horses and squires. The knights normally travelled separately from their horses, but when an assault landing was to be made the armoured knights and the harnessed and saddled horses sailed together in the transports. The transports were equipped with

c

large ports through which the horses could exit and enter and portable bridges by which the land or shallow water could be gained. The transports were flat-bottomed so that they could approach closely to the land.[53]

The small ship hired by Joinville in 1248 to take some twenty knights and their horses to Egypt was somewhat differently constructed. It had a large door through which the horses entered. After the horses were in the hold of the ship the door was closed and made watertight because it would be under water when sailing. This apparently means that the ship took on enough passengers, cargo, and ballast to make it ride much lower in the water. It must have been much more difficult to disembark the horses from this ship than from the Venetian transports used in the Fourth Crusade. Presumably the horses' port had to be brought back above the water level by unloading and lightening the ship before the horses could be brought ashore again.[54]

A rare example of the land transport of horses occurred when the Emperor Henry IV passed over the Alps in the winter of 1077. The horses were unable to travel on the ice and steep slopes so some were moved by machines, presumably some form of block and tackle or levers, while others with their hooves tied together were turned on their backs and dragged and pushed over the snow and ice.[55] (See below, p 90).

Other animals, such as cattle and sheep, transported themselves in the seasonal movement called transhumance. The usual form of transhumance could be termed altitudinal, and consisted of allowing the animals to follow the vegetation in the spring as it advanced up the mountain slopes and then to return to the lowlands for the winter. Another type of transhumance might be named latitudinal, and entailed following the northward movement of the grass as it sprang up after the seasonal retreat of the snows.[56] In Spain, such migratory sheep farming had existed from time immemorial and wide tracks (*canadas reales*) were set aside for the seasonal movement of millions of sheep between the northern and southern limits of the peninsula. By the late Middle Ages the sheepmen formed a great association (the *Mesta*) which was normally supported by the Crown to the detriment of the settled farmers.[57]

GOODS AND MATERIALS

Gallo-Roman transport of goods could be characterised as not very advanced technically but extremely well organised. Corporations existed which offered various specialised transport services. *Utricularii* were persons who carried goods on rafts supported by inflated skins. *Ratiarii* handled wooden rafts which ferried people and vehicles across streams. *Navicularii* were sailors who operated vessels on the seas and large rivers. There were men who pulled boats upstream by heavy ropes slung over their shoulders. They used a type of cane or stick to maintain their balance. *Nautae* handled water transport on the smaller rivers and the lakes. There is no trace of any organisation for land transport in Gaul, although there are numerous bas-reliefs showing wagons loaded with goods being pulled by mules. From this two assumptions are possible: first, that there were organisations specialising in land transport but that no records or inscriptions have survived testifying to their existence; or, second, that groups such as the *nautae* and *ratiarii* transported goods by land between bodies of water when necessary as a task incidental to their main occupation of forwarding merchandise by water. Gallo-Roman water transport was cheap but slow.[58]

In Italy, except for the Po valley where the *cursus publicus* used boats (see above p 28), there were few navigable rivers and inland water transport was difficult to arrange. Special efforts were made for the city of Rome itself where a compulsory gild or corporation of *caudicarii* carried the all-important grain supply from Portus (Ostia) up to Rome by barge. Sixty men (*navicularii* or *lintriones*) were organised in another gild which transported wood to heat the Roman public baths, undoubtedly deforesting the countryside for miles around.[59]

Although there are no indications that animals were used

to haul boats up Gallic rivers, in Italy oxen with ropes fastened to their necks were used to pull barges fifteen miles up the Tiber from Portus to Rome. The road (really a towpath too narrow for wagons) was smooth and no sails or oars were used.[60]

In the conditions prevailing after the collapse of effective Roman government in the west, it is likely that both the population and the animal power available for transport were greatly reduced. The old Gallo-Roman organisation of transport disappeared. Under such conditions it could be expected that transport would confine itself only to the movement of necessities and that the transport of luxuries would decrease. This did not happen. The aristocracy, both lay and clerical, continued to insist on their perquisites and niceties, while the mass of the population was usually left to fend for itself and provide for its own survival. Such being the situation, the goods transported ranged from light, luxury articles, such as precious metals, jewellery, furs, and silks to heavy, bulky commodities such as salt, grain, wine, and fish. Luxury articles could normally be carried on the person or on pack animals, which could negotiate any type of terrain, but occasionally articles of a precious nature reached large proportions and posed problems for transport.

Plunder from war was sometimes both bulky and valuable. The Avar treasure, which had been slowly accumulated over hundreds of years by raids and tributes, was suddenly liberated by Charlemagne's troops, who penetrated the Avars' defences of concentric ringwalls and broke their power. The spoils, consisting of gold, silver, precious stones, and silk, required fifteen wagons, each drawn by four oxen, for transport to Charlemagne at Aachen.[61] The effects of the sudden access to wealth were felt at once. The hoard was disseminated with a lavish hand, but its beneficial effects went beyond the few nobles and clergy who received most of it and increased the prosperity of the whole realm, making possible the encouragement of art, learning, and literature.[62]

Other extremely heavy articles whose nature was more

spiritual than material were sometimes transported over surprising distances by people whose technical sophistication is little-known or suspected. The megaliths making up the inner circle at Stonehenge were transported hundreds of miles in prehistoric times. The capabilities of the Romans are better known. They were able to bring Egyptian obelisks, carved from single stones, to Rome in large ships and set them up vertically with no apparent technical difficulties. When one of the same obelisks was moved a few feet in Renaissance times it was accomplished only with the greatest difficulty and was acclaimed as a superb technical feat.[63] One of the Romans' secrets was the use of extremely powerful draught animals. Elephants were used at Rome to move a colossal statue of Nero.[64]

That engineering skill did not disappear completely during the so-called Dark Ages is shown by the movement of the 276-ton monolith capping the tomb of Theodoric from Istria to Ravenna.[65] Although the workmen of Charlemagne were not capable of making art objects equal to those of the Romans, they were able to transport them. Not only choice mosaics and marbles, but large columns and even a colossal equestrian statue of Theodoric (or the Emperor Zeno) were brought to Aachen.[66]

Similarly, when Abbot Desiderius built a basilica on top of Monte Cassino in 1066, he brought columns, bases, and marble from that great quarry, the ruins of Imperial Rome, shipped them from Portus Romanus at the mouth of the Tiber to the Garigliano river, brought them by boat up to Suium, and transported them from there to Cassino by wagon. The first column was brought up the mountain on the backs of local people fired by religious fervour.[67] When Abbot Suger was planning the rebuilding of the church of St Denis around 1140, he considered bringing marble columns from the palace of Diocletian in Rome by ship through the Mediterranean, around the Iberian Peninsula, through the English Channel, and up the Seine. He was spared the immense labour and expense by the discovery of suitable stone close at hand near Pontoise.[68] The nature of these materials precluded their being dismantled and transported in small loads, and required that they be moved *in toto*. The accomplishments are noteworthy, even though not only the methods of transport but the routes followed often remain a matter of speculation.

Once the shortage of wood and the desire and necessity for permanence and protection had made itself felt in western Europe, cathedrals and castles were built of stone. Skills in stone cutting and shaping were revived or redeveloped and the material was brought to the building site. At times, religious enthusiasm persuaded the population to replace draught animals in the transport of heavy materials, as in the construction of Chartres cathedral. The nobility, both men and women, harnessed themselves to wagons and dragged wine, grain, oil, stone, and wood to the site.[69]

It must have been more usual to employ all the available animal-power (such as draught oxen when not required for ploughing) and to develop new techniques to cope with the new problems. Although the finished cathedrals were magnificent in conception and often tremendous in size compared to any buildings with which the populace was familiar, it was customary to keep the blocks of stone as small as possible. By doing most of the shaping at the quarry, the amount of unnecessary weight to be moved was reduced as much as possible.[70]

Local stone was not invariably used, and particularly famous and desirable types of stone were moved long distances. The stone of Caen in Normandy was transported to England for the construction of Battle Abbey at Hastings and the White Tower in London and to the rest of France in connection with the religious building fever of the eleventh century.[71] Wherever possible, water was preferred for the transport of building stone. It was much easier to exploit a quarry which was located near a usable water-course.[72]

The increased use of stone after AD 1000 had beneficial effects on transport. Roads had to be repaired or constructed so that the stone could be moved. The chipped and broken stone, which was a by-product of the quarry, was a natural and efficient material from which to construct the roads. Such an improvement in roads was conducive to an increase in traffic. More goods moved more rapidly. More efficient harness, better vehicles, and more draught animals, particularly the faster horse, were called for. The simpler roads made of broken stone, or cobbles laid on sand, were better for the conditions of medieval traffic than the Roman roads had been. They were easy to repair, gave good footing to horses shod with iron, and were not broken up by frost.[73]

The culture of the vine was widespread in Gaul from the time of the late empire. The conquering Franks soon developed a taste for wine and came to consider it a necessity rather than a luxury. It was a necessity for Christian religious services. Consequently, the spread of Christianity required the supply of wine to areas like England and eastern Germany where cultivation of the wine had not been introduced by the Romans. The solution of the problem appeared to depend either on transporting the wine or in extending the range of the grape. Attempts were made to raise vineyards in all areas of western Europe, even those with an inauspicious climate such as England, Pomerania, and Poland.[74] It has been said that the early medieval climate was more conducive to raising the vine in northern Europe.[75] Others feel that the climate was not warmer but that only poor wines were produced in northern Europe.[76] In any case, vine growing in the north continued only in those areas which had southward facing slopes and considerable sunshine. For most of northern Europe, if wine of good quality was to be consumed, it had first to be transported from some more fortunate area.

In classical times and in the Mediterranean area, wine was transported in pottery vessels (*amphorae*). In Gaul and in other well-wooded areas of western Europe, wine was commonly transported in wooden barrels. In the funerary bas-reliefs barrels are much more common than *amphorae*.[77] Archaeology is able to provide innumerable sherds of *amphorae* but very few remains of barrels because of the nature of the materials used. The bas-reliefs show not only barges but also mule-drawn vehicles loaded with barrels. Local transport of wine for personal consumption was in containers made of animal skins. Because of the scarcity of wood, skins rather than barrels were used in the Mediterranean area in the early Middle Ages for transport of wines and other liquids.[78]

The distinction between wine in *amphorae* and in barrels may have been geographical and due to availability of materials, or it may have been a matter of quality, with the common cheap, local wines kept in barrels and the choicer, more expensive wines stored in *amphorae*.

In Merovingian times wine was transported from Orleans by boat on the Loire.[79] English merchants purchased wine at the St Denis fairs from the mid-eighth century.[80] Wine was brought across the English Channel to London from Rouen between 991 and 1002. Land transport of wine was mentioned at Saint-Vaast d'Arras in 1036 where *carrus, careta et tonellus vini* are spoken of, indicating that barrels are associated with land vehicles in the transport of wine.[81] The probability is that barrels were developed originally for the storage and transport of beer and wine, but became useful for the transport of loose goods such as salt, fish, and preserved meat. Their leak-proof propensities made them useful in more ways than one. They also protected and preserved their contents from contamination and moisture. As their useful qualities became more apparent their range of contents grew more extended. Such items as silver pennies, arrows, and even the rolls of the Exchequer were transported in barrels.[82] Even the pickled remains of Crusaders were sometimes moved in this way. The Emperor Frederick Barbarossa furnishes an excellent illustrative example. After he was drowned in Asia Minor in 1190, his intestines were buried at Tarsus. The remainder of his body was preserved in vinegar and carried along with the army. He did not keep well, and all but a few bones had to be buried at Antioch. The bones continued on towards Jerusalem but got only as far as Tyre where they seem to have disappeared without trace.[83]

Salt provides a convenient example of the transport of heavy bulky material. A necessity rather than a luxury, its uses were numerous—to improve the taste of food and to preserve meat and fish. It could be produced either by the mining of rock salt, the evaporation of brine in salt pans, or the burning of peat and the leaching of the ashes. While the salt trade was extremely profitable to the North Sea coast, the burning of peat destroyed agricultural land and raised the water table and eventually had to be stopped.[84] The presence of salt production is often indicated by place-names such as Salzburg (German) and the older Halle (Celtic). Salt merchants plied their trade by sea, river, and land. By the late Middle Ages whole fleets gathered to carry salt from the Bay of Bourgneuf in southwest France. In the Merovingian and Carolingian periods frequent mention is found of salt boats floating down the Moselle (see above p 29) or passing the tolls on the Danube ('Raffelstetten Tolls', MGH, *Capit. Regum Francorum,* II, No. 253). The growing prosperity of Venice in the ninth century may have been largely due to the salt trade. (See *The Cambridge Economic History of Europe,* Vol II [Cambridge, 1952], Chap IV, Michael Postan, 'The Trade of Medieval Europe: the North', 128-9, for material on the salt trade.)

For the land transport of salt perhaps the clearest information is from the English sources. By the time of Domesday Book the termination *-wich* had come to mean salt-works, although its original meaning had been 'row of houses' or 'village' like the Latin *vicus* from which it was derived. Because of its granular nature salt is divisible into packs of any size, so it is adaptable to many methods of transport. From Cheshire *-wiches* salt was carried away by all available means, including carts drawn by two or four oxen, packhorses, and even the backs of men. The evidence makes some deductions possible. In 1065 carts were still normally drawn by oxen; horses were pack-animals. From the tolls charged, it seems that a man carried one quarter of the load of a packhorse and each ox in a cart team pulled a weight equivalent to twice the load of a packhorse. Since men and animals varied individually in strength there was a tendency to try to build up the loads as much as possible, but this was countered by the heavy fines charged if the axle of a cart or the back of a horse was broken.[85]

The establishment of toll stations by various jurisdictions and the records of the toll houses themselves are indicative not only of the types of goods carried but even of the relative volume of various items. The increase in the number of tolls on particular routes reduced the amount of goods which otherwise would have passed and limited the distance which goods could travel economically. In such a situation, alternative routes with less onerous charges were sought. The most drastic solution, but one which was discouraged with severe penalties, was smuggling. Those who attempted to sell weapons and hauberks to the Slavs and Avars had their goods confiscated.[86] If a free merchant attempted to pass a tollplace with his ship without paying, the ship and the merchandise were to be taken from him.[87] Cases of concealment of identity were treated less harshly. Merchants attempting to pass as pilgrims were only required to pay the established tolls before proceeding.[88]

INFORMATION AND IDEAS

The Church had much to gain by fostering communication. To be effective, such a universal organisation required something more accurate and 'official' than could be provided by oral instructions. Once a decree had been made or a doctrinal point settled in writing, the parchment remained as a witness to past action and a precedent for the future. Taking as a text Daniel 12.4, 'Many shall run to and fro, and knowledge shall be increased', the Church organised special congregations which repaired roads, built bridges, set up messenger relays, and established hostels for travellers. In such ways the Church attempted to fill the void left by the slow decay of the *cursus publicus*. Entire pilgrimages could be arranged through the Church, including the furnishing of horses or asses for the journey and the safeguarding of valuables during the pilgrim's absence. Unreclaimed wealth went, of course, to swell the coffers of the Church.

The reasons the Church had for encouraging communication were sufficient to cause the lay authorities to discourage it. Oral communicatons were enough for the effective control of small areas, and subjects could best be protected from dangerous ideas by isolating them from their neighbours in adjoining feudal territories. A consequent tendency was to extend one's territory only as far as effective control could be maintained. Little effort was made to provide facilities and encouragement for the passage and dissemination of the communications of universal concern promulgated by the Church.[89]

Early medieval messengers were often only people who happened to be going where someone wanted a message carried. More control and a better system were obviously needed, and Pope Gregory the Great had the necessary talents for organisation and administration. Christianity itself was transported to the Anglo-Saxons in Britain in 597 by Gregory the Great's emissary, St Augustine. St Boniface, in the eighth century, used priests to carry his numerous letters from Germany to England and Rome. In the tenth century the Abbey of Cluny created a messenger service to link it with the daughter houses.[90]

Not only were the letters of St Boniface transported, but they carried within themselves references to items of an intellectual nature whose transport was either requested or reported. While in Germany, St Boniface received books from Abbess Eadburga in England.[91] He wished to be informed of anything in the library of Abbot Duddo which might be useful to him.[92]. He wanted a copy of the *Epistles of St Peter* written in gold letters so as to impress his congregation with honour and reverence.[93] Late in life he needed a copy of the Prophets, written out in large letters and without abbreviations, because of his failing eyesight.[94]

Relics and other objects of religious significance were frequent articles of transport. Being usually small in size and light in weight, they posed little problem, but their spiritual significance far outweighed their physical dimensions. In consequence, they required (and received) pious attendants who joined in joyous and reverent procession to accompany them in their translation from place to place.

Einhard arranged to have the dust and ashes of the martyrs, Marcellinus and Peter, stolen from their graves in Rome and brought over the Alps to Germany. The body of St Marcellinus was lifted from his tomb by night, wrapped in fine linen, and taken to a house in Rome for concealment. On another night, soon after, the limbs of the martyr Peter were removed from the tomb and placed in a silken bag. The remains of both saints were sealed in caskets (probably small ones) and taken to Pavia clandestinely. They were brought over the Alps (probably concealed in saddle bags), not by the usual route, but by St Maurice. Once the Alps had been passed, the fear of retribution from Rome and the need for concealment came to an end. The bodies, well broken and jumbled by this time, were placed in a single casket, although still in separate linen packages, and carried openly on a bier by the inhabitants of the localities through which they passed. Increasing numbers of rejoicing people accompanied the bier to Strasbourg where it was transferred to a boat for the journey down the Rhine to a convenient landing place (Portus?—perhaps near modern Mannheim). From there a great multitude brought it by a five-day journey to the Odenwald. By various manifestations the saints chose their own final resting-place at Seligenstadt. The last leg of the journey was made easy by divine intervention. Although there had been hard, uninterrupted rain, there was little mud and the streams which had to be crossed did not rise as a result of the storm.[95]

Mortuary rolls announcing the deaths of well-known religious people and asking for prayers for their departed souls were widely circulated. Each was carried by a wandering priest. At every religious house where he paused additional notes were placed on the scroll, adding to its length and eventually making it more difficult to transport. The most extreme example is the roll of Count Wilfred of Cerdana, who died in his monastery in the Pyrenees in 1050. His mortuary roll was carried throughout France. It accumulated memorial inscriptions, many of great length, from 133 religious houses. The dates and locations given make it possible to reconstruct the route and estimate the speed of the messenger, but there are no clues as to his mode of transportation.[96]

Heresy was one type of information whose dissemination the Church did not wish to encourage. Nevertheless, in its early stages when it was merely doctrinal discussion, before it was officially characterised as heresy, it did circulate through normal Church correspondence channels. Such an intellectual type of heresy really did little more than sharpen the wits of churchmen and help them attain a unified doctrinal position. Far different were the popular types of heresy, whose distribution and dissemination are more difficult to trace. Traders and travellers from the lower social classes were the most likely carriers of such heresies. Like St Willibald, they showed an amazing ability to make themselves understood in distant lands. Much distribution of heretical ideas was probably only oral. Few heretics are likely to have been able to write Latin, or any other language. The vernacular languages, whether written or oral, were unsatisfactory instruments for international communication because they varied too much from place to place to be mutually comprehensible.[97] Nevertheless, heresies spread surprisingly. Sometimes whole groups, or occupations, like the weavers, were suspected of heresy, regardless of their location. The Albigensian heresy of southern France probably resulted from contacts made by early crusaders with heretics in the Balkans.

DISEASE

Some of the most influential of medieval travellers were invisible. These were the disease-bearing organisms which accompanied man and his animals wherever they journeyed. Lack of effective sanitation and increased traffic on the roads facilitated the spread of disease. Local isolated communities, which had developed their own immunity to certain diseases, were exposed to new strains and types of disorders by the coming of travellers from afar. A little was understood of the method by which disease spread. A ship coming to Marseille from Spain was blamed for the introduction of a disease into Merovingian Gaul.[98]

Suspicions of this nature may have contributed to a distrust and dislike of strangers and led to attempts to preserve isolation and achieve economic self-sufficiency. Such attempts were countered by the pressures of material and spiritual advantage to be gained by increased intercourse. It is possible that the comparative isolation and difficulty of access enjoyed by Britain in the early Middle Ages may have made her less subject to epidemics than was the rest of Europe.[99]

Although something was suspected of the transport-mechanism of disease, it was more usual to couple the coming of an epidemic with natural phenomena, such as earthquakes and comets. The appearance of a comet presaged a famine, and famine was followed by pestilence.[100] Monks seem to have been particularly vulnerable to epidemics. They were among the very few members of the general population who lived close together in sizeable groups. The movement of the monks from one monastery to another served to spread disease.[101] These factors, rather than any weakness resulting from abstemious diet, were the most likely causes of the high mortality among monks.

Visible as well as unseen plagues were likely to follow the roads. After five years in Carpitania (a province in Spain near Toledo), locusts followed the great highway to a neighbouring province. They covered an area of fifty by a hundred miles.[102] The black rat, which was the effective carrier of the bubonic plague bacillus, undoubtedly used both sea and land transport in its destructive course through Europe. The time of its introduction is uncertain. It may have come with the barbarian migration of the fifth century or it may have been brought back by some of the early Crusaders.[103] Although the

Middle Ages were aware of the influx of rats, no connection was recognised between the rats and the plague. Even if the connection had been known, no satisfactory means of extermination was at hand. The Pied Piper of Hamelin belongs only to legend.

Notes to this chapter are on pp 183-90

2

Land transport

THE MEANS OF transport and the route have a reciprocal effect on each other. Walking men require little in the way of a path; men on horseback or driving pack-animals need a route which is wider and better prepared; vehicles generally require still wider roads and much maintenance of the road surface.[1] The Romans were perhaps the first in western Europe to make the entire roadbed permanent and so channel the traffic for its entire course. Earlier peoples had only kept to a specific route when they were constrained by such geographic limitations as passes in mountain areas and good footing across marshes. A permanent pathway was sometimes assured through swampy land by the construction of corduroy roads by laying logs side by side or by the building of stone causeways.[2] The Celtic peoples usually built with wood, the Romans with stone.

Much has been written of the Roman roads, but little was written by the Romans themselves. The best evidence regarding the roads and their theory, purpose, and details of construction, is provided by archaeological investigation of their remains.[3] The description in Vitruvius, which has often been quoted to illustrate Roman road construction is, in actuality, a description of the building of a masonry floor for a dwelling.[4] A similar system may or may not have been used in road-

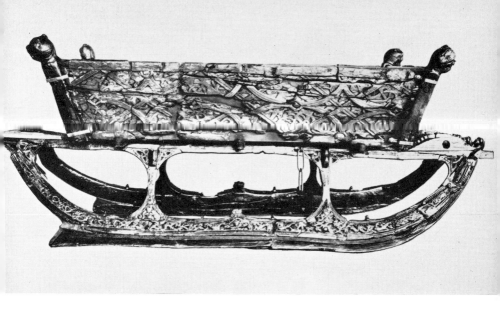

Page 49 (*above*) Oseberg sled, Norway AD 800-50; (*below*) Irish coracle

Page 50 Bayeux Tapestry c 1070: *(right)* man-drawn four-wheeled wagon; *(below)* mule plough-ing and horse harrowing, showing whippletree

PORTANT:ARMAS: ADNAVES: ETHIC
TRAHVNT:CARRVM
CVM VINO.ETARMIS:

building, but there is certainly no warrant for transposing the terminology and naming the road layers after those used in making house foundations. There is a literary description of road-building c AD 90 by Statius (*Silvae*, IV. iii) which uses different terminology than Vitruvius and is perhaps too poetic to be technically precise.

The roads themselves show a great variety and a lack of standardisation in their construction. They were not, as is sometimes said, rigid works of masonry laid across country like walls placed on their sides. Instead, they were composed of relatively plastic layers laid over each other, the superposition often indicating repairs rather than conscious design. Instead of tearing up and replacing an old road surface, a new surface was laid on top of it.[5]

Neither the construction of the roads, nor the direction in which they ran, was as inflexible as is often maintained. The roads were built for a purpose, which was to provide communication with Rome and to make possible the rapid and efficient shifting of troops. Use of them by the general public and for the transport of goods for trade was only incidental. They were intended to provide a way which was less subject to interruption from climatic and geographic causes than a natural route.

Although the Roman roads provided a surface which was usable under most climatic conditions, it is unlikely that many users found them comfortable. It is probable that even the legionaries, inured to hard marching and provided with hobnailed sandals for foot protection, preferred the side of the road for marching under many conditions. Stone, either crushed or flat, provided an inflexible and uncomfortable surface to marching feet under hot and dry conditions. When the surface was wet, the stone became slippery. Conditions which were bad for pedestrians were worse for horsemen. As it seems that most Roman horses were unshod, it is likely that hooves would soon deteriorate when used on a stone surface. Vehicles and their draught animals were even more out of place on a hard surface with extremely steep gradients.

D

Inflexible wheels and unsprung wagon-bodies bearing directly
on a non-yielding surface must have resulted in excessive and
rapid wear on both the vehicles and the roads. Lack of braking
power and inefficient harness must have discouraged the use
of vehicles on steep ascents and descents.

When the Roman state lost its power and pressure was no
longer felt moving outward from the capital of the empire,
some of the advantages of the Roman road system became
liabilities. The roads, which had provided routes for efficient
and rapid deployment of troops to the borders to meet emergencies, became routes for the rapid movement of invading
marauders, who frequently surprised their victims as a result of
the breakdown of Roman internal communications. Perhaps
learning the lesson they themselves had taught, the Saxons in
England settled in dispersed hamlets without regard to the
Roman road network. They may have feared marauding plunderers.[6] The resulting isolation hindered the development of
an effective government which was the only real solution to
the problem. In addition, the work of the Church in converting
and educating the rural dwellers was unduly hindered. Not
only the political rulers but also the religious leaders required
good communications for the dissemination of ideas as well
as for maintaining order.

The Roman roads were unsuitable for medieval conditions
not only because they facilitated the inroads of plunderers and
provided an uncongenial surface for horses shod with iron but
also because they no longer led where people wanted to go.
The lack of large political units meant that men's horizons
were limited. They found it difficult to conceive of any good
coming from a distant political authority. There was little
economic incentive for them to maintain a route which only
passed through their area and brought no benefits to their
immediate vicinity. In addition, changing times and conditions
encouraged a reorientation of the interests of western Europe.
The focus of political power and economic attraction moved
away from the Mediterranean towards the north and west,
whether owing to climatic changes, to man's adaptation to the

climate, or to the relative weakness of western Europeans in the face of the advance of Islam.

The Roman roads had served as channels for the spread of early Christianity. Church missions had moved along them and expanded into the countryside from them.[7] However, the establishment and development of new shrines, such as that of St James at Compostella, in locations where no Roman roads led, indicated the inadequacy of the Roman roads for new conditions.[8]

The fate of the Roman roads was various. Some were used; some abandoned. Some became sources of building stone for the adjacent population; some became boundaries. Others were ruined by the combination of hard usage to which they were unsuited and lack of maintenance.

After the barbarian invasions, the much-reduced scale of traffic meant comparatively little wear on the road surface. It is estimated that the main highways would stand up under the onslaught of unshod hooves and iron-tyred wheels for seventy to a hundred years.[9] The lack of organised maintenance must have been a greater factor in the deterioration of the roads. Evidence for the lasting ability of the Roman roads is provided by Procopius (*Gothic Wars* 5.14.11) who saw the Appian Way eight centuries after it was built and noted that, after so long a time and having been traversed by many wagons and animals, the paving blocks had not separated at the joints or worn down. Despite the contention of Lynn White, jr, that the Roman roads were too costly to maintain even for the wealthy Byzantine and Islamic empires,[10] there is evidence that the Byzantines, at least, improved as well as maintained the road system they had inherited.[11] The Crusaders in 1097 made good use of the roads in the Balkans, particularly the Via Egnatia from Durazzo towards Constantinople, and even found the roads in Asia Minor in relatively good condition although the area was no longer under Byzantine control. That this situation continued is clear from the statement in William of Tyre (Book 21, 12) that in Asia Minor *c* 1175 there were broad and open roads well adapted not only for the passage of the army but for the transport of their masses of baggage and impedimenta of all kinds.

The Arabs, breaking out of their peninsula in the seventh century, fell heir not only to much of the land and wealth of the Byzantine and Sassanian empires but also to their well-developed highway systems. To the Arabs, conditioned to a harsher environment, the highways seemed unnecessarily elaborate. In their eyes it was more efficient to transfer their familiar desert transport techniques to their new territories. They allowed the Byzantine and Sassanian roadways to decay through lack of maintenance and were content to have simple trails marked by posts driven into the ground to guide their camels and pack-mules. This does not mean a diminution in the amount of transport or in the quantity of goods in circulation. On the contrary, Moslem trade grew to proportions hitherto un-dreamed-of.[12] The Moslem techniques gave them unexpected mobility. The desert was their friend—their sea—a congenial element to which their camels and horses were well adapted. They needed neither roads nor horseshoes to master this environment and could appear out of the desert without warning, to the consternation of settled peoples. Their methods did not often need to be so heroic as that of Khalid who made a legendary 200-mile dash across a waterless desert in 635 by taking along a herd of camels as a portable water supply. The gorged camels were slain systematically at each stop to provide water for the horses.[13] Certainly the problem of road mainten-ance was simpler in the southern climes. In the north and west, the alternation of freezing and thawing was particularly detri-mental to the unmaintained roads.[14]

The best-preserved of the Roman roads were those which were soonest abandoned. Any masonry structure tends to sink into the sub-soil. Those which were unused soon acquired a protective coating of vegetation and soil.[15] In remote areas they were often untouched by the reduced population and remained undisturbed from the time of their abandonment until the coming of modern archaeologists.

In areas where people remained they found more immediate

uses for the stones of the roads, which became quarries.[16] The stones often found their way into town buildings and walls.[17] Locally, it was more important to have shelter and protection than transport channels to remote places.

Abandoned roads remained conspicuous features of the landscape. In England they seemed far beyond the capabilities of ordinary men, and their construction was ascribed to fabulous giants.[18] On the Continent it was more usual to consider them as creations of Julius Caesar or Queen Brunehilde. Many abandoned roads returned to their original function as boundaries. During their construction the surveyors of the fields (*agrimensores*) and the engineers of the roads had worked together, so that the public roads marked the boundaries of estates. The word *limes* denotes both road and boundary.[19] Even in their abandonment the roads remained prominent and permanent and served as natural dividing lines. Part of the border between the kingdoms of Alfred the Great and the Dane, Guthrum, was formed by Watling Street, a renamed Roman road.[20]

As the Middle Ages advanced and the invasions of the Saracens, Magyars, and Vikings came to an end in the tenth century, traffic on the roads increased. Population was growing and trade was quickening but, in addition, changes in transport had come about which were much more destructive of those Roman roads which still remained usable. Transport began to move faster, at the pace of the horse rather than the ox. Horses were now commonly shod with iron. This not only preserved their hooves but made it possible for them to dig into the road surface, get a better purchase, and exert more strength. The adoption of the horse-collar and more efficient harness multiplied the weight a horse could move and made teams of many horses possible, arranged one behind another (*tandem*) as well as side-by-side. Finally, more horses were available than before. Their use for work became common. They were no longer exclusively for the aristocracy. The combination of more loads, larger loads, and sharp, shod hooves was final and fatal for the Roman roads which had remained in use.

Opinions vary as to how long the Roman roads lasted. They kept their importance to the Merovingian epoch, then were often abandoned.[21] They were in use in Gaul until *c* 650 and disappeared gradually in the next century.[22] They still covered the countryside in 800 but were little used.[23] Charlemagne was still able to use them for both horses and oxwagons.[24] 'Nothing could have been worse than the condition of the roads from the 9th century. All that remained of the admirable network of Roman roads now finally disappeared.'[25] The Roman roads were maintained and gave good service to trade.[26] The Roman roads broke down only in the tenth and eleventh centuries on the Rhine, Rhone, and Danube after centuries of use and because no one any longer understood how to maintain them.[27] The frequent swift journeys of the Vikings in England make it probable that the Roman roads there were still usable at need in the ninth and tenth centuries.[28] The roads undoubtedly survived longest where they were least used. They could stand the ravages of nature better than the continued traffic of man.

Late medieval maps show many routes in northern France and the Low Countries which are labelled as Brunehilde roads (*Chaussées Brunehaut, Strata Brunechildis, Cauchies Brunehaut,* etc). The presence of such names on the routes has led to the supposition that Queen Brunehilde of Austrasia, who was killed in 614, was responsible for a tremendous road-building and repairing project in the late sixth century. Brunehilde is even spoken of as a wise and beautiful queen who made great contributions to the development of Merovingian Gaul.[29] Such a characterisation of Brunehilde is strongly at variance with the impression she made on her contemporaries. To St Gall she was evil incarnate, a second Jezebel.[30] There is no contemporary evidence that Queen Brunehilde constructed or repaired roads. Realising the difficulty of attributing the 'Brunehilde' roads to the Austrasian queen, an attempt has even been made to ascribe them to a medieval Brunehilde, Duchess of Flanders.[31] This is nonsense, of course, since Flanders was a county and was never ruled by a duchess, or by a Brunehilde, for that matter.

A very thorough study of Queen Brunehilde has been made by Jules Vannerus.[32] Evidence which he has collected leads him to believe that roads were not named after Brunehilde until the beginning of the thirteenth century.[33] The roads were much older, frequently of Roman construction, but they bore other names such as *calceia,* or *via publica,* until they were attributed to Brunehilde.[34] Vannerus also notes that the poem *Auberon* was written in the early thirteenth century. *Auberon* is the only *chanson de geste* which mentions Brunehilde. The *chanson* is doubly interesting. It couples Brunehilde and Julius Caesar in a (mythical) family relationship and attributes road-building to both of them. According to the poem, Julius Caesar was the son of Brunehilde and the emperor of Rome. *Auberon* was apparently written by someone from Artois. This was also the area where some of the 'Brunehilde' roads made their earliest appearance.[35]

The thesis of Vannerus, based on this evidence, seems convincing. If there were no earlier uses of the term it would be conclusive. But there are earlier references.[36] The existence of this material—more solidly based historically than *chansons de geste*—indicates that there is possibly a link between the historical Brunehilde and the roads that bear her name.

In general, the early Middle Ages were not a time of road-building. If it was necessary to go between points not having a prepared road, the passage of travellers, over a period of time, would make a path of sorts. If the way became impassable, the bad spots could be avoided, or a new route chosen. The road was more an abstract right of passage than an actual strip of land. Everyone had the right to pass into the neighbouring farmland if the road had impassable holes.[37]

At times, however, and in certain places, it was necessary to construct roads. Orderic Vitalis, writing in the twelfth century and possibly using an early version of the *chanson de geste* 'The Song of William ', tells us how, in 806, Count (St) William Courtnez of Toulouse built a road to his new monastery, St Saviour in the Cevennes. Whether the account reflects

twelfth- or ninth-century practice in road-building, it still
represents a rare early view of road construction methods.
'Count William made a road to the monastery by a sharp and
difficult ascent to the steep hills, cutting rocks with hammers
and pickaxes and other iron tools, and with the fragments
laid the base of a causeway along the river.'[38] It is possible
that the salt industry found it necessary to construct new roads
during the early Middle Ages,[39] since the producing areas were
not connected to the new consuming areas by the old Roman
road network. Further impetus to road-building came from the
construction of water- and windmills which required new routes
to bring grain for milling. The Lombards took an early interest in better land transport and restored the *Via Francigena,*
which remained their most important highway throughout
the Middle Ages.[40] In Denmark, good paved roads for non-
winter transport were in use in Roman times and the Scandinavian road system was extended in the later Viking period.[41]
Despite this familiarity with the roads, a unique case was provided by the Norse settlement of Iceland in the ninth and
tenth centuries. Here no roads were built, but only bridle paths.
All travel was on foot or horseback and there was little heavy
material to transport, or much need for vehicles.[42] Packhorses
provided the usual method of transporting goods until the
late nineteenth century.

Considerable impetus was given to road-building by the construction of stone cathedrals and castles in the eleventh century
and later. Prepared roads were necessary for the movement of
heavy loads of stone, and the waste material from the quarries
was an excellent substance with which to pave them. In other
road-building activity of the time, Godfrey de Bouillon built a
road from Nicomedia to Nicea in Asia Minor during the First
Crusade. Three thousand men with axes and swords hacked
a route over a steep mountain 4,000 feet high and marked it
with crosses of metal and wood.[43]

Compared with its Roman predecessor, the medieval road
was very simply made. No great supply of labour, such as the
Roman slaves or legionaries, was available. The elaborate

foundations constructed by the Romans were eliminated and stones, crushed or in blocks, were laid directly on the soil. The method was cheap and repairs were easy to make. The surface [illegible] than the Roman. While it would be extreme to say that the medieval roads were better than the Roman, it is correct to say that medieval roads were appropriate to medieval conditions of transport.[44] The medieval road was more suitable for vehicles and horses with shod hooves than the Roman roads which were built primarily for marching.[45] In summary, the Roman roads were over-built. They wasted both material and labour. They were based on the idea that the road itself had to bear the weight of the traffic. The medieval roads were closer to the modern idea that the subsoil bears the load and is the best foundation. The road should be just a wearing surface and a roof to protect the subsoil from moisture.[46]

The problem of bringing a road across a river was differently met in various periods. Both fords and bridges were known at all times but, in general, the Romans were often content with fords at locations where the men of the Middle Ages preferred to erect bridges. A possible reason was that the Middle Ages moved a greater proportion of its goods on wheeled vehicles and required a dry crossing so as not to wet the goods.[47] Without bridges, medieval carts and wagons would have had a very limited range.

Fords were sometimes natural crossings used by animals, and were discovered by hunting or observing animals.[48] Fords were often artificially improved. It was Celtic practice to construct wooden platforms and immerse them in the river. The Romans paved the fords with stone. The location of fords is frequently marked by the finds of many coins in the river. It is likely that the coins were tossed in deliberately as offerings to the river god and were not lost by accident.[49]

The Celts built their bridges of wood. The Romans normally used stone, and made the bridge narrower than the road it was supposed to carry. This was economical in material but meant that vehicles could not pass on the bridge.[50] Roman bridges were also constructed with semi-circular arches—the wider the span, the higher the arch—consequently, steep ramps, difficult for vehicles, were required for the bridge approaches.[51] Some of the Roman stone bridges, such as that over the Mouzon at Pompierre (Vosges), survived into Merovingian times.[52] Some are still in use. Frankish practice reverted to the use of wood. Leudast was captured when his foot slipped between two planks while he was trying to flee over the city bridge at Paris.[53] Houses were destroyed near the river Oust in order to obtain material for the construction of bridges.[56] Charlemagne built a wooden bridge over the Rhine at Mainz. He intended to replace it with a stone structure but died before he was able to do so.[55] The condition of bridges in the late tenth century is well described by Richer (*Histoire de France*, ed. Latouche, Vol. II, 224-30). The bridge at Meaux was full of large holes but horses were brought over it by bridging the holes with a shield and loose planks which were moved forward ahead of the horses. The use of stone bridges became common again in the eleventh century along with the building of stone cathedrals and castles.

THE MEANS AND METHODS

The undersurface of the foot is marvellously adaptable in providing its own tough protection by the development of callosities, but many situations arise owing to conditions of weather or terrain where additional protection for the feet is required. The early saints prided themselves on their ability to go barefoot under the most adverse conditions. Toughness of foot was correlated with constancy of faith and the idea of self-torture was acquired from the early desert fathers. But shoes and thoughts of comfort were not unknown. Because of poverty, Gallus, an uncle of St Gregory of Tours, often went on foot the forty miles from Clermont to Brioude. Having taken off his shoes because of heat, he stepped on a thorn in the grass which required a miracle for its removal.[56]

Man can be an effective beast of burden. The Roman

legionaries, who called themselves the 'mules of Marius', had shown that humans could carry heavy weights rapidly over long distances and difficult country.

War captives and slaves were frequently beasts of burden. From the standpoint of the slave dealers it would have been inefficient for a slave to transport only himself, so the captives and slaves acquired by the Jewish merchants in the Slav lands and brought across Europe to Spain by way of Verdun served also as sumpter-beasts during their journey, except in those rare cases where their beauty represented a premium which it was worthwhile to preserve.[57]

Other medieval pedestrians carried merchandise over the Alps from the Rhine to the Po valley in the eleventh century on their own backs or in primitive wheelbarrows.[58] Still others worked as *haleurs*, vulgar boatmen, who with the aid of a shoulder harness and a cane to steady their feet, hauled loaded barges slowly up various streams. Their pictures can still be seen on Gallo-Roman bas-reliefs.[59]

Piety, rather than economy, seems to have been the motivating idea behind the practice of walking barefoot on pilgrimage, or as a penance. The mother of St Godric of Finchale, for example, wore her shoes to London, but then went barefoot to Rome and back.[60] Various types of footwear were widely available. Custom, geography, price, and the availability of suitable materials dictated the choice of footwear. Open sandals of fibrous matter were appropriate for Mediterranean lands and hot dry climates.[61] In moister, more northerly latitudes, full foot-coverings of leather with cross-gartering to the knees were required.[62] The far northern peoples adapted themselves to severe winter conditions, and foot transport was even enhanced during the winter months by the use of skis and snow-shoes over the countryside, and bone runnered skates on frozen streams and lakes.[63] Because of the low coefficient of friction, foot travel was not only more practical but more pleasurable during the far northern winter. The peoples of the temperate zone were more likely to be hampered by winter conditions, which usually meant rain, mud, and cold for them, rendering the roads difficult or impassable. When severe northern conditions reached them on occasion, they were more likely to be ill-prepared, lacking in winter techniques, and generally paralysed into inactivity by the unusual cold.

Special means of pedestrian travel were available to some men of the temperate lands. The messenger is frequently represented carrying a spear or long pole. This can be considered first as a mean of identification, a badge of office. Such was the custom in the Roman empire where the *beneficiarii* and the *speculatores* carried broad-headed spears when they carried messages or conveyed shipments. Here the lance of the *beneficiarius* seems to have been a symbol, rather than an actual weapon for defence. The medieval messenger's spear had another very practical use. The messenger represented the authority of his lord and anyone who interfered with his progress was subject to heavy fine. In the course of his travels he had the right of way and was empowered to make short cuts across any man's fields or crops.[64] While making such short cuts the spear was of frequent use as a vaulting pole to clear small streams and low hedges.

A unique method of pedestrian travel available to medieval man was the use of stilts. While stilts were customarily used in swampy country such as the Landes in Gascony, Flanders, and the English fen country in Lincolnshire, there was nothing to prevent their use as real 'seven-league boots' in any sort of terrain. Their use in the swampy areas seems to have existed from time immemorial. They are shown in the medieval MSS.[65] The failure to use stilts on a large scale during the Middle Ages was perhaps a lost opportunity. They could have been used for fast cross-country message-carrying, and no prepared road would have been needed.

Another area in which little progress was made was in the use of light, wheeled vehicles for personal locomotion. The Romans had children's toys which resembled a two-wheeled scooter. There are similar medieval representations.[66] They seem to have been little used for personal transport. Such vehicles could have used the force of gravity during the decent of hills and, consequently, lessened the consumption of human energy.

For those men unable or unwilling to transport themselves, the backs of animals were available. It was even possible for one human to carry another. The legendary St Christopher, recently removed from the calendar of saints, who is supposed to have lived *c* AD 250, carried men across a river.[67] In this connection, think also of the Robin Hood of the ballads being carried over the stream on the broad back of Friar Tuck. This system was sometimes the only one available to the aged or infirm. St Godric of Finchale was accustomed to carry his mother on his shoulders across fords and rivers when she made her barefoot pilgrimage from London to Rome and back referred to above (p 61).

Swimming as a means of transport was probably not practised as frequently as in classical times. When escaped slaves had to cross a river they swam on their shields, indicating a need for additional support (Gregory of Tours, *History,* III, 15). The hero Beowulf swam for seven nights encumbered by armour and weapons (Beowulf, VIII-IX). In a less legendary vein, Charlemagne was noted for his skill at swimming (Einhard, *Vita Karoli,* 22).

Aerial transport has only a small place in the Middle Ages. Eilmer, a monk of Malmesbury, glided quite successfully from a tower and would doubtless have done even better if he had only provided a tail.[68]

Transport by ass was common, particularly among early clergymen, and the use of the ass was widespread throughout Europe. The ass was small enough and tractable enough to be ridden safely by unskilled riders and there was little need for the use of stirrups, bits, or spurs, even if they had been available. St Gregory of Tours regarded ass-riding as a sign of asceticism, like eating barley instead of wheat or drinking water as a substitute for wine.[69] In the mid-eighth century St Sturm, after vainly seeking by boat for a site for what became the monastery at Fulda, saddled his ass and set out alone from Hersfeld. His description of his travels is much like that

of early pioneers in America. He made his way through a pathless wilderness and cut trees each night to make a circular
fence to protect his ass. He even encountered the equivalent of
aborigines. When he came to where the road from Thuringia
to Mainz crossed the Fulda river, he observed 'stinking Slavs'
washing in the ford.[70] This is probably an extreme example of
the penetration of the ass beyond the limits of the old Roman
Empire and contradicts the assertion that Germany was too
cold for the ass.[71] The most famous of the medieval asses was
probably that ridden by Peter the Hermit during his preaching
of the First Crusade. As an object of veneration it was second
only to its master and since its hairs made good relics it was
soon quite bare.[72]

The mule, that unique biological invention, had an essential
but unhonoured role in the medieval economy. Although he
had 'neither pride of ancestry nor hope of posterity' (quota-
tion attributed to Ignatius Donnelly in a speech in the Minnesota legislature in 1860), he was tougher, more disease-resist-
ant, and had a longer work life than the horse and was stronger
than his father, the ass.[73]

The mule, perhaps because of his mixed ancestry, occupied
a position in popular esteem generally between that of the
horse and the ass. He was used as a beast of burden, as a
draught animal, and for riding by people inferior in status to a
knight. In classical Rome the mule had occupied a prominent
and respected place. Most of the vehicles in cities were pulled
by mules. Canal boats moved by mule power.[74] Even great
ladies did not disdain having their vehicles drawn by mules.
The mules were often ornamented by having their hooves
gilded.[75] Medieval mules were not so pampered, but were
most often used as pack-animals, surefootedly making their
way along narrow trails and through dangerous mountain
country.

It is possible that equivalent results could have been obtained
by selective breeding of the ass, with the additional benefit of
a self-reproducing race. For asses, like horses, vary tremend-
ously in size and strength, with specimens ranging from the

size of a large dog to fifteen hands (sixty inches) at the shoulders.

The ox was the most common draught animal and its harness the most rationally devised. Nevertheless, comparisons of capability with modern draught cattle are difficult to make because the animal appears to have been much smaller and weaker in ancient and medieval times. A grown ox was little larger than a present-day calf.[76] Oxen were normally driven in pairs. If the animal was so small and weak there was probably little to be gained by developing a yoke or other harness for a single ox. During the First Crusade, when their horses died while crossing the Anatolian desert, knights were forced to proceed on foot or use oxen as mounts. The Crusaders even used goats, sheep, and dogs as beasts of burden.[77]

The horse had the greatest speed of the common draught animals. Nevertheless, it was not customary for the horse to work.[78] It is contended that there is no document which indicates that horses were used for work in Roman Gaul.[79] Work, in this context, must mean that horses were not used in heavy transport, for the evidence of the Theodosian Code and numerous funerary reliefs indicates that horses were used for light, fast transport on the Roman roads in addition to their primary use as luxury riding animals and drawers of display vehicles and racing chariots.

The horse seems to have become and remained a relatively scarce animal throughout most of the early Middle Ages in western Europe. It is probable that the raising of horses in Gaul was at least hampered, if not brought to a virtual halt, by the coming of the Germanic peoples in the fourth and fifth centuries. The Franks, the most numerous of the new peoples, were renowned as infantry and only the leaders were commonly mounted. The ancient Germans seem to have had more of a taste for the flesh of horses than a preference for them as riding animals.[80] The comparative rarity of the horse is seen in the fact that six of them were regarded as a suitable number for a king.[81] A story is told that Clovis himself, after the battle of Vouillé, gave the horse he had ridden to the monastery of

St Martin at Tours, but, soon realising that a good horse was a rarity, wanted to take it back in exchange for fifty silver marks. The monks took the opportunity to hold out for more and Clovis had to part with double the price, which prompted him to mutter in his beard that St Martin served his friends well but sold his services a little dear.[82]

In 758 Pepin the Short changed the Saxon tribute from 500 cows to 300 horses.[83] This indicates the growing importance of cavalry. Even under Charlemagne, who well understood the value of cavalry and owed much of his success to it, the horse remained in short supply. An epizootic in Pannonia killed off most of his cavalry.[84] He rebuilt his cavalry strength from conquests in Spain which provided enough animals for him to send gifts of Spanish horses and mules to the king of Persia.[85]

The change in esteem for the horse can perhaps be seen in the rise in status of the marshal (*mariscalcus*). Originally a servile stable-man (Lex Salica, x, 4), he becomes one of the great officers of a kingdom and eventually a hereditary noble-man. From the time of Charlemagne, the horse of good quality can be considered a noble animal and primarily a possession of the aristocracy which commenced horse-breeding on its own stud farms.[86] It would be a matter of several hundred years before the increased supply of horses, and the adoption of horse-collars and iron horseshoes, made them commonly available for non-noble riders and for the pulling of vehicles and agricultural implements. The horse continued to be an attribute of the aristocracy and primarily a riding animal for the armoured knight.

The need for more horses was met by systematic breeding of horses and mules in the Moslem countries. The increased number of horses supplied the enlarged market and brought the price of horses and mules down to a lower level after the tenth century and made possible their use on a larger scale.[87] One of the consequences of the introduction of the three-field system of crop rotation, particularly after the end of the Viking and Magyar invasions, was an increased production of oats which also helped to feed a larger supply of horses.[88] Henri

Page 67 Bayeux Tapestry: (*above*) horse transport by sea; (*below*) landing horses from a ship

Page 68 (*above*) Detail from the bronze door of Novgorod Cathedral, *c* 1154, showing an early whippletree; (*below*) detail from the font of Winchester Cathedral, *c* 1180, showing an early central stern rudder

Pirenne speaks of an improvement in draught horses in the tenth century.[89] The impression of increasing numbers is heightened by the large number of horse purchases revealed by eleventh-century charters.[90]

A horse which could carry an armoured knight was also capable of greatly increased effort in other activities. The increase in the number of horses led to a familiarity which reduced their prestige. The heavy charger descended by degrees over the centuries until he became the heavy draught horse. Shortly after the Norman Conquest, the Bayeux Tapestry shows a horse drawing a harrow.[91] Plough horses are mentioned in 1095 in the Statutes of the Synod of Clermont, where Pope Urban II preached the Crusade.[92]

The introduction of the horse-collar and harnessing in file, coupled with the common use of iron horseshoes, made it possible for horses to exert increased strength and move heavy weights more rapidly than had been possible with the draught ox. The use of horse-drawn carts and heavier wagons became common, and more goods could be transported greater distances. By increasing the distance over which perishable goods could be transported without spoilage, the horse assisted in the support of the population of growing cities.

The Romans, with their access to Asia and Africa, were able to make various experiments in the use of unique and exotic animals for transport. Probably no one has since gone to the lengths of the Emperor Heliogabalus. He used teams of naked young girls to pull his carriage, as well as experimenting with the use of such unusual draught animals as leopards, tigers, lions, and stags.[93] It is a tribute to the skill of Roman animal-trainers that they were able to harness such bizarre beasts successfully, but it is to be doubted whether any of their experiments resulted in any advance in the theory and practice of transport.

The camel finds a certain place in transport in Merovingian Gaul. Caravans of camels laden with gold and silver were captured in southern France.[94] A bishop who visited Bishop Aurelian in Uzes had a camel to carry his luggage.[95] The old Queen

E

Brunehilde was placed on a camel and paraded in mockery before her enemies before being bound to the tails of wild horses and dragged to her death.[96] The parading of criminals on camels was also practised in Visigothic Spain.[97] Little more is heard of camels in Europe. The Moslems reintroduced them to Spain in 1019 and to Sicily in 1058.[98] The adaptable Crusaders made good use of captured camels after the battle of Dorylaeum in Asia Minor in 1097.[99] Since the camel is physically unsuited to most of Europe, it is doubtful whether any importations had much more than curiosity value.

Elephants found uses in peace-time as well as in war in the ancient world. The colossus of Nero, a statue supposed to have been a hundred feet high, was moved by the power of twenty-four elephants.[100] The ownership of elephants was restricted to the emperor and they were used to draw huge chariots with images of the gods and emperors.[101] Elephants seem to have disappeared with the empire in the west but they lingered on in the eastern empire and were still to be found in Constantinople in the reign of Constantine Monomachos around 1050. In medieval times elephants were not utilised as draught animals but were esteemed for their curiosity value and as symbols of good fortune. (See above, pp 31 and 32, for the transport of medieval elephants.)

Attempts to tame and utilise exotic animals did little for the progress of transport. With the possession of the ox and the horse (suitably modified by castration), western Europe had the most powerful and tractable draught animals the world had to offer. The elephant, while more powerful, is slow and can work only four hours a day. The use of the water buffalo is limited to suitably wet areas. In the New World, the North American Indians had only the dog as a draught animal, and South America had to make do with the limited load-carrying capacity of the llama. Northern Europe had some success using reindeer and even elks as draught and riding animals.[104]

Late Roman vehicles. From a cursory survey it would appear that much is known of Roman vehicles. Dozens of types of vehicle are mentioned in the surviving literature. A corresponding number of vehicle types are represented in funerary reliefs, triumphal columns, mosaics, and Pompeian wall-paintings. However, nowhere is the type of vehicle named along with its graphic representation. Certain deductions can be made but careful scholars admit that while we have the names of the vehicles and pictures of vehicles, it is hazardous to attempt to apply the one to the other.[103]

Scholars were not always so cautious. Older books on classical antiquities are embellished with line drawings, usually taken from existing monuments such as Trajan's column but occasionally derived from the delineator's imagination, all carefully and confidently identified with type-names of vehicles drawn from the literature. The man responsible for much of the confidence and certainty with which most scholars have treated Roman land transport was Johann Christian Ginzrot, whose elegant drawings have been reproduced countless times in classical dictionaries, encyclopedias, and other works.[104]

Ginzrot did not stop with drawings of the whole vehicles but even included detailed sketches showing the construction and functioning of various wagon components based, in part, on his own vast experience as a master coach-builder. He is still quoted as *the* authority in the Smithsonian Report for 1934[105] and even more recent scholars have echoed his praises.[106] The warning given by Lefebvre des Noëttes that Ginzrot, Grivaud de la Vincelle, and the French Encyclopedia had merely repeated old errors remained largely unheeded.[107]

Because of the perishable nature of the materials used in making vehicles, archaeology is of little help in providing actual vehicles to the student of Roman transport. Beyond the remains of a litter (*lectica*) excavated at Rome on the Esquiline hill in 1874,[108] and a few wheels unearthed at Newstead in Scotland (see p 76 below) and the Saalburg in Germany in the early twentieth century, little exists of the remains of actual vehicles.

It is a curious fact, but linguistic analysis reveals that a surprising number of the Latin names for vehicles and their parts are borrowed from the Celtic.[109] The conclusion seems inescapable that the Romans borrowed not only the names but the vehicles themselves from their Celtic conquests, and that the Celts, not the Romans, were the master carriage-builders of early Europe. A Swiss historian states that while the Celts provided the vehicles, the Romans furnished roads suitable for them to run on.[110] It is probable that the Celts easily made the transition from building chariots for war to constructing freight wagons for peacetime.[111]

The Theodosian Code, promulgated in the fifth century, regulates the loads which can be transported in various vehicles and specifies the number of draught animals to be used. Solicitude is even shown for the animals. '. . . No person shall use a club in driving, but shall employ either a switch or at the most a whip in the tip of which a short prick has been inserted, by which the lazy limbs of the animals may be tickled into action, and the driver must not force the animals to exert themselves beyond their strength . . .'[112]

The limitations placed on the weights to be carried, i.e. 1,000lb on a carriage (*reda*), 200lb on a two-wheel vehicle (*birota*), and 30lb on a posthorse,[113] seem absurdly low and have long been a puzzle to scholars. Various conjectures have been made in an attempt to explain the reasons for the limitations. Among the theories advanced are: concern for the roads to prevent their breaking up, small size and lack of strength in the draught animals, inefficient harnessing and lack of horseshoes, and solicitude for the health and wellbeing of the animals.

The number of draught animals is also specified for various vehicles. For example: 'Eight mules shall be yoked to a carriage, in the summer season, of course, but ten in the winter. We judge that three mules are sufficient for a two-wheeled conveyance.[114] Not only are the weights to be carried absurdly low, but the number of animals provided is exceedingly high. As the Romans are not supposed to have understood harnessing in file (*tandem*—but see p 81 below), they must presumably have harnessed side-by-side. It is highly unlikely that eight (or ten) mules harnessed side-by-side drawing one wagon, with a 1,000lb payload, could have been accommodated on even the widest Roman roads. Similarly, three mules pulling a 200lb load in a two-wheeled vehicle posed problems of control as well as of harnessing. Although the nineteenth century furnished examples of twenty-mule teams driven by one man, the animals were harnessed tandem in pairs and not all ranged side-by-side. The problems of control, while difficult, were successfully accomplished by the highly-skilled professional drivers with the aid of extremely long whips and colourful vocabularies. Animals harnessed in file are constrained to follow the manoeuvres of their fellows while those harnessed side-by-side have more opportunity to be individualistic. In the situation envisaged by the Theodosian Code perhaps only a few of the animals were harnessed to the vehicle at one time, the others being led along without loads for use as reliefs or to assist in difficult passages.

It seems that more solicitude was felt for the animals than for the soldiers. Each legion, while on the march, was only allowed to appropriate two postwagons (*Angariae*) with two yoke of oxen for each and these vehicles were only for the sick.[115]

The load limit of 30lb to a post-horse seems particularly low because here, at least, the question of inefficient harness throttling the horse should not arise. If the horse was saddled and ridden by a courier, as seems from other provisions to have been the case,[116] the total weight borne by the horse reaches reasonable proportions; but if the animal was merely led as a supplementary post-horse (*parhippus*) or packhorse, the load is ludicrous.

The seemingly wasteful provisions of excess animal power may indicate only that the possession of surplus horsepower for status and display purposes is not just a contemporary phenomenon. The imperial authority even found it necessary to place limits on the size of vehicles. Those workmen who made vehicles larger than the prescribed norm were subject to severe punishments, exile for the free and perpetual labour in the mines for the slave.[117]

That the 1,000lb payload is not the only factor to be considered is made clear by the limits placed on the number of riders. Not more than two men, or three at the most, can be conveyed on each wagon and they must be custodians and official escorts.[118] Heavier weights are allowed on the post wagons which are ox-drawn. Here the load limit is 1,500lb.[119] This is a refutation of the theory that it was only in harnessing the horse that the ancients were inefficient. It has been held that the ox yoke was rational and efficacious.[120] The 1,500lb limit for ox-drawn vehicles is an indication that ox harness was little more efficient than equine. Perhaps the smallness and weakness of the draught cattle is responsible for the low limit. The evidence of the Theodosian Code is not satisfied by any of the theories which have been advanced.

This problem has been studied intensively by Henri Polge (*L'Amelioration de l'Attelage*, 28-34), who advances several reasons for Roman difficulties with heavy transport. By adopting paving with large blocks the Romans made traction difficult for the draught animals and increased the likelihood of vehicles slipping. By using extremely steep gradients they increased the difficulties of ascent and made descent practically impossible. The Romans had neither adequate bits to control a horse in a steep descent nor sufficient drags or brakes to control a heavily loaded vehicle on a steeply slanted and slippery pavement. To take proper advantage of the camber (the bulge in the centre to provide proper drainage) of the Roman roads it would have been necessary to use dished wheels—concave wheels with the tyres wider spread than the hubs when mounted on an axle—but dished wheels were not invented until the fifteenth century (at least in Europe, but see Joseph Needham, *Science and Civilisation in China,* Vol 4, Part II, (Cambridge, 1965), 76-8, where 'dishing' is said to be found in China in the fourth and third centuries BC). Polge also states that since the Romans did not have pivoted front axles, they could only turn their four-wheeled vehicles with difficulty by sliding them around corners. The Romans were also limited by having no solution, such as ball or roller bearings, to the problem of friction between the hub and the axle. All these factors, then, as well as the inferiority of ancient horse-harness, tended to limit drastically the loads that could be drawn over the Roman roads.

Another point brought out by Polge (op cit 35-6) is that the *cursus publicus* had an obligation to maintain a certain speed. With this in mind, the loads allowed by the Theodosian Code are seen to be comparable with those prescribed for similar services in France in 1776. The real improvements in speed and capacity, according to Polge, come in the eighteenth and nineteenth centuries rather than the Middle Ages, and consist of improvements in road construction, lessening of gradients, improvements in vehicles, better organisation of posting facilities, rationally bred draught cattle and horses, improved suspension and brakes, ball and roller bearings, and lubrication.

The Edict on Prices of Diocletian, published in 301, provides additional evidence for Roman practice by establishing prices for various types of transport, vehicles, and even parts of vehicles. Whether or not these prices were observed, the data do give some insight into Roman materials and practices concerning transport. Prices are established for the wooden parts of vehicles, including axles, hubs, spokes, seats, forks, and wagon tongues. Higher valuation is set on turned than on unturned pieces.[121]

The detailed enumeration is convincing evidence that wood was the primary material for ancient vehicles, contrary to the opinion expressed by Kreisel that ancient vehicles were executed in bronze and decorated with noble metals while medieval vehicles were made of wood.[122] (Kreisel perhaps took the ornament for the substance or accepted bronze votive offerings as truly representing the real vehicle.) The types of vehicles listed in the Edict include freight wagons, four-wheeled passenger wagons, wagons for sleeping, four-wheeled travelling wagons, four-wheeled wagons with yoke, and two-wheeled freight wagons with yoke. The importance and value given to good wheels is seen in the fact that wagons with the fellies (the wooden parts making up the circumference of the wheels) in one piece sold for nearly twice the price of wagons whose wheels had fellies made up of joined pieces.[123]

The construction of a felly in one piece presupposes considerable ability in woodworking. It is not likely that the felly was cut out whole from a large piece of timber (this would be extremely expensive and entail the spoilage of much timber), but rather that a piece of wood was bent to form a complete circle. Steaming is the most likely process to be employed for this purpose. In addition, it seems that the wheels were furnished with iron tyres, for the prices of the tyres and ironwork for the vehicles were computed separately.[124]

As already mentioned, wheels from Roman times actually exist. Two nearly complete wheels, which closely parallel the description in the Edict, were found at the excavation of the frontier post at Newstead in Scotland. The wheels are three feet in diameter with a thick hub fifteen and a half inches in depth. The felly is made from a single piece of ash bent by some process entailing artificial softening and the ends of the piece of ash are bolted together with an iron plate. The wheels contain eleven spokes each and are probably made of willow. The hub is quite elaborate, made of elm, probably turned on a lathe, and lined with an iron ring to protect it from wear. The wheels have iron tyres three-eighths of an inch thick and one and three-quarter inches wide. In addition, the remains of a larger wheel, three feet five inches in diameter, were found. This wheel was coarser and heavier in type, with twelve spokes. It had no iron mountings and its felly was made up of six sections joined together with wooden dowels.[125] The clever use of different woods for different purposes should be noted.[126] This must have come as a result of long experience and great familiarity with the properties of the materials used. Great skill is required in the making of wheels identical with each other. Certainly one of the earliest examples of standardisation is the making of a set of wheels for a vehicle.

The material of which a load is composed has some bearing

on the size and weight of the load. The length and width of
a vehicle bed prescribe two of the measurements of a load, and
practical considerations, such as the height of an underpass
or the balance of the loaded vehicle, limit its height. Materials
of high density may make up a load without filling the space
available, while light materials reach the limits of available
space before approaching the weight limit. Some indication
of this is found in the Edict. Both a standard wagon-load of
goods and a wagon-load of wood are limited to 1,200lb, while
a camel can carry 600lb of goods but only 400lb of wood.
Judging from the tariffs charged, an ass-load of general goods
should equal one half of a camel-load, or 300lb, while an ass-
load of wood would be only 200lb.[127] The bulky nature of the
wood made it impossible to reach the weight limit which the
pack-animal could have carried.

In a disreputable section of Pompeii a very curious vehicle

Fig 2   Wine wagon from Pompeii, AD 79

is depicted.[128] It is actually a great wine skin which has been fitted to an oddly shaped four-wheeled wagon. The painting has been characterised as 'a slovenly daub in the original',[129] but line drawings have been made from it which make it possible to say something of the technical construction of the wagon. The artists, either of the original or of the line drawings, had difficulty in understanding the details of construction and also encountered difficulties in rendering perspective correctly. The picture has frequently been adduced as proving that the Romans had pivoted front-axles, but this is not certain from the drawing. The wheels are placed under two inverted truncated pyramids which hold the frame on which the wine skin is cradled. Parts of all four wheels show, but neither the right front nor the left rear wheel is really connected by an axle to the body. The space between the front and rear truncated pyramids has been called an opening to permit the front wheels to turn corners, but this is not necessarily true, because the wheels, as represented, are too high to pass under the body frame. Unfortunately, owing to the lack of precision in the drawing, it is not possible to reach definite conclusions about this vehicle. In fact, from the upward slanting position of the horse yoke, it is evident that the yoke is free to move in a vertical plane. For it also to move in a horizontal plane, a sort of universal joint would be required and this would represent more technical sophistication than a pivoted front-axle.

Little need be said of other Pompeian vehicle representations, which are frankly of a purely imaginative type. The vehicles are conventional two-wheeled chariots but the motive power is unusual. Chariots are shown drawn by pairs of hinds and gazelles, with wheels which lack axles or other attachments to the cars, and with only the hand-held reins serving to connect the animals with the chariots.[130] Other chariots are shown drawn by swans, a lion and tiger team, and a griffin.[131] The most fantastic of these pictures shows a chariot pulled by a green parrot, hitched by a red collar to shafts, and driven by a grasshopper holding the parrot's reins in its mouth.[132]

More serious representations of Roman methods of land transport can be found in the bas-reliefs on certain sepulchral monuments such as those of Arlon in Belgium, and Igel and Neumagen on the Moselle in Germany. An Arlonese fragment shows only the front half of a team of horses. Nothing is seen of the vehicle to which the horses are attached by solid shafts kept in place by a belly band and what is possibly a sort of neck collar.[133] Another fragment shows a light, two-wheeled vehicle whose body is in the form of a wickerwork basket. This cart is drawn by a single horse attached to the body by solid shafts.[134] The falsity of the belief that the ancients did not know how to harness animals singly but only in pairs is shown by this fragment. (Other examples are reproduced in Needham, *Science and Civilisation in China,* Vol. 4, Part II, Plates CCX, CCXI.)

A large barrel containing about 106 gallons (or 400 litres) mounted on a four-wheeled wagon frame is represented on a bas-relief in the Museum of Langres.[135] The wagon has an undercarriage but it is difficult to determine whether the front wheels pivot. The vehicle is drawn by three fat mules with neck bands, but other details of the harnessing are not clear.

On the west side of the Secundini monument at Igel near the top (*Attika*) is a bas-relief of a light two-wheeled cart drawn by two mules and carrying two persons.[136] This vehicle is pictured as a *cisium* in Daremberg-Saglio.[137] While the cart accords well with literary descriptions, the designation is by no means certain. Again, a solid shaft leads from the cart body along the right-hand side of the nearest mule terminating in a collar which is mounted high on the animal's neck. The reins also pass through rings on the collar. The rest of the harnessing is problematical. Whether there is a shaft on the left side of the animal or shafts for the other mule is unknown.

On the lower part of the west side of the pedestal is a vehicle of a different type. This is a four-wheeled freight-wagon with an undercarriage, heavily laden with large bundles carefully secured with ropes. The wagon is pulled by three mules of which the nearest wears a neck collar and is connected with his partner by a yoke. Neither traces, shafts, nor pole are visible. The harnessing method used for the third mule is not seen nor is it clear why he is there. Possibly he is only accompanying the others to act as a relief or to assist over difficult stretches. He may even be one of the supplementary post-animals spoken of in the Theodosian Code.

Similar harnessing arrangements are seen on the monument of Lucius Securius at Neumagen.[138] Here again are three mules, two of whom pull, while the third carries his head high. As only a portion of the relief remains, no trace of the vehicle and only the front half of the team is seen. While the neck collar seems to be placed too high for effective pulling, this is an apparent, rather than real, impediment. The mules with their heads down are pulling effectively. It is clear from the relief that they are exerting pressure against the yoke and not against the collar. With their heads carried low, like oxen, the yoke is actually quite efficient, and the pressure is not against their windpipes but against the bony structure of their shoulders. The collar acts merely as a support for a ring through which the guiding reins pass. It channels the reins and brings them more conveniently to hand.

A vehicle with no visible means of propulsion is also seen at Neumagen.[139] This is a special-purpose vehicle like that at Langres, made up of a large barrel laid lengthwise on the platform of a four-wheeled wagon. Both the draught animals and the wheels are missing, apparently broken off. Some details of the undercarriage are visible. It consists of two axles connected by a long pole, which is necessary to provide stiffening for two supports which rise from each axle to hold the wagon platform. Unfortunately the front axle is almost completely effaced, making it difficult to determine whether the front wheels swivelled. If the front axle duplicated the rear, as seems likely from what remains, then it was non-pivotable.

Although mules seem to be the usual beast of burden, enough horses are found to cast doubt on the assertion of Duval that horses were not used for work in the Gallo-Roman period.[140] Additional doubt is caused by the representation of a reaping machine *c* AD 200, pushed by a single horse or mule.[141]

As might be expected from its position closer to the frontier (*Limes*), Roman remains are rarer, cruder, and more fragmented in Roman Germany than in Roman Gaul. Few representations of vehicles exist. Among them is a tablet from Vaihingen, preserved at the museum of Stuttgart, which shows a four-wheeled wagon with light, eight-spoked wheels, loaded with an indeterminate large object, driven by a man seated on its front, and drawn by three horses with their heads held high.[142] No details of the wagon or harness are discernible. There is also a grave monument from Baden-Baden in the Karlsruhe museum showing a four-wheeled wagon, with the front and rear axles connected by a pole. The spokes of the wheels, while not clear, are very numerous, numbering at least twelve per wheel. The wagon is heavily loaded and is drawn by two horses while the driver holds a whip in his right hand. The sides of the wagon-box are staked rather than solid.[143] Technical details of the vehicle and its method of attachment to the horses are not visible.

A unique representation was found at Langres in 1849. It consists of fragments which, when fitted together, show a four-wheeled wagon being drawn by four horses, arranged in pairs, with one pair harnessed in front of the other. This relief, dating perhaps from the second century, AD, is the only known representation of tandem harnessing under the Romans. There is no doubt as to the stone's authenticity, or of the manner in which the fragments have been fitted together. Details of harnessing are not clear, but the reins for all four horses seem to be guided through rings set high on the necks while the weight of the load is probably sustained by a collar placed on the lower neck or shoulders.[144] If this relief is a true representation, it casts serious doubt on the assertion that the Romans could only harness animals side-by-side, and lends practicality to the provisions of the Theodosian Code referring to the number of animals to be used in pulling certain vehicles.

Early medieval vehicles. Certain of the sources for the study of transport, such as the funerary bas-reliefs, are brought to a conclusion by the end of Roman rule. Nevertheless, enough material exists to prove that there was never a complete cessation of wheeled traffic in western Europe. Archaeological remains are very few. The Dejbjerg wagon found in Denmark belongs to antiquity (first century BC), but is an enduring tribute to the skill of the Celtic wagon-builders who exported it to Scandinavia. The wagon found with the Oseberg ship in Norway (ninth century AD) is the only genuine early medieval vehicle that still exists. A comparison of the two is worthwhile.

Both vehicles were found only in pieces, hence the vehicles as seen today owe much to the skill of the restorer. Deductions made from the vehicles as they now exist must therefore be tinged with caution. However, it is certain that the Dejbjerg wagon is of a slim and elegant cast with extremely light and modern-looking wheels. The whole vehicle is of very skilful workmanship. The hubs were turned on a lathe and, what is even more surprising, transverse grooves were found inside the hubs. Opinion is divided as to the purpose of these grooves. Some hold them to be receptacles for wooden rods to act as roller-bearings between the hub and the axle.[145] Since flat strips rather than rollers were found in the hubs at the time of the excavation, these do not appear to be primitive roller-bearings. The opinion is expressed that the grooves perhaps held greased leather or wool or rag packing.[146] The efficacy of such an arrangement is, at best, doubtful. As restored, the pole for the draught animals is attached firmly to the chassis. If the restoration is correct, this severely limits the manoeuvrability.[147] The consensus is, however, that the undercarriage was intended for turning.[148]

The Oseberg wagon, although built approximately eight hundred years later than that of Dejbjerg, seems much heavier and more pedestrian in its running gear. The wagon body, which is the usual focus of attention, is very richly and skilfully ornamented with carvings, but the wheels are thick and clumsy with none of the Dejbjerg refinements. It is claimed that the Oseberg wagon is incorrectly restored and cannot be used to prove the existence of a pivoted front axle in medieval times. [149]

The perishable nature of the materials used in wagon-building and the hard usage to which most vehicles were subjected militate against their survival. The spread of Christianity brought with it a decline in the practice of burying goods and valuables with the deceased and so limits the number of survivals. As a result, no actual remains of the vehicles pictured in the illuminated manuscripts and the Bayeux Tapestry have survived.

A survey of methods of transport in western Europe after the end of the Roman Empire in the west should be instructive. In Ireland, never conquered and little affected by Roman influence, a continuance of pre-Roman, Celtic culture and wagon-building techniques can be expected. In Merovingian Gaul, the preponderance of the Celtic substratum in the population should result in some survival of Celtic technical skill as well as some trace of Roman organisational ability. The case of England may be somewhat different, as Romano-British techniques may have been largely replaced by those of the Anglo-Saxon invaders.

Despite the claims of Giraldus Cambrensis that there were no roads in Ireland,[150] it seems that the Irish were well furnished with roads and vehicles before and after the introduction of Christianity.[151] The Irish were the last of the Celts to continue the use of war chariots, which were employed in battle as late as AD 637.[152] The war chariot had the same structure as the travelling chariot but was embellished with scythes, spikes, points, and sharp edges.[153] The Irish chariot had a wooden frame, which was covered with wickerwork and sometimes adorned with tin, two shafts projecting to the rear, a pole with a single yoke for two horses, and two wheels, sometimes made completely of iron or brass, but when made of wood always tyred with iron.[154] Two-wheeled chariots are shown on a ninth-century cross at Clonmacnois, one with six-spoked wheels, the other with eight-spoked wheels. The chariots appear to be drawn by single horses but no details of harnessing are visible.[155] Little mention is made of farm and work vehicles in the Irish literature but they were coarsely built, drawn by oxen, and probably furnished with cheaper, solid wheels.[156]

The literary sources have occasional references to vehicles throughout the early medieval period but it is seldom possible to derive much information concerning types of vehicles and details of construction from such occasional mentions. The reference to St Columba (*c* 520-95) being scandalised at the sight of a cleric in Ireland, sitting in a car, gaily driving over the plain of Brega[157] is more typical than items which give technical details, such as, St Columba rode safely in a carriage whose wheels had not been secured by linch-pins.[158] The presence of linch-pins presupposes wheels that turn on the axle, rather than wheels which are fixed to the axle and turn with it as a unit. Vehicles were in use even on the small island of Iona where St Columba established his mission. In the summer in which he died, he was drawn in a wagon to the little western plain of Iona.[159] No mention is made of what draught animals were used.

On the continent around 575 food was brought to St Columba's near namesake, St Columban, at Anegray, in a horse-drawn wagon.[160] This is noteworthy as being an early use of the horse for work, rather than for the transport of the aristocracy. Usually the draught animal is not specified in the literary sources. In one instance a litter (*basterna*) carried by untamed bulls was driven off a bridge in order to drown a girl.[161]

The sick Sigivald was lifted in a litter (*basterna*) and carried to another villa on the advice of a bishop.[162] Ecdicius, a relative of Apollinaris Sidonius, transported over four thousand poor and starving people to his house by horse and wagon *(cum equitibus et plaustris)* and fed them during a famine in Burgundy.[163] In this passage, it should be noted that the horses did not necessarily pull the wagons. It is likely that two different means of transport were utilised. That even Merovingian armies did not live completely off the land as they moved is seen by their use of baggage wagons which were left behind with the less important people (*cum populo minori*) when a rapid strike was made.[164]

Transport was not neglected in Charlemagne's army. Ancient custom was formalised and each man was required to furnish food for a three months' march and arms and clothing for six months.[165] Carts were to be provided for the equipment of the king, bishops, counts, abbots, and nobles. Flour, wine, pork, and victuals in abundance were to be carried as well as mills, adzes, axes, augers, and slings. Stones for the slingers were to be carried on twenty beasts of burden, if necessary.[166] Waterproofed carts, covered with sewn-together skins, were supposed to be furnished to the army, so that rivers could be crossed without damaging the contents.[167]

More detailed instructions are given to Abbot Fulrad: the carts are to contain axes, planes, augers, boards, spades, iron shovels, and other utensils needed by an army. Discipline was also to be enforced so that the men would not ravage the parts of the realm they marched through. The men were to march with the carts and horsemen, always controlled by a leader, and taking nothing from the countryside but fodder, wood, and water.[168] The Avar treasure was brought to Charlemagne at Aachen in fifteen wagon-loads, each drawn by four oxen. The information concerning the number of wagon-loads and the draught animals comes only from late sources, but probably represents a genuine tradition.[169]

Vehicles were known and used by the Anglo-Saxons. It is difficult to say whether they learned of the use of vehicles from the Celtic inhabitants of Roman Britain or whether they developed their vehicles independently. Pictures of vehicles are found in illuminated manuscripts of the Anglo-Saxons. These include two- and four-wheeled vehicles pulled by men as well as by animals, and even strongly built travelling wagons with leather roofs intended for long journeys.[170] The value of such illustrations as evidence is limited both by the capability of the artist to represent accurately what he has seen, and his frequent

F

lack of understanding of the relations and functions of component parts. One of the vehicles represented is a two-wheeled chariot drawn by two horses and driven by a woman.[174] Unfortunately, details are lacking. The wheels are not connected to the body, nor are the horses harnessed, but only linked to the chariot by the reins. Such a method of connection would require not only Herculean arms on the driver but mouths of iron for the horses. The artist is evidently not worried about such minor points, but is confident that he has conveyed the essence of the vehicle and that anyone familiar with horses and chariots will be able to fill in mentally the requisite harness, axle, and so on.

Among the more unusual Anglo-Saxon vehicles is the one represented in the manuscript of Aelfric's translation of the Pentateuch (British Museum, Cotton. Claudius B. IV fol 60R). It seems to be a four-wheeled wagon with two poles rising from the axle-trees with a hammock slung between them. But is this what the artist really intended? He has represented a four-wheeled wagon by showing only two wheels. May not his two posts and hammock hooks really indicate the presence of four—one at each corner of the wagon? If so, the ride would certainly not be quite so uncontrolled and would approach the swaying comfort of a litter. The manuscript is variously assigned to the ninth, eleventh, and twelfth centuries, with modern opinion favouring the first half of the eleventh century.[172] Whatever may be its true date, it is one of the earliest medieval attempts to mitigate the shocks of the road for a passenger by means of suspension. A possible predecessor of this system is that reconstructed and described by Ivan Venedikov from archaeological finds of the late Roman period (third century AD) in Thrace.[173] (See below, p 122). If this Anglo-Saxon drawing actually represents a real vehicle, its only parallel is the tenth-century report by an Arab source of a large suspended carriage used by Slav rulers in south-east Europe[174] (see below p 123).

The Anglo-Saxons even built vehicles for special purposes. In the Life of St Godric of Finchale a very sick man had a bier made on wheels to which horses were hitched as if to a chariot. He had himself placed on the bier and was brought to the sepulchre of St Godric, where he was cured by a miracle. He walked away in perfect health leaving the bier-wagon as a witness to the miracle which had been performed there.[175]

The Bayeux Tapestry shows a four-wheeled wagon being used to load Duke William's ships for the invasion of England. It is pulled by two men harnessed by shoulder straps. The wagon has unique eight-spoked wheels, each spoke with its own felly. The staked body is loaded with a large wine barrel. Helmets surmount each body stake and lances are also stacked vertically in the wagon.[176] That vehicles were not lacking in early Norman England is seen by the fact that the body of King Malcolm of Scotland, killed in 1093, was brought to Tynemouth on a cart by two natives.[177] Another mention of vehicles is found in a charter of Cluny at about the same time, during the rule of Abbot Hugh, when the lords of Beresi speak of the *plaustrum* which they have in Peronna.[178] Professor Ganshof suggests that in this context *plaustrum* probably refers to the right to command transport from the inhabitants of a certain place, but it also implies the existence of some sort of vehicle to be used for the transport.

After his murder in the New Forest in 1100, the body of William Rufus was brought to Winchester in a horse-drawn vehicle by a few country people.[179] This passage is illuminating for two reasons. In classical Latin a *rheda* signified a luxurious, four-wheeled travelling wagon. Here it designates something much simpler, probably a rustic cart, possibly even a form of litter. This is only one of many similar illustrations where the classical vocabulary is still used to identify objects which no longer bear a close resemblance to their antique counterparts. The passage also indicates that the use of horses has spread to the lower orders of society and that horses can be used for work as well as for aristocratic transport. This dovetails well with the evidence offered at nearly the same time by the Bayeux Tapestry's picture of a horse harrowing and Pope Urban's mention of plough horses (above, p 69). Horses were becoming more numerous, even when allowance is made for the increase in human population. Their availability, and the development of more efficient harness, made it possible to use them in tasks prevously thought inappropriate for horses. The increased supply and the reduced price made horse-owning more common and lessened the aristocratic prestige surrounding the beast.

At times unusual uses are made of medieval vehicles. A prefiguring of the Hussite wagon-fortresses is seen in the Gothic Wars of Justinian, where wagons were used by John's soldiers at Ostia to form a barricade around the camp. This adoption of the *Wagenburg* by the imperial forces would probably not have taken place had it not been for the fact that the wagons could not be used to transport supplies to Rome because the oxen were half-dead from hunger and the road was rather narrow.[180] The *Wagenburg* has a long history among the wandering Germanic tribes and the Central Asian nomads. The Visigoths used it in the form of a perfect circle at the battle of Adrianople in 378.[181] A much earlier use of this technique among the Hebrews may be found in 1 Sam xvii. 20 and 1 Sam xxvi. 5, 7. English translations usually give the word 'trench' but German versions often have *Wagenburg*, from a Hebrew word in the margin which may be transliterated 'magal' —wagon. Another extraordinary use of vehicles was made by the citizens of the north Italian cities, who mounted their standards on the *carroccio,* a large, four-wheeled platform drawn by oxen. This unique conveyance was a morale factor and rallying point rather than a real war vehicle.[182]

That extremely useful invention, the wheelbarrow, seems not to have been in existence in antiquity, but to have been a medieval innovation. No Roman remains or representations of wheelbarrows exist. Linguistically and historically, its origins remain a puzzle.[183] Its Latin name *birota* (still to be seen in the French *brouette*) is found as far back as the Theodosian Code,[184] but there it means a two-wheeled, animal-drawn cart. The name *birota* indicates that the wheelbarrow as first used had two wheels, but no pictures exist of such vehicles.[185] We would expect that the earliest attempts would result in small, hand-drawn, load-carrying carts of the rickshaw variety. But the wheelbarrow is distinguished from other wheeled vehicles in that it is the only one which is habitually pushed rather than pulled and, from its earliest depictions, it has only one wheel.[186] Early representations are among the sculptures of the church of Saint-Spire at Corbeil, constructed in the twelfth century during the reign of Louis VII, on a glass window of Chartres cathedral from about 1200,[187] and in a Bible of the thirteenth century from the abbey of Saint-Bertin, which shows a king, a bishop, and a commoner seated in a wheelbarrow, being pushed to Hell by a devil with one wooden leg, who is assisted by another demon harnessed to the front of the barrow and playing the bagpipes as he leads the way.[188]

While the origin of the wheelbarrow remains obscure, it is a reasonable speculation that men, who must frequently have had occasion to pick up the shafts of two-wheeled carts and push them about in order to hitch them to draught-animals, should have conceived the idea of a smaller, man-sized cart which could easily be handled and would be convenient for transporting small loads. The first men who tried the new vehicle would immediately realise that efficiency and economy could both be enhanced by dispensing with one of the wheels (always a complicated and expensive item when made by hand tools). A one-wheeled barrow is much easier to turn and manoeuvre and requires only a narrow track. Another possible derivation for the wheelbarrow would be the replacement of the front man carrying a stretcher or litter by a single wheel.[189] In western eyes, this would dispense with the need for the additional man, and they may never have conceived the Chinese idea of taking away all load-carrying duties from the remaining man and using him only for balance and propulsion as in the Oriental balanced barrow.

The sledge is a wheel-less vehicle usually thought of as being useful only when the ground is covered with snow, but in fact sledge-type vehicles can be effectively used over bare ground under many conditions.[190] In steep terrain they are more easily controlled than wheeled vehicles. They slide easily over wet grass. During the transitional period from winter to spring the roads can be spared hard usage and consequent rutting and repair by the use of sledges over unimproved ground. The tax on wheeled vehicles was sometimes avoided by the use of sledges. When sledges were used on roads, water was often splashed in front of and beneath the runners in order to lessen friction and prevent ignition of the runners. Various forms of grease and whale oil were also used to coat the sliding surface and make passage over city cobblestones easier. When the temperature was sufficiently low, the water coating became ice and reduced friction to a very low figure.[191]

In the colder climate of Scandinavia, winter was actually the time when transport was easiest. By long acquaintance with frigid conditions, the inhabitants were able not only to acclimatise themselves but also to take advantage of their temporary ascendancy over friction. The use of skis and snowshoes was known from early times and enabled individuals to transcend the normal limitations imposed by rocky and uneven paths. The snow not only levelled the inequalities but preserved the underlying land from harm when it was passed over. Snowshoes enabling man to spread his weight over a larger area and so cross soft snow without sinking are found in Norway at least as early as the tenth century[192] (see above, p 61).

That people outside Scandinavia could also travel in winter is shown by the Alpine crossing of the Emperor Henry IV in the winter of 1077 (see above, p 34). The transit was as unusual as it was unexpected. Although a winter passage of the Alps was then unheard of, ingenuity as well as audacity saw the party through. The difficulties are vividly described by Lambert of Hersfeld (Annales, under 1077). The men slipped, rolled, and fell on the slippery snow and ice. The queen and her ladies sat on ox skins and were drawn down the mountain. Some horses were moved with the help of machines, others had their hooves tied together and were slid on their backs, but many died or were badly hurt. Few survived the ordeal in sound condition.

SOME DIFFICULTIES AND LIMITATIONS

The effects of climate often limited but seldom prevented transport. Sudden changes in weather were expected and regarded as inevitable. Discomfort was an expected fact of travel; only its degree was changed by climatic fluctuations. Medieval man may occasionally have objected, but he was still able to travel when events made it necessary. In an incident in Merovingian times, the king's command forced the bishops to meet at Metz in November. The bishops travelled despite heavy rains and unbearable cold. The roads were deep in mud and the rivers were in flood.[193]

The coming of winter to the more temperate parts of western Europe usually put a stop to the efforts of many transporters and brought isolation to most of the inhabitants. Neither clothing nor equipment was adequate to the task of winter travel. Wheeled vehicles were unsuited to snow. Their weight was concentrated on too small an area to be supported by the snow surface. Consequently, both vehicles and the draught animals sank deeply and moved only with great difficulty. Ice, while it might support great weights, brought such almost frictionless conditions that equilibrium was affected and traction lost. Even horseshoes were of little use in snow and ice.

On the other hand, in localities where a hard winter was normal, it was a time of opportunity and was eagerly awaited for the performance of certain tasks. A deep snow cover made the whole land a highway for sledges, snowshoes, and skis. The cold congealed the sap in the trees and made winter an ideal time for lumbering operations. The slight friction of sled runners on the snow allowed for the transport of enormous loads with the expenditure of little energy. Logs could be brought to the woodworker or left on a stream bank to await the spring thaws and easy water transport downstream on a watercourse augmented by the melting snow.

Travel to such localities as Novgorod in Russia was easier in the winter and the Greek and Arab traders came there on dog sleds loaded only with themselves and the coins they brought for trading.[194] Presumably they returned the way they came with sleds loaded with goods from the north, such as furs. The freezing of streams, lakes, and even arms of the sea at times, converted them into routes usable for various types of land transport. In a bad winter in Merovingian Gaul the people crossed the streams as if they were bare ground.[195] The Vandals were able to surprise the Romanised population of Germania by crossing the frozen Rhine in the winter of 406. Transport and communication were occasionally possible across the frozen Kattegat from Denmark to Sweden.[196] In 1323, the coldest year ever recorded, even the Baltic between Sweden and Germany was crossed regularly by horses and sleighs.

The advent of spring was eagerly awaited even though it turned the snow and ice back into water, flooding the streams and bringing mud to the roads. The first travellers and traders to venture forth in the spring ran the greatest risk of being stuck in the mire. However, the urgent needs of customers after their winter isolation and the possibilities of greater profit to those first to arrive with goods combined to put the traders on their way as soon as possible. Fodder for the horses, which had limited winter travel, became available again as the grass grew beside the roads.[197]

Western Europe is a small area, but it contains many examples of the types of geographical feature that condition and limit transport. Mountains, plains, swamps, and rivers are likely to meet in chaotic combinations interposing many difficulties to land transport. To the modern eye mountains may appear beautiful, but to medieval man they were only inconvenient obstacles which had to be surmounted or which necessitated long and circuitous journeys.

The Roman network of roads had shown how a uniform system of government could be maintained over a wide area despite natural obstacles. With the decline of an effective centralised government with its systematic road maintenance, the roads lost their power to unify. The successor states had to return to the direct use of natural conditions as they found them. If there was no longer a serviceable road over the mountains there were, nonetheless, weaknesses in the mountain barrier. There were places where pack-animals could cross even if vehicles could not, where men could climb when even beasts failed.

Swamps which had been crossed by Roman causeways became obstacles again when the causeways were broken or sank in the mire. New swamps arose when the drainage culverts of the old Roman roads were allowed to become clogged. The interruption of an aqueduct or the failure of land drainage ditches contributed to swampy conditions. The geographical obstacles which arose in this manner were often more numerous and annoying than they had been before the Romans came.

Streams and rivers, despite their merits as carriers of water transport, must be regarded as interruptions and hindrances to the course of land transport. Individual travellers and their mounts could frequently achieve a crossing where a wagon loaded with perishable goods could not. Charlemagne attempted to improve this situation by the construction of waterproof carts (*Capitulare de villis, c* 64). An individual might swim, use his shield as a raft, or cross with the support of an inflated skin bag. If the depth was not excessive, the banks too steep, the current too swift, or the footing too loose, he might ford the stream, using the shaft of his lance to steady his feet. If he was fortunate, a strong peasant like St Christopher might be available to carry him dry-shod or a small boat might be for hire to ferry him over.

These methods did not usually suffice for the man attempting to cross with goods which might be spoiled by immersion in the water. He needed a dry passage above the water. The bridge was more necessary to the medieval tradesman than to the Roman because medieval goods were more frequently carried by cart.[198] A unique method of water crossing was reported of the Huns. They carried portable rafts on wagons for use in swampy areas.[199] With such a device they could make their crossings without being dependent on fords, boatmen, or bridges.

They were probably able to ferry their wagons, their animals, and themselves across on the raft, reload the raft onto the wagon, and continue their advance.

Some areas were much better favoured by nature than others for land transport. Merovingian Gaul had comparatively easy gradients to surmount and slow rivers to cross. Travel within the territory was less subject to geographical obstacles than passage over the mountains to Spain or Italy. In addition, Gaul had a legacy from the Romans of a road network and many stone bridges, which gave passage over otherwise difficult streams. Spain, in contrast, had a much more difficult terrain. The peninsula was crossed by numerous formidable mountain ranges and its rivers were so swift as to make fording or bridging difficult, and boating impossible.

The most ubiquitous artificial limitation on medieval trade and transport was the toll. The idea of the toll came to the Middle Ages from the Romans but, as frequently happens when a less sophisticated group succeeds to the control of affairs, the purpose of the regulation was forgotten and ignored. Instead of the toll proceeds being devoted to the maintenance and improvement of the road they were diverted to the coffers of the collectors.

It is not too extreme a generalisation to say that there were tolls everywhere on everything.[200] Even the simple pedestrian (if he was not a pilgrim) was subject to *peage*. Conflicting regulations bedevilled the harassed transporter. In Germany, anything which fell from a wagon could be seized by the local lord under the *Grundruhrrecht*. This encouraged the use of small wheels to lessen the likelihood of spillage.[201] On the other hand, if the axle touched the ground, the wagon was considered part of the land and belonged to the lord. To avoid this, large wheels were advisable. The rule of *Strassenzwang* compelled transporters to use certain routes. As an example, merchants going from Polen to Leipzig fair were required to travel by way of Glogau and Posen, which was three times as far as the direct way.[202] Some lords were suspected of having hidden holes dug in these routes to cause breakdowns. If a merchant tried to avoid these holes, he could be assessed for damage done to the grass by his wagon wheels. If he tried to use a ford he could be forced to cross a bridge and pay its toll. If his boat passed under a bridge, he was required to pay the charge for crossing it. Ropes were stretched across the stream to interrupt boat traffic and collect tolls. If a merchant was unlucky enough to be wrecked, under the *Strandrecht* the ship belonged to the owner of the shore.[203] Such artificial constraints, which originated from lack of centralised control, abetted by irresponsible local rulers, greatly raised the prices which consumers had to pay and so limited the quantity of goods which could find a market. Perishable goods were often spoiled by the delays occasioned by such shortsighted toll policies.[204]

Among the few likely to be exempt from toll were the members of the religious community. All travellers were examined but legitimate pilgrims were allowed to pass free. Certain monasteries were given toll exemptions.[205] The income from some tolls was assigned to particular monasteries.[206] The monastery of Corbie was given the privilege of free transport from the Fos toll to the monastery in 716,[207] and the abbots of Cormery, St Mesmin, Fleury, St Benoit, and St Aigrain had free navigation on the Loire.[208]

It was only a short step, and one often taken, from toll collection to brigandage. Only a rare lord could see beyond the advantage of the moment and comprehend the benefits to be derived from the fostering of increased economic activity. Collective action, such as the formation of merchant companies capable of self-defence while in transit, was one answer. Another was the negotiation of treaties with each authority along the route.

Neither method was likely to be successful with foreign invaders like the Magyars, Vikings and Saracens. The Vikings frequently found quicker profits in pillage and robbery than in trade. The Saracens, from their base at Fraxinetum on the Riviera, fanned out to interrupt trade and traffic in the area between the Mediterranean and Lake Geneva from 888 to 972 and were only eliminated when they outraged the public conscience by kidnapping and holding for ransom the Abbot of Cluny.[209]

IMPROVEMENTS—TECHNOLOGICAL CHANGE AND DEVELOPMENT

In assessing medieval land transport technology, it would be convenient to start from a complete knowledge of the state of Roman technology at the beginning of the medieval era. Unfortunately, the data, while much more numerous for the Roman than for the later period, are not as conclusive as was once thought. We have already seen (above, pp 70-71) how older scholars confidently took the names of vehicles from literature and matched them with the representations of vehicles on triumphal columns, wall-paintings, and funerary bas-reliefs. Living in a period of horse-drawn transport, they transposed their knowledge of how vehicles were in the eighteenth and nineteenth centuries to how they must have been in the time of the Romans. The outstanding example of this transfer technique was furnished by the master coach-builder, Johann Christian Ginzrot.

In a few cases identifications can be safely made. The *currus,* frequently described in literature as a racing-chariot, can be equated with the often-pictured vehicle used in the races in the circus. *Biga* and *quadriga* indicate the number of horses used in pulling particular vehicles. A *birota* is a two-wheeled vehicle, but so many varieties are pictured that it probably refers to a class rather than to a specific vehicle. There are also linguistic clues in the vehicle names borrowed from the Celtic. The *petorritum,* for example, derived from a Celtic word meaning four-wheeled. Positive identifications are rare and the labelled pictures in classical dictionaries, many of which derive from Ginzrot, should be accepted only with caution.

The sources for medieval land transport technology are scanty and consist of scattered references in the literary sources, illuminated manuscripts, seals, tapestries, and archaeological finds. The literary sources such as chronicles, charters, and saints' lives, are difficult to use because Latin words drawn from a classical vocabulary are often used to describe vehicles which no longer bear a resemblance, either in appearance or function, to their Roman namesakes (see above, p 87).

Early medieval illuminators often lacked the skills to repre-sent details of vehicles and harness in an accurate and practical manner. Vehicles may have no visible connection with their wheels, or horses may have nothing other than the reins to hitch them to a wagon. Such representations are of little use in forming firm opinions on the technology of early medieval transport. Artistic licence and convention result in such ve-hicles as that of the Trier Apocalypse (*c* 800), in which a round wagon, shaped somewhat like an Irish *coracle*, is placed above four wheels of varying size, with varying numbers of spokes. The size of the wheels may be only the artist's attempt to adjust the slanted vehicle-bed to the level ground rather than proof that the front wheels swivel. If he was attempting to indicate a pivoted front-axle (as suggested by Lynn White, jr)[210] it is apparent that much is lacking in the representation. There are no axles. There is no connection between the pair of horses and the front wheels and the team has no other link to the wagon than two straps from the left side of the near horse to the wagon-bed. This improbable connection would have yielded as much sideways as forward motion. The artist, then, omits a great deal in the hope (or assumption) that the eye of the beholder will comprehend.

Seals are usually too small to show much in the way of technical detail. The medium is so limited that even skilled engravers had difficulty in rendering recognisable designs. Even as late as 1396 varying perspective makes it difficult to see a wagon in the seal of Francesco of Carrara.[211] The vehicle is viewed from above but the wheels are represented as round. The effect is that of a wagon which has been crushed or flattened with the wheels laid out flat in the same plane as the wagon-bed. If this is a definite pivoting front axle, as claimed by Bertrand Gille, it is difficult to see why the almost identical rock carving from the Swedish Bronze Age has not as good a claim in which case the invention of the pivoted axle can be carried back to between 800 and 500 BC.[212] The problem then would be not to invent the pivoting axle but to determine if it survived (see below, p 118).

The Bayeux Tapestry is a unique and extremely valuable source for late eleventh-century armour, weapons, and living conditions—a time when horses had green legs, blue bodies, yellow manes, and red heads, and all the people were double-jointed[213]—but it shows little of land transport. A small four-wheeled wagon pulled by men and loaded with a wine-barrel and spears is shown at the loading of the ships for the invasion. (See above, p 87.) Coats of mail were slung on poles carried between two men. The gathering of materials for the ships and supplies for the expedition must have required a considerable effort in transport but it probably was not considered germane to the subject of the Tapestry and was not recorded by the embroiderers.[214]

The materials of which vehicles and harness are made militate against their long survival. Wood and leather are subject to frequent breaking in use and deteriorate rapidly in the moist European climate when discarded. Sometimes valuable possessions were interred with the bodies of wealthy pagans, presumably for their use in an afterlife, but this custom largely disappeared with the coming of Christianity. Consequently, archaeology reveals most about western Europe during pre-Christian times, or in areas where Christianity was late in coming, such as Scandinavia. St Boniface converted the Germans and changed their burial habits just in time to confuse the picture of the introduction of the stirrup to that area.[215] While metal pieces, particularly brass, outlast the wood and leather with which they once were joined, it is not often possible to reconstruct such articles as horse-harness from surviving metal ornaments and buckles in a way that will satisfy all scholars.[216]

Technology can assist transport by devising better methods of harnessing and controlling draught animals, and ultimately by 'improving the breeds' of the animals by selective controlled mating. It is doubtful whether the ox changed significantly during the early medieval period in respect of size, strength, or method of harnessing. The shoulder-yoke for pairs of oxen was known in antiquity and its use continued throughout the Middle Ages. Whenever it was necessary to do heavy hauling, the ox was available. The shoulder-yoke was well suited to the anatomy of the ox, and he was able to exert a significant portion of his strength continuously, with no such circulatory or respiratory restrictions as attended the use of the same type of yoke on a horse. Oxen were slow, but no faster means of heavy transport was available until a more rational horse-harness was developed. The oxen that pulled the heavy freight wagons of the Roman *cursus publicus* would have felt equally at home bringing the Avar treasure to Charlemagne, or hauling stone for cathedral construction in the twelfth century.

Oxen's lack of speed and phlegmatic disposition made them relatively easy to guide and control. Only a pointed stick or goad was necesary. It was also possible to yoke oxen over the horns. This method was developed in late antiquity. It made it possible for the oxen to hold back when descending hills but it is doubtful whether it made the oxen capable of pulling any greater weights.[217] A unique system of ox guidance is seen in an early-eleventh-century illuminated manuscript from Monte

Fig 3 Tandem harnessing of oxen, *c* 1100 (Bibliotheca Laurentiana, Florence)

Cassino.[218] The illustration shows a four-wheeled wagon being drawn by a yoke of two oxen. The oxen are driven and guided from the wagon body by reins which lead from the seated driver to the horns of the oxen. The effectiveness of this device is questionable. Oxen are usually controlled from the ground by voice and goad. It is doubtful whether enough leverage could be exerted against an ox's horn by pulling on a rein to turn or stop him. The artist's representation may be only fanciful. The question of tandem-harnessing of the ox seems bound up with that of the horse. It may have been introduced as early as the first century BC.[219] Even if introduced so early, it is doubtful whether the system of hooking one yoke of oxen in front of another became widespread until the introduction of the heavy plough into western Europe, which may not have taken place until the eighth or ninth century. Tandem-harnessing with pairs of oxen was a simpler process than it was with horses and required only that the rear of one yoke-pole be fastened to the front end of another. Systematic breeding was not practised for oxen during the early medieval period and the animal remained small and comparatively weak.

While the geographical range of the ass was extended throughout northern and western Europe by the activities of merchants and Christian missionaries, no change was made in his mode of employment or harnessing. He was primarily a pack or riding animal at this period and seldom used for drawing vehicles. His hybrid offspring, the mule, resembled the horse in strength and size but retained the patience and endurance of the ass. The mule was a great favourite as a pack-animal. The great disadvantage of the sumpter-beast, of course, is that it has to be unloaded each night in order to give it a rest and a chance to roll. A vehicle can be left loaded. The mule harness was identical with that of the horse and changed along with it. The comparative intelligence of mules made it possible for them to do work which would have been impossible for horses. The mules of Roman Gaul are praised by Claudian. He describes one muleteer controlling several mules, each individually harnessed to a cart, by his voice alone. Each mule obeyed the commands intended for him and hauled his rumbling cart unguided by a rein.[220] Ginzrot interpreted this passage as meaning that the mules were hitched in single-tandem one in front of another, all attached to the same cart.[221]

The animal whose effectiveness was most improved by technology in the early Middle Ages was the horse. Changes made him better to ride, more controllable, and able to exert greater force. Horses became more numerous, lost their status as purely aristocratic transport, and were introduced to many types of work. It is probable that the horse was the first animal of the Middle Ages to be improved by systematic breeding. Even the maligned Merovingians raised horses on their estates (Gregory of Tours, *History,* VIII, 40) and, presumably, they took some care in their matings. That Charlemagne watched horse-breeding closely is clear from the *Capitulare de villis* where *c* 13, 14, and 15 are concerned with the care and breeding of his horses. An exceptional Spanish stallion was given to William of Normandy by King Alphonso. We even have a picture of this horse.[222] If great care was taken to import exceptional stallions, less attention was given to the selection of mares for them to mate with. Nevertheless, the size and strength of horses was increased, making it possible for them to bear the increasing weight of armoured knights.

The introduction of a padded, form-fitting saddle with stirrups did much to increase the safety and comfort of horse-riding. The Greeks and Romans usually rode bareback, or on simple saddle-cloths. The resulting seat was insecure and prolonged riding without stirrups to support the feet led to serious and lasting discomfort in the legs. Mounting was a difficult process and required the assistance of others, blocks or pedestals to mount from or considerable vaulting ability. The Roman roads were furnished with mounting blocks as well as milestones (Plutarch *C. Gracchus.* 7). Equestrianism was thus effectively restricted to the young and athletic.

A form of saddle without stirrups made its appearance in the west in the first century AD.[223] This marked only a partial solution to the problem of riding. Comfort was increased but

G

mounting was as difficult as ever. The rider's steadiness may have been somewhat improved by placing straps or handles on the front of the saddle for grasping during sudden emergencies.[224] Romans did not have the bronco-buster's aversion to 'clawing leather'. The achievement of a really secure seat had to await the introduction of the stirrup.

Much has been written concerning the introduction of the stirrup to western Europe and its consequent effects on methods of warfare.[225] Lynn White, jr, concludes, on the basis of archaeological finds, modifications in language, and changes in weapons, that the stirrup came to western Europe in the early eighth century. Pictorial representations only begin to appear in the next century.[226] It may be possible to propose somewhat earlier dates even without additional archaeological information.

Julius Pollux of Naucratis (fl. AD 200) wrote of stirrups in his *Onomasticon*. The objection here is that all manuscripts of the *Onomasticon* are later in date than the ninth century and contain late interpolations which are impossible to identify (*Oxford Classical Dictionary*, s.v. Pollux). The stirrups may or may not have been found in the original, but the author shows considerable insight into the function of the stirrup. I translate freely from *Onomasticon*, I, 11, 15: 'When you sit on a horse you must put your weight on your feet in order not to injure the horse's front legs. In so far as possible you should have the position of a standing person, because the stirrup serves more for standing than for sitting.'

Professor White (*Medieval Technology and Social Change*, p 27) says that in the early eighth century the words *insilire* and *desilire,* indicating leaping on and off a horse, began to be replaced by *scandere* and *descendere,* stepping on or off the horse. But similar words were used earlier. Clovis *ascenso equite* in 507 (Gregory of Tours, *History*, II, 38). In 578 Duke Dragolen was unseated and hung helpless from his horse (. . . *suspensumque de equo sursum* . . . Gregory of Tours, *History* V, 25). This may mean that his foot was caught in a stirrup.

The stirrup brought changes beyond warfare. Ease of mounting and support for the feet while in the saddle permitted the extension of horse-riding to a large group of people. It no longer required the efforts of a vigorous athlete to attain and keep a seat on a horse. The aged, the clergy, and women could now safely ride. More speed in travel was attained with the expenditure of less exertion. With the rider firmly in his seat it was possible for him to devote more of his attention and strength to the control of his mount. Although there was nothing new in the idea of a bit in the horse's mouth for his guidance[227] and spurs on the rider's heels for his stimulation,[228] the rider had hitherto not been in a position to apply these aids effectively. The saddle with stirrups gave the rider a mechanical advantage sufficient not only to control ordinary mounts but also adequate to dominate the larger horses developed to carry armoured warriors. Similarly, stirrups made it more practicable to use spurs. Pricking-up a steed was a very dangerous procedure for a bare-back rider. The horse might be stimulated to more rapid movement, but control was lost. We should not expect rapport between the medieval horseman and his mount. The horse was a tool and a means of transport. The knight, particularly, required perfect control and instantaneous obedience over a beast in which spirit was valued. Severe curb bits and cruel rowel spurs gave him such mastery. Geldings might be preferable for farm work and transport, but for prestige and a fighting spirit to match his own, a knight must have a stallion (see numerous examples in the Bayeux Tapestry).

Horses of good quality were a perquisite of the aristocracy. When St Sturm sought a site for the abbey of Fulda *c* 743 he encountered a man in the wilderness leading a horse for his master from Wetterau to Grapfelt. From this it would appear that a servant did not dare to mount a horse, even when out of sight of his master, deep within a forest.[229] Horses of lower quality were always in existence, although their numbers were probably less, proportionate to the population, than they had been in Roman Gaul. Three grades of horses are listed in the eighth century Lex Bajuvorum: *marach*, probably a horse suitable for war; *wilz*, a middle grade; and *angargnago*, a horse which could not be used in the army.[230] Lower quality horses were used, like mules, as pack-animals.

Packhorses can carry approximately 220-330lb on their backs.[231] Problems of balance, however, require the load to be split into two equal portions. Only materials which are divisible into small and light loads can be transported efficiently in this manner. Problems of loading and tying can be simplified by the use of a properly designed pack-saddle. Pack-animals can be used in difficult country which is unsuitable for wagons or carts, but, unlike vehicles, they must be unpacked each night.

Horses seldom pulled vehicles after the decline of Roman power in the west. Funerary bas-reliefs from Roman Gaul indicate that the use of the horse to draw light wagons was common under the empire. Vehicles not only carried people but were loaded with goods and even barrels.[232] Only in Ireland, which had been little influenced by Rome, did the Celtic chiefs continue to travel in horse-drawn chariots. Aristocrats in other areas preferred to travel on horseback. The Roman technique of harnessing horses, inefficient though it may have been, fell rather suddenly into disuse after the coming of the Germanic invaders to Gaul. It is probable that systematic horse-breeding in Gaul stopped, at least temporarily, with the invasions.[233] The relatively few horses still remaining became mounts for the nobility or, if they were of too inferior a grade, were associated with mules as pack-animals. There are few incidents to match the horses who drew a wagon loaded with food to the starving St Columban at Anegray, *c* 575. The circumstance is the more remarkable in that the horses were unguided. They are recorded as having found their own way in the dark.[234]

If the horse was to have much of a future as a draught animal, some innovations were necessary to improve his efficiency. One area in which improvement was needed was in the care and protection of his hooves. The Greeks had recognised this and Xenophon (*On Equitation* iv. 3-4) recommended that cobblestones be provided in the stable and yard so that the hooves would be hardened. An early example of improvisation to meet a specific emergency is also found in Xenophon (*Anabasis* iv. 5.36) where socks were tied around the horses' feet to prevent them sinking into deep snow. This may have been the predecessor of the *hipposandal* used by Roman veterinarians to protect the hooves of injured animals and allow opportunity for healing (Columella, vi. 12.2). Rich and prominent Romans like the Emperor Nero and his wife Poppaea gilded and silvered the hooves of the mules attached to their carriages (Pliny, *Natural History* xxxiii. xlix. and Suetonius, *Nero* 30). The *solea ferrea* was apparently a metal shoe attached to a boot, probably attached temporarily on rough journeys where protection was needed (Suetonius, *Vespasian*, 23).

Perhaps we should look, not among the Romans where horses were always comparatively rare, but among the Celts—wagon-builders, blacksmiths, and horsemen *par excellence* of Europe—for early examples of true horseshoes. There is evidence to support such a pre-Roman dating. A unique find of nine horseshoes was reported by the Marquis de Cerralbo[235] at Aguilar de Anguita in the province of Guadalajara, Spain, in a Celtiberian necropolis dating from *c* 300 BC. The Celtic provenance of horseshoes is extended by Fritz Heichelheim[236] to Gaul and the Alpine regions, ie they were common to the whole Celtic area. This attribution to the Celts in their pre-Roman phase is maintained by M. Hell[237] and Thomas W. Africa.[238]

If this is the case, then the Romans could be expected to bring their *hipposandales* with them in their expansion and to encounter the better, permanently mounted, Celtic horseshoe in their new territories. *Hipposandales* have been found in Roman excavations in Britain and Germany. Around a dozen were found in Verulamium (St Albans) and were characterised as easily adjustable and removable. As an indication of the transition they could be expected to undergo to meet new environmental conditions, some of them were fitted with ice nails. One example found at London and now in the British Museum is a true combination—a *hipposandal* with a normal

horseshoe attached to it as a secondary sole.[239] Other examples
from Roman Britain include true horseshoes whose location in
sealed deposits dating clearly from Roman times leaves little
possibility of medieval intrusion.[240] On the Continent finds are
particularly numerous in the Saalburg, the Roman fort in the
Taunus mountains, on the Limes Germanicus.[241] Albert Neuburger (*The Technical Arts and Sciences of the Ancients,* 52-3)
states that many horseshoes are found in Roman settlements
and that they were mass-produced.

If horseshoes were relatively common in Celtic times and in
the areas where Roman government replaced Celtic localism,
we should wonder what happened to them in the period from
the replacement of Roman rule to nearly 900 (when even the
most convinced sceptic must admit the existence of horseshoes). In Ireland, never a part of the Roman Empire, the
use of horses in large numbers continued longer than in the
barbarian-conquered Roman Empire, and the horses may have
continued to be equipped with shoes. Despite the difficulty of
dating Irish epics, it would seem that a passage in *The Intoxi-
cation of the Men of Ulster,* 'What causes the quantity of sods
which their horses send from their shoes, so that it is pitch
dark to the mighty air over their heads?' (T.P. Cross and C. H.
Slover, *Ancient Irish Tales,* 224) refers to an early period.

On the Continent perhaps we should see a slow surfacing,
or percolating upwards, of knowledge about the horseshoe
from the doubly submerged Celtic substratum of the population rather than the activities of the burrowing rodent (so
humorously presented by Professor White) who greedily
seizes recent horseshoes to drag them down to the depths of
his capacious abode for deposit alongside his other treasures—
such as coins of Vespasian—to the eternal confusion of
classical and medieval archaeologists.[244] Some indications of
the continued use of horseshoes are found. The remains of
such a shoe were found in the tomb of Childeric (father of
Clovis) who died about AD 460. A picture of the shoe, completely restored in his own inimitable fashion, is found in
Ginzrot.[243] St Eloi (Eligius), the well-attested patron saint of

goldsmiths and blacksmiths, who lived *c* 588-660, is credited in later legend with miraculous feats of horseshoeing—he cut off the hooves, shod them, and put them back on the horse.[244]

Iron was not the only material, nor horses the only animals, that were involved in protective shoeing. Esparto grass was a favourite from classical times for covering the feet of draught animals. Similar straw sandals were used for horses in Japan until the nineteenth century. Police spies of Paris used leather horseshoes in relatively modern times to muffle their approach against criminals (Ginzrot, op cit, II, 515) and rubber shoes were used by draught horses on cobbled city streets. Aristotle (*History of Animals,* ii. 499a.30) and Pliny (*Natural History,* II. 45) write of boots or shoes for camels. Although it was considered laughable, peasants at the time of the First Crusade shod their oxen as if they were horses, harnessed them to two-wheeled carts and set out for Jerusalem.[245] Shoes for oxen were used especially in mountain areas (Ginzrot, op cit, II, 518). The horseshoes counterfeiting the tracks of cows (supposed to have been used by marauding medieval barons) which Sherlock Holmes encountered in *The Adventure of the Priory School* (. . . it is a remarkable cow which walks, canters, and gallops') had actual counterparts. *Strand Magazine* in May 1903 reproduced a photograph of an ancient horseshoe recently found in the moat at Birtsmorton Court, near Tewkesbury, which imitated the mark of a cloven hoof.[246]

There is no question that the iron horseshoe was known in western Europe by the ninth century and its use rapidly became common. The iron shoe brought several benefits to horses. It protected the hoof from injury and made it possible for the horse to cover longer distances more comfortably and operate efficiently over surfaces such as mud and ice which would have been otherwise impossible. Not only riding horses but even packhorses and mules benefited from the new shoes. Their footing in steep terrain was improved and they could negotiate mountain paths with more certainty and heavier loads. In addition, the horseshoe paved the way for renewed use of the horse for pulling loaded vehicles.

With the new shoes the horse was able to point his toes, dig into the ground, and exert much more strength than he had hitherto. This would not have aided him in the pulling of heavily loaded vehicles unless new methods of harnessing had been introduced. The epoch-making work of Joseph Needham is the best source for references for developments in the west as well as the east (see *Science and Civilisation in China,* Vol. IV, Part 2, Section 27 (f) Power-sources and their employment (I), Animal traction, 303-30). The horse-collar proved to be the most successful method. (For other methods see below, p 110). The horse-collar made it possible for the animal to

Fig 4   Horse-collar, *c* 1170 (Herrad of Landsberg, *Hortus Deliciarum*)

exert his full strength in pulling without constricting his breathing or limiting his blood circulation as the ancient throat and girth harness had done. Like the stirrup and the horseshoe the horse-collar developed and spread in an obscure fashion.

It makes its appearance in linguistic, pictorial, archaeological, and literary evidence around the ninth century.[247] The derivation of the word *hames* (the rigid side-pieces of the collar) from a Turkic dialect of Central Asia, the finding of metal horse-harness mountings in ninth-century Swedish graves, and the mention of ploughing with horses in Norway in the *Orosius* (i. 18) translated by King Alfred (with contemporary material added by the king), indicate a possible introduction of the horse-collar by the Vikings from their Russian contacts.

Although the technique of using the horse-collar may have been familiar to ninth-century Scandinavia, its dissemination and widespread use in the rest of western Europe seems to have been strangely delayed. A Monte Cassino miniature from 1023 shows a light, two-wheeled cart being pulled by two horses, but no horse-collars are in evidence.[248] The harness is still of the antique type (Needham, *op cit,* 316-17, calls this breast-strap harness) and the vehicle is probably intended for pleasure driving rather than heavy hauling. It seems more like an aristocratic conveyance than a work vehicle. A possible reason for the delay in introducing the horse-collar was the rarity and expense of horses and mules. A contrary view is expressed by Lewis Mumford (*Technics and Civilization,* 113): that the reinvention of rational horse harness, by increasing the usefulness of horses, gave an incentive to increase the number of horses, which fitted in with the shortage of human labour.

The efforts of the Carolingians to increase horse production by repeatedly forbidding the export of stallions seem to have had little success.[249] One possible solution was the institution of large scale systematic breeding of horses and mules for export attested for Moslem Spain after 1000 (see above p 66). This helped make horses available for purposes other than riding. The horse-collar seems first to have been applied to farm work. Harrowing and ploughing by horse would have been impractical without its use. Much evidence from the middle and late eleventh century shows horses and mules engaged in farm work.[250] No precise dates for the introduction of the practice are to be found in the sources but it became more common as the twelfth century advanced. There was occasional opposition to the introduction of the new horse-power. Welsh law forbade the use of horses for ploughing.[251] This may have been indicative of a continuing scarcity of horses, conservatism, or a lingering feeling that it was just not right so to employ a noble animal. The application of the horse-collar to transport soon followed. As we have seen (above, p 87) English peasants in 1100 had a horse-drawn vehicle on which to transport the body of William Rufus. By the late twelfth century, horses for the cart, dray, or plough were sold at the Smithfield Market outside London.[252] The application of the horse to heavy transport could not have been undertaken unless the horse-collar had been available to increase the horse's pulling power.

The horse-collar is not the only effective means of harnessing the horse. At various times in history differing types of breast bands have been used. As usual, the earliest unambiguous evidence of a new method comes from China. There is some evidence that the Chinese were already changing and improving the throat-and-girth harness as early as the fourth century BC and a great deal of evidence that an efficient breast-strap harness was universal in China by the second century AD.[253] That it was efficient is seen in the fact that single horses between shafts have enough power to draw carts containing several people, whereas horses yoked in pairs were normally necessary to draw lighter loads with the old throat-and-girth harness. The late Roman Empire also experimented with harness modifications with some success. As seen above (p 79) they were able to harness single animals between shafts but only to light vehicles with limited load-carrying capacity. They seem not to have achieved a truly effective breast-band harness.[254]

Linguistic analysis and the discovery of new evidence has done away with the contention of Lefebvre des Noëttes that the horse-collar appeared in western Europe before the breast-strap harness. On philological grounds, André Haudricourt maintains that the *bricole* (breast-strap) was known in the west in advance of the dispersion of the Slavs before the sixth century, was used in Merovingian Gaul, and was adopted early for agriculture, whereas the horse-collar (*Kummet*) is a Germanic borrowing from the Turkic, dating from the eighth or ninth centuries, after the dispersal of the Slavs.[255] As confirmation of the earlier date for the breast-strap harness, a scene from the base of a cross at Ahenny, Tipperary, Ireland, is offered. It shows two horses pulling a light two-wheeled cart carrying two persons. The near horse appears to be wearing an unsupported breast-band connected directly to the vehicle (see reproduction in Singer, *History of Technology,* II, 544, fig 490). It is difficult to accept this as an actual method of harnessing and more difficult to accept its date as eighth century. Irish sculpture in stone only begins about the middle of the eighth century and the earliest examples are usually very simple. Such elaborate carving should logically be dated considerably later. It is doubtful whether this stone deserves credit as the earliest European representation of the breast-strap harness. A better example is seen in the tapestry found in the early ninth century Viking ship-burial at Oseberg.[256] Dr Needham (op cit IV, 2, 316) feels that this type of breast-strap, rather than the horse-collar, was used by the Vikings in ploughing by horse (*King Alfred's Orosius,* ed H. Sweet (London, 1883), i. 18). The breast-strap harness is certainly nearly as efficient as the collar-harness, but despite the fact that it was known and used in the west throughout the medieval and modern period, it saw its main use in light hauling and never had the popularity and wide dissemination of the collar-harness.

The problem of effective horse-harness was never completely solved. It was only held in abeyance by the popularisation of motor-vehicles in the twentieth century. The nineteenth century had been filled with controversy as to the most effective methods.[257] As late as the beginning of the twentieth century, the British Artillery switched from the horse-collar to the breast-strap harness.[258] Straps proliferated in the harness of the nineteenth century, often with contradictory functions. The martingale held the horse's head down, while the checkrein held it high, making a fine display but preventing the horse from effectively using his strength.[259]

To meet the problem of harnessing the horse to a cart, the Middle Ages developed several innovations which had been unknown, or little used, in antiquity. The chief of these were the use of shafts, tandem-harnessing, and the whippletree.

While the Romans normally harnessed horses in pairs with a pole between them, enough examples exist to prove that they were familiar with the use of rigid shafts for single horses and light loads.[260] The Chinese had, of course, been using shafts since the introduction of the breast-strap harness (see above, p 110). The horse-collar multiplied the effective pulling strength of the horse four or five times.[261] Consequently, after the use of the horse-collar became widespread in the eleventh century, it was feasible to move quite heavy loads (over 2,000lb) with a single horse harnessed between shafts. This brought other advantages. The horse was able to back with the load as well as go forward. This made the vehicle much more manoeuvrable. In addition, the horse could hold back against the rigid shafts and exert a braking effect while going downhill. It is doubtful if the Roman variety of breast band would have had much braking effect in the same situation. There is no apparent continuity between the Roman and the medieval use of shafts. The shafts of the Oseberg wagon are extremely narrow and could hardly accommodate any type of draught animal. The Romans had used shafts only in light carts; medieval horses were able to pull heavy loads.

Like the use of shafts, the harnessing of horses in front of one another rather than side-by-side was probably reinvented in the west during the Middle Ages, even though the Chinese had occasionally used this method much earlier (Needham, op cit, IV, 2, 247-8). Although only one representation of tandem harnessing is known from Roman times (see above, p 81), there are several references in the literature which indicate the probability that the tandem method was known. Plough teams of eight oxen are mentioned.[262] There is no practicable method of harnessing by which eight oxen placed side-by-side could pull a single plough. Nor were Roman roads wide enough to yoke eight mules side-by-side to pull one carriage. In all probability, they were arranged in tandem by pairs.[263]

There is no great difficulty in placing one yoke of oxen in front of another. Yoking oxen in tandem by pairs was probably practised at least occasionally from antiquity until the introduction of the heavy plough to western Europe, perhaps in the eighth or ninth century, at which time it became the common method of yoking. The fifteen wagons each drawn by four oxen which brought the Avar treasure to Charlemagne were probably harnessed in this manner.[264] Harnessing horses or mules in tandem is a more difficult proposition. The Romans, using harness similar to the ox-yoke, found it necessary to use eight or ten mules to pull comparatively light loads.[265] No further mention of horses being harnessed in tandem is encountered until after the popularisation of the horse-collar in the eleventh century. Not only tandem harnessing, but the use of horses in general, became very rare in western Europe from the fifth to the eleventh century. Once the horse-collar had become common, it became desirable to harness several horses together, thus increasing the available power, so as to haul really heavy loads. As horses moved faster than oxen, the new method not only increased capacity but also reduced journey time. The simplest method was to harness several horses side-by-side. This worked well until the team had so many animals that it became wider than the load. When this happened, the outside horses applied their force on a tangent rather than straight forward.

A better solution was to place the horses ahead of, rather than beside, each other. Medieval tandem harnessing differed from the probable Roman method in that horses were harnessed singly in file rather than in pairs. The tandem harness is not mentioned in the literary sources but it begins to make its appearance in illuminated manuscripts in the twelfth century.[266] The horse nearest the vehicle was frequently harnessed between rigid shafts, but the lead horse was harnessed by flexible traces or ropes, giving the impression that the attachment may have been temporary, used only as an expedient to climb difficult gradients or to get through particularly muddy stretches. By harnessing the horses in tandem all the available power was used for forward motion and none was wasted in tangential pulling. Discipline in the team was improved. The horses had less opportunity for individual misbehaviour. The harness encouraged them to follow the lead of their fellows. The flexible traces made it easy for the horses to change direction. When the team turned, even a four-wheeled wagon without a pivoted front axle was bound to follow. Even a slight looseness of the wheels on the axles was enough to make it possible to turn in a reasonably short distance without breaking the spokes. The outstanding difficulty with tandem harnessing was that the horses could not hold back or back up with the flexible traces.

At least one of the innovations included in the complex of techniques that made horse-drawn transport feasible is unique to the Middle Ages. This is the whippletree, a wooden bar whose ends are hooked to the horse's traces and whose centre

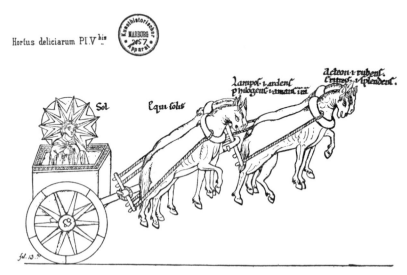

Hortus deliciarum Pl.V bis

Fig 5   Horse-collar, whippletree and tandem harness, c 1170 (Herrad of Landsberg, *Hortus Deliciarum*)

is connected to the front of the vehicle. Claims for earlier whippletrees do not seem well-founded. The reconstruction of the early Iron Age plough from Vebbestrup, Denmark, does not seem to have a true whippletree,[267] Haudricourt (*L'Homme et la charrue,* 185) disagrees with Steensberg, the reconstructor, and does not accept this early (500-100 BC) example as a genuine whippletree.

Needham feels that the whippletree is a sort of transmigrated yoke, which, being no longer necessary with the collar-harness, was moved by stages to the rear of the horse, eventually becoming the whippletree (op cit IV, 2, 328) and that it had been used by oxen in third-century China. This interpretation is difficult to accept. The word used, *chhiu,* has other meanings such as swing and equine crupper-strap (Needham, op cit, IV, 2, 260, 309, 328, and 376) and the whippletree is singularly inappropriate to the nature of the ox. Its function is to cushion the shock caused by the rapid movements of the horse in taking up the strain of a load and to equalise the stress on the traces when making a turn. The more deliberate movements of the ox require no such cushioning device. Under certain conditions, such as the first ploughing of new lands, oxen remained more satisfactory than horses. As an example, the early Dutch settlers in the New Netherlands requested 'yoke-oxen for the plough, inasmuch as in new lands, full of roots, oxen go forward steadily under the plough, and horses stand still, or with a start break the harness in pieces . . .'[268]

The whippletree is known by many names. In English alone it is called whippletree, whiffletree, splinter bar, swing bar, and swingletree. When two horses are harnessed abreast, their singletrees are attached to the ends of a doubletree, whose centre is connected with the vehicle. The German language has at least three names for the whippletree, *der Schwengel, der Schwenzel,* and *das Ortscheit* (from which derives the Polish *Orczyk*). In French it is *le palonnier* (which in more modern times became the rudder-bar for an aeroplane). The multiplicity of names indicates a widespread dissemination of the whippletree in western Europe. Its English names of whippletree and swingletree make it derive linguistically from a whip. This must be based on its appearance, because it is extremely unlikely that such a relatively fragile and flexible instrument as a whip could ever have been used as even an experimental whippletree. The whippletree, because it is connected to the vehicle by a single link, makes it possible for the team to change direction easily. The whippletree is subject to frequent breakage (hence splinter bar), particularly in the centre where all the force is concentrated. To prevent breakage of the bar it may be desirable to make the iron connecting hook somewhat weaker than the bar so that it will give way before the bar breaks. It is much easier to change hooks than to replace the whole whippletree.

The whippletree came to be a distinguishing feature of horse-harness, just as the yoke is characteristic of the ox-harness. The use of a whippletree is suspected by Lynn White, jr, in the mention of harrowing by horsepower in *Ruodlieb* (V, 468-9). This is a logical deduction since harrowing (dragging a heavy unwheeled frame with spikes over ploughed land to break up heavy clods) is just the sort of work—bouncing and jolting, with frequent starts and stops, and sharp turns—for which the whippletree with its flexibility and cushioning effect is most appropriate.[269] Confirmation of this early use of the whippletree is seen in the Bayeux Tapestry (*c* 1077) in which (Stenton, *The Bayeux Tapestry,* Plate 12) a mule-drawn plough follows a horse-drawn harrow. (This is not contrary to actual practice—the tapestry is to be viewed from left to right; consequently, earlier events appear at the left.) The mule is attached to the plough by an indeterminate round blob, which represents a whippletree seen end-on. The embroidering artist realised the lack of clarity and showed the harrow in the following scene as viewed from the top. This gives a better view of the whippletree, although only one end of it seems to be connected to the horse's traces. A nearly identical harrow and whippletree is seen more plainly in the Holkham Bible (*c* 1330), which makes the method of attachment clear. Artistic representations of the whippletree begin to appear in the twelfth century. An early whippletree is seen on the bronze doors of Novgorod Cathedral, made at Magdeburg *c* 1154.[270] Observe the difficulties of the sculptor. He has harnessed both the horses to a single whippletree, with only one trace leading to the right side of each animal. This is an unlikely and inefficient method of attachment and is not likely to represent the real connection.

From the archaeological evidence it seems that the craft of wheelmaking lost some of its skill after the Germanic invasions of western Europe. The wheels found with the Dejbjerg cart and in the excavations of the Roman fort at Newstead are slim but strong. The materials are carefully selected and well adapted to the functions for which they are used (see above, p 76). The Dejbjerg and Newstead wheels were probably used on horsedrawn vehicles and were probably made by Celtic craftsmen. When the fashion or custom of driving horses went into disfavour after the coming of the Germans there was little market for such wheels and the skills disappeared. Wheels for ox-drawn vehicles were not subject to the strains of rapid motion and could be built in a heavier and clumsier style. The wheels of the ninth-century Oseberg cart were probably built by native Scandinavian craftsmen and seem very heavy and awkward compared with the Celtic product.[271] The fellies are very thick and there is no evidence of iron tyres. The cart would not have withstood prolonged or fast movement. There was little incentive to improve wheels until horse-drawn transport became common again in the eleventh and twelfth centuries.

Two-wheeled ox-drawn carts were common throughout the early medieval period. Few changes were made in the two-wheeled cart until it was adapted to the horse, probably in the eleventh century, by substituting lighter, stronger wheels and adding shafts. The two-wheeled cart, with its wheels revolving on the axle, was easy to turn but suffered from the disadvantage that the bed was tilted when the team was unhitched.

As we have seen (p 89), the idea of the wheelbarrow, a notable medieval invention, may have suggested itself to men

H

who picked up the shafts of a light, two-wheeled cart to shift it about. Such an origin fits in well with the Latin name of the wheelbarrow, *birota*, which indicates that it originally had two wheels. However, no pictures exist of such wheelbarrows. From its earliest appearances, it has only one wheel.

Like the two-wheeled carts, four-wheeled ox-drawn wagons were used throughout the early Middle Ages. With a four-wheeled wagon the load was not shifted when the team was removed, but remained level. The ox-drawn wagon often gives the appearance of being a box with wheels at the corners.[272] The horse-drawn four-wheeled wagon usually has an under-carriage which gives the impression that the vehicle may have originated by hooking two two-wheeled chariots together by pinning the pole of one to the centre of the axle of the other.[273] If this was the case it was not necessary to invent a pivoted axle. It was there already, and all that was needed was to attach a wagon-bed above the two linked chariots. Such a body would be quite stable, being supported at its rear end by the axle of the rear chariot and at its front by the pole with its link-pin.

The difficulty of turning a four-wheeled wagon without a pivoted front-axle is obvious. Tangential force applied to such a vehicle would have broken a rigid wagon-tongue and sub-jected the wheels to severe sideways strain.[274] Nevertheless, on the surviving evidence, the existence of the pivoted front-axle is uncertain. There is no literary evidence for it from either antique or medieval sources. The pictorial evidence is often crude and unskilful and cannot be trusted.[275] Neither the Pom-peian wall-painting nor the Gallo-Roman bas-reliefs give un-equivocal evidence for the pivoted axle (see above, pp 70-80).

The belief that the Romans had a pivoted front-axle is widespread.[276] In most instances this belief can be attributed to the influence of Ginzrot, who not only stated that the front wheels of the Roman wagons could swivel but also included a drawing showing details of the front axle's construction and a listing in four languages (German, French, Greek, and Latin) keyed to the drawing and giving the names of the component part.[277] Ginzrot's chief authority was Julius Pollux of Naucratis, a tutor of the Emperor Commodus, who flourished in the second century AD. Pollux was the author of an *Onomasticon*

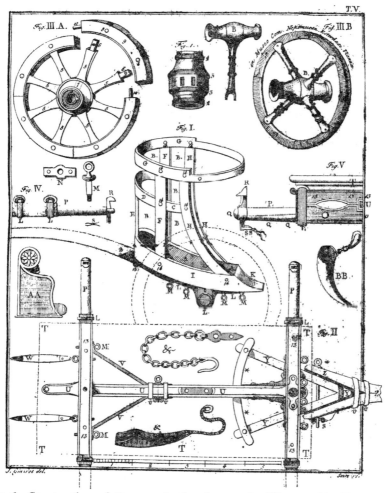

Fig 6   Construction of Roman pivoting front axle (Ginzrot, *Die Wagen und Fahrwerke der Griechen und Römer*)

which listed, among many other things, the names of vehicles and their parts.

Confronted with such authority, it is worthwhile to examine

Pollux more closely. In the first place, none of the manuscripts of Pollux is older than the ninth century and all of them contain late interpolations which cannot be separated from the original material.[278] Unknown to Ginzrot, some of the material he used from Pollux may have been considerably later than

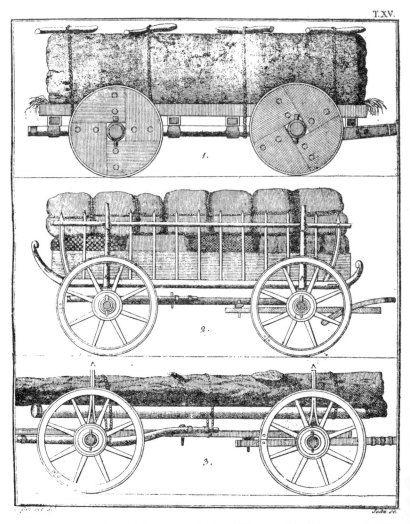

Fig 7 Construction of Roman vehicles (Ginzrot, *Die Wagen and Fahrwerke der Griechen und Römer*)

the Roman period. A more damning indictment results from Ginzrot's translations. As an example, the most essential part of a swivelling front-axle is the kingbolt, which descends from the front of the wagon-bed and fits into a hole in the centre of the front axle and so provides the connection which supports the wagon body, and the pivot upon which the front axle turns. Ginzrot's drawing includes a kingbolt (appropriately labelled 'X'). In his listing of the component parts of the front assembly, 'X' is rendered in Latin as *estor*. Certainly, if Latin had a word for kingbolt, the Romans must have possessed the pivoted front axle. Pollux uses the term *hestor* but defines it as a 'key which adjusts the yoke to the pole'.[279] This, of course, is not a kingbolt but merely a device for connecting the horses' yoke to the front of the pole of the chariot. This definition is confirmed.[280] Ginzrot's front-axle drawing is purely imaginary, and useless as a proof that the Romans had swivelling front axles. Laudatory comments on Ginzrot should be tempered with caution.[281] Ginzrot's method of working can be seen from his own statement, 'Table XV, Fig 2, shows the method of constructing such a wagon, as I imagine it, because I have nowhere found a picture on ancient monuments which would be suitable for this' (translated from *Die Wagen und Fahrwerke der Griechen und Römer*, I, 246).

A possible, although unlikely, confirmation for a late Roman swivelling axle was found in 1888 in Hungary, where an object which has been described as a kingbolt was discovered among excavated iron and bronze wagon parts dating from the third century AD. (See illustration and description in Mötefindt, *Die Erfindung des Drehschemels am vierrädrigen Wagen*, 37-40.) There is considerable doubt as to whether this is actually a kingbolt.

A society that regarded the saddle of a horse as a more honourable place than the seat of a wagon devoted little effort to ways of making wagon travel more comfortable, such as the suspension of carriages. Even the Romans, who were able to write in shorthand while travelling in chariots,[282] seem not to have conceived the idea of suspending their carriages to lessen road shocks.[283] Nevertheless the materials from which all vehicles are constructed have a certain amount of elasticity. Completely rigid poles or shafts for draught animals would be brittle. Litters, whether carried by animals or humans, have flexible poles which have some effect in cushioning the ride. Replacing the bearers with wheels would result in a slightly cushioned vehicle. Early chariots sometimes obtained a similar effect by placing the driver somewhat ahead of the axle on the pole so that his ride would partake of the springiness of the pole. This type of 'suspension' is represented in such vehicles as the medieval *Federbrettwagen* and the American pioneer's buckboard wagon. Classical times seen not to have progressed beyond this concept. (I must regard the pictures of swinging chariot seats in Jürgen Smolian's *Vorgänger und Nachfolger des gefederten Wagens*, 157, plates 16 and 17, as purely theoretical reconstructions.)

A possible progenitor of a true suspension system is seen in the work of Ivan Venedikov (*Trakijskata Kolesnica*, Sofia, 1960), who studied the remains of approximately forty wagons found in archaeological excavations in Thrace dating from *c* AD 300. In his reconstruction of the wagons, he decided that about one-third of them had bodies suspended transversely by straps from four vertical posts rising from the axles. Although I have not seen the condition of the remains from which the reconstruction was made, certain comments would seem to be in order. The vehicle itself seems to be of a standard late Roman type; that is, four large, equal-sized wheels with close spacing between the pairs indicating no swivelling front axle. The reconstruction seems mechanically unsound. There is no indication of a carriage underbody connecting the axles to give firm support to the poles, and the straps which provide the suspension seem too short to give effective cushioning. Even slight sidewards movement would bring the hanging body into contact with the posts with probable danger of breakage.[284] Neither the earlier Dejbjerg wagon, with its excellent craftsmanship, nor the later Oseberg cart, with its fine ornamentation (above, p 82), shows any signs of a suspension system. I believe we must look later for our earliest true suspension systems.

The Arab geographer Al-Bekir, writing in the eleventh century, and quoting from the tenth century Al-Masudi, says that the kings of the Serbs travelled in large, high, four-wheeled wagons which had four posts from which the body of the vehicle was suspended by chains.[285] The Anglo-Saxon 'hammock wagon' (see above, p 86), if it had four posts, as seems likely, was probably a smaller version of the royal Serbian vehicle. This vehicle probably saw little use. Such vehicles had little effect on the transport of their times.

A larger vehicle which better illustrates the probable construction of the Anglo-Saxon hammock wagon is seen in Rudolph von Ems' *Weltchronik* dating from *c* 1340. (This is not, incidentally, a new discovery pushing the first suspension of a wagon body back another hundred years, as believed by Smolian [*Vorgänger und Nachfolger des gefederten Wagens*, 146 and 159-50].) A picture of this vehicle was published in the nineteenth century by Joseph Zemp, *Die schweizerischen Bilderchroniken und ihre Architektur-Darstellungen* (Zürich, 1897), 8, fig 4, and its significance was recognised by Wulf Schadendorf, *Zu Pferde, im Wagen, zu Fuss* (Munich, 1959), where a fine reproduction in colour serves as frontispiece, and by Marjorie Nice Boyer in 'Medieval Suspended Carriages', *Speculum*, 34 (1959), 363-4. No concern should be felt that both the Anglo-Saxon hammock wagon and the south German vehicle in Rudolph von Ems' *Weltchronik* ostensibly represent Biblical times. This is a good illustration of a medieval artistic convention. These do not represent actual vehicles in prehistoric Palestine, but contemporary customs, costumes, and vehicles which the artist felt would be more comprehensible to his viewers. It is only in the later Middle Ages that suspended carriages come into widespread use.[286]

The Romans were probably more familiar with lubrication than were the early medieval peoples. Cato the Elder recommended the boiling of olive lees to the consistency of honey. The resulting concoction was good for greasing axles and preserving leather.[287] Pig fat was also used for axlegrease.[288] It is also possible that sometimes the Romans did no more than throw water on the wheel hubs when they began to smoke. (See the circus mosaic from third century Gaul (Musée de la Civilisation Gallo-Romaine, Lyon), reproduced in Moses Hadas, *Imperial Rome* (New York, 1965), 54-5, where a figure in the upper left is about to throw water towards the track. Probably his function is to prevent burning axles; possibly he is doing no more than laying the dust.)

The wandering tribes of the great plains of Eastern Europe were unable to move silently. When the Quman hordes moved in the twelfth century 'the heavy wheels of their carts squeaked and squealed on the wooden axles.'[289] That this situation was not soon improved is seen in the account of a Prussian king's journey from Berlin to Breslau some centuries ago, when the peasants along the way had to stand with buckets of water ready to splash his wheels as he passed and prevent fires starting from the friction of the hubs on the axles.[290]

Notes to this chapter are on pp 190-206.

3

Water transport

MEDIEVAL MAN PREFERRED to use water transport whenever possible.

An outstanding characteristic of medieval water transport was the use of extremely small, even intermittent, streams for the carriage of goods. Every watercourse that could be used was brought into service, frequently with very minor man-made improvements in its course. The use of such small streams seems so unlikely and unprofitable to modern eyes that it has been postulated that the flow of rivers was more full in medieval times than now.[1] It is possible that a greater forest cover at that time may have had some effect in controlling the flow and keeping the level more constant, but the main factor affecting the flow must have been the rainfall. Dry as well as wet years are often reported by the chroniclers. It is unlikely that the rainfall was consistently and significantly greater than at present. It is probable, rather, that the medieval boatmen seized their opportunities and moved their goods wherever and whenever possible, floating where they could and portaging when they could not, sometimes successful in reaching a market and sometimes not.

When St Sturm first sought a site for the abbey of Fulda, c 743, he and two others, starting from Hersfeld, rowed up the river Fulda for three days. This is far above the usual navigable limits of the river. Bebra, about fifteen miles below Hersfeld, is the present-day head of navigation. In St Sturm's day the area around Fulda was real frontier territory. It was heavily wooded, largely unknown, and little populated. When St Boniface sought title to the land for the abbey from King Carloman, the king did not know the extent or location of his holdings in the area. A few Slavs lived in the vicinity. The river marked the western limit of their penetration. Probably the only road was that from Thuringia to Mainz which crossed the Fulda by a ford. For the most part, the territory was characterised as a pathless wilderness inhabited by dangerous beasts.[2] The Fulda, at this period, was a stream in its natural state. St Sturm's navigation of its upper stretches was probably due, not to its containing more water than at present, but to its lack of artificial obstacles and to the smallness of St Sturm's boat, an oared craft seating three.

The larger streams were more likely to be usable on a habitual basis. Rivers are characterised as *chemins qui marchent*.[3] Unfortunately this road moves in only one direction. A great variety of goods can move downstream efficiently and relatively quickly, but the journey upstream is difficult and slow. (In recent times flatboats have gone down the Rhône from Lyon to Avignon in two to five days. A comparable journey upstream took nearly a month and required large numbers of oxen or horses for towing.)[4] Even large rivers in their natural state were sometimes difficult to use. The Scandinavians, on their way down the Dnieper towards Byzantium in the ninth century, encountered both natural and man-made difficulties. Cataracts on the river made portages necessary. The portage points made them vulnerable to attack from land-based raiders. The Petchenegs often laid ambushes where they knew the Scandinavians had to carry their boats. The rowlocks and oars from old boats were re-used, but new boats were carved by the Slavs each winter from single tree trunks.[5] This indicates that the Scandinavians made no attempt to ascend the river by boat, but merely salvaged useful parts and brought them back overland for re-use.

The situation of the city of Rome was unique in that most of its river-borne traffic had to move against the current of the Tiber. The difficulties encountered by the Romans in maintaining communication with the sea by means of the Tiber are instructive and indicative of the smaller-scale problems experienced by other localities. The population of ancient Rome was so great that it could not be supported by local land and water transport from its hinterland. Consequently, imports from distant areas, primarily brought by sea, were required to provide livelihood for the many and luxuries for the few. The problem was to move the imports from the harbour (Ostia, later Portus) at the mouth of the Tiber up the river to the city. The Tiber is a relatively small river. It is about 330 feet wide and three to four feet deep at Rome. By constant dredging it is possible to maintain a channel four feet deep for the fifteen miles from the city to the sea. The river is subject to great seasonal fluctuations. It has frequent floods but becomes very low in the summer. It is doubtful if its characteristics and measurements were markedly different in antiquity.

The navigational season on the river is in conflict with that of the sea. In classical times the Mediterranean was closed to shipping from November to March, which was the period when the river was at its best for navigation. Perhaps some materials could be stockpiled at the river mouth and brought up during the high water of winter, but many goods had to be delivered more rapidly. To accomplish this, strenuous efforts were required. Dams were built on the upstream tributaries to store water, which was to be released to help summer navigation. White buffalo (or oxen) pulling from towpaths on the river banks brought seagoing vessels up to the city. In the late afternoon winds were usually favourable, so sails could be used to lessen the strain on the oxen.[6]

At the time of the Gothic wars of Justinian, oxen were still used for this purpose, although they seem to have pulled special barges rather than seagoing vessels.[7] When Portus and the barge road (towpath) were held by the Goths, Antonina (the wife of Belisarius) contrived with great difficulty to supply

Rome. She and the army commanders took small boats from the ships, fenced them in with high planks for protection against the Goths, and manned them with archers and sailors. When the wind was right they sailed up the Tiber. If it was not, they rowed against the current. By making many such trips they were able to provide bare necessities for the city.[8]

Passengers as well as goods were carried on the rivers of Merovingian Gaul.[9] In 755 several means of transport were used to bring St Boniface's body back from his martyrdom by the Frisians. A boat with his body was drawn up the Rhine, apparently from a towpath along the bank, as far as Mainz. From there a boat with the body was rowed up the river Main to Hohleim on the banks of the Moyn from whence it was carried to Fulda.[10] Charlemagne frequently travelled by boat on various rivers. In 793 he travelled by ship from Regensburg to the canal he was attempting to dig from the Altmühl to the Rednitz. Then he descended the Rednitz and the Main to Würzburg where he spent Christmas.[11] In 943 Liutprand of Cremona went downstream from Pavia to Venice in three days. Such an account seems nearly incredible, but skilled oarsmen can add considerably to the speed of the current.[12] In the eleventh century the Thames was so improved that it was possible to ship goods as far up as Oxford.[13] The Roman network of irrigation and transport waterways in Lombardy was revived around 1100. Impetus was given to river transport by the revival of Roman law in the Peace of Constance in 1183. Feudal law had considered rivers to be the private property of the nobles through whose territory they passed. The lords' penchant for controlling, impeding, and plundering river transport had hardly been conducive to progressive development. In Roman law, however, rivers were regarded as public property.[14]

Artificial waterways were little used in early medieval times. The Romans had constructed aqueducts for water supply and ditches for drainage and reclamation of marshes, but they had seldom constructed long canals for navigation. Horace wrote of travel by canal through the Pontine Marshes of Italy.[15]

The cutting of a two-mile canal from the Rhine near Arnheim to the Yssel was mentioned by Tacitus.[16] Pliny the Younger planned to link a lake near Nicomedia to the sea, when he was provincial governor in Bithynia for Trajan.[17] The most grandiose projects of this sort were proposed, as might be expected, by the Emperor Nero. He planned to cut a direct canal from Ostia to Rome which would enable seagoing ships to sail directly up to Rome. Nothing came of this, or of his other scheme, to cut through the Isthmus of Corinth, for which he even ceremonially dug and carried away the first basket of earth.[18] The largest project the Romans seem to have considered was a connection between the Saone and the Moselle (Tacitus *Annales* 13.53) which would have required a canal of about forty miles in length by the most practicable route (that of the modern Canal de l'Est) passing over a height of land about 130 feet higher than the Moselle and descending to a Saone over 300 feet lower than the Moselle. The engineering difficulties are obvious, and such a canal was not built until modern times.[19]

The most noteworthy early medieval attempt to make a major artificial waterway was that of Charlemagne, who tried to dig a canal connecting tributaries of the Danube and the Main and so to link the North Sea with the Black. He gathered a great crowd of workmen and made a strenuous attempt, the remains of which are still visible. The project was never completed because the marshy ground filled in again as fast as a channel was dug.[20] Even if the digging had been successful, Charlemagne would probably have had difficulties with the different levels of the two streams. Surveying techniques were not well developed, and if the two streams had been brought together, the lower would have drained the higher. The same problem had been foreseen by Trajan who feared Pliny's canal would empty the lake near Nicomedia rather than provide communication with the sea. If the Romans were unable to solve the problem of differing water levels in a canal, it is not likely that Charlemagne's engineers would have been successful.

Given the state of technology at the time, the probable solution would have been to bring ditches from the two tributaries towards each other, but to leave a dike between them to keep the waters from mingling. This would have necessitated either transhipping the goods from one level to another, or actually shifting the boats from one canal to the other over a prepared way or by crane. The Greeks accomplished the crossing of the Isthmus of Corinth by the *diolkos,* remains of which were discovered in 1956 near the Corinth Canal. Boats were actually hauled over the four-mile isthmus on special wagons which ran in prepared parallel tracks or ruts, dragged by their crews or draught animals.[21] This method was in use until the ninth century AD. A similar system would have been suitable for Charlemagne.

More practical methods of changing from one water level to another were developed early in the Low Countries. A precursor of the chamber-lock was the *porte d'eau.* This was a dam with a gate which could be opened to let a boat through. Boats going downstream would be carried by the current of the released water, but those headed upstream must have had a more difficult time, having to wait for the levels to equalise and the current to slow. Such dams were mentioned as early as 1080-85 in a charter of Philip I of France. All that was needed to develop the modern lock-chamber was to put two such *portes d'eau* together, leaving enough space between them for the vessel which was changing levels. Rather than this, what developed was the *overdraghe,* an inclined plane of wood barring a river. Water constantly ran down the *overdraghe,* so boats could slide down the inclined plane or be hauled up it by cable and capstan. The *overdraghes* date from the twelfth century.[22] In England, Henry I recut the Roman Fossdyke in 1121. It was used both for drainage and transport.[23]

Perhaps the easiest and safest water transport was that which took place on lakes and inland seas. The freshwater sailors did not have to contend with the currents of the river boatmen or the waves, tides, and severe storms of the deep sea mariners. An intermediate range of difficulty and danger was encountered in coasting—sailing on the salt seas but remaining in sight of the land.

Coasting was the favourite method of the small scale sea trader in both Mediterranean and Atlantic waters throughout antiquity and the early Middle Ages. It was a difficult proposition. Winds could not be depended upon to carry small boats with limited manoeuvrability in the desired direction along a coast and long delays were frequent. Any attempt to gain directional control by adding rowers limited the cargo space and made nightly landings necessary to rest and feed the crew. In northern waters particularly, storms were more violent and fogs more frequent so that it was not possible to rely on visual landmarks. The unsatisfactory alternative was to go by sounding—constantly testing the depth of the water and bringing up samples of the sea bottom. It would take the accumulated knowledge of centuries to develop this method to a satisfactory stage. Neither the necessary techniques nor the capability of recording results for future seafarers were available to the illiterate sailors and traders. With no regular system of beacons for night sailing or sound signals for guidance in fog, wrecks were frequent. Since, by definition, it was not a wreck as long as a human being, a dog, or a cat survived, the local lord of the shore frequently saw to it that there were no survivors in order that he might legally seize what was left of the ship and cargo.[24]

The best area for coastal shipping was probably the North Sea coast of Belgium, Holland, and Germany where there were shallow, sheltered waters between offshore islands and the mainland. Here, and in England, there were coastal changes, sometimes sudden, brought on by storms, sometimes more gradual from silting and subsidence, which aggravated the problems of the coastal seafarer. Frequently it would have been safer and faster to use the open sea where there was more room to manoeuvre and seek favourable winds. But for most of the early Middle Ages neither the technology of shipbuilding nor the techniques of navigation were equal to the problems of open-sea sailing. Two exceptions to the usual custom of coasting are found: the pious Irish who neither knew nor cared where the winds and waves carried them, and the violent Vikings who knew very well where they were going—often over the open sea directly to an unprotected monastery like Lindisfarne where they could obtain riches with little effort.

The logical progression from coastal navigation to sailing on the open seas was accomplished in prehistoric times, but many difficulties remained to plague ancient and medieval mariners. The lack of visual contact with the land raised problems of navigation which were only slowly mastered. It was no longer possible to put in to shore to avoid a storm or tie up for the night. Boats had to be stronger and capable of self-sufficiency for longer periods. The lore of the sea had to be learned and transformed into custom. Mediterranean navigation under the Romans normally ceased from 10 November to 10 March and was considered completely safe only from 26 May to 14 September.[25] The Geniza documents reflecting eastern Mediterranean conditions from the tenth to the thirteenth centuries contain no instances of ships setting sail from November through March.[26] The sailing seasons considered not only safety but also the direction of the prevailing winds.

The Mediterranean sailing season also coincided with the blowing of the Etesian winds, which usually took ships quickly from Italy to Egypt between 15 July and 1 September. Seasonal winds could sometimes be of use for two-way travel. About AD 50 it was discovered that one could sail from Egypt to India on the monsoon and return a short time later on a reverse monsoon.[27] Occasionally ships ventured to sail the Mediterranean during the winter season, but they often encountered discouraging delays which convinced them of the wisdom of the old customs. In 726, St Willibald's voyage from Tyre to Constantinople (p 15 above) took the whole winter, from 30 November to the week before Easter.[28]

The Vikings were more venturesome in more dangerous seas. It was customary to plant in the spring and then go raiding in the summer. A return was made to gather the harvest, and then they went autumn *viking* until one month into the winter.[29] Oddly enough, the closed season in the Baltic and North Seas was shorter than in the Mediterranean. The hardy northerners only stopped sailing from 11 November to 22 February.[30]

Experience and ingenuity sometimes led to the use of the peculiar characteristics of the sea. During the Gothic Wars of Justinian, the flow of the tides was used to provision Ravenna. Boats which were loaded with supplies in deep water rode the inflowing tide up to the city.[31] The reverse current of the ebbing tide may have been used to bring the boats back out to sea again. Such uses of the tides were possible even in the landlocked and comparatively tideless Mediterranean. The northern seas had much greater changes in level to contend with, or utilise.

THE MEANS AND METHODS

Once man had glimpsed the potentialities afforded by waterways, he was obliged to devise means by which they could be used. The simplest and most primitive method was swimming. Both the legendary Beowulf and Charlemagne were noted for their skill in swimming.[32] However, unaided man could carry little extra weight while swimming. Pack animals could support some small loads while swimming but the practice was dangerous and frequently destructive of the contents of the pack. In any case, the quantity of goods that could be transported across water by swimming was extremely limited.

Better results could be obtained by the use of flotation gear. The idea was primitive and many methods were used. In Roman Gaul, inflated skins were used as rafts to transport goods across the rivers, by men called *utricularii*.[33] The Huns aptly combined water and land transport by carrying portable rafts on wagons for use in crossing swampy areas.[34] Shields could even be pressed into service as floats or boats. In Merovingian Gaul, escaping slaves swam a river on their shields.[35]

I

A double-purpose method of water transport, which has continued throughout history, is the flotation of logs downstream. The logs can not only be floated individually, but can be formed into rafts which can carry men and cargo downstream. Upon arrival at the destination, the cargo can be sold and the raft can be broken up and the logs sold. Occasional rafts of this type, which had been lost, have since been recovered by archaeologists. One found at Utrecht dates from the third century AD.[36] Limoges on the Vienne received its wood in this manner from the twelfth century. It was the occasion for a seasonal fete, which broke the monotony of daily life and provided work for many people.[37] The broad, sluggish rivers of Lithuania, Poland, and Galicia were peculiarly fitted to this type of transport and big timber rafts carrying huts to live in, as well as cargo, were frequently floated downstream to market by the Slavs.[38]

Boats were safer than rafts and had a larger capacity in relation to their size. In areas with great supplies of timber it was often possible to find single tree-trunks large enough to make good-sized boats when hollowed out. The boats used by the Scandinavians in their trade with Byzantium were of this type. Each winter the Slavs made dugouts from large logs for the eastern Vikings. The resulting boats were light enough to be carried around rapids and seaworthy enough to sail on the Black Sea.[39]

The Irish and Scots from the fourth to the ninth centuries made much use of light frame boats covered with wickerwork which, in turn, was covered by hides. Boats of this construction—round *coracles* for the rivers and elongated *curraghs* for the sea—were surprisingly seaworthy and were used for saints' voyages as well as pirates' raids.[40] Despite their light construction, these vessels sometimes carried both sails and oars. Cormac sailed due north for fourteen summer days and nights in a skin-covered ship which had full sails set and oars available.[41] The Welsh, also, have long used boats of such construction. There is an account in Giraldus Cambrensis, *Description of Wales*, dating from 1188:

The boats which they employ in fishing or in crossing the rivers are made of twigs, not oblong or pointed, but almost round, or rather triangular, covered both within and without with raw hides. When a salmon thrown into one of these boats strikes it hard with his tail, he often oversets it, and endangers both the vessel and its navigator. The fishermen, according to the custom of the country, in going to and from the rivers, carry these boats on their shoulders; on which occasion that famous dealer in fables, Bledherc, who lived a little before our time, thus mysteriously said: 'There is amongst us a people who, when they go out in search of prey, carry their horses on their backs to the place of plunder; in order to catch their prey, they leap upon their horses, and when it is taken carry their horses home again upon their shoulders.'[42]

It was more common in western Europe to build boats by cutting, shaping, and joining timbers. In the winter of 858-9 such a vessel was built at Ferrières. Twenty trees were requested from the wood of Marnay. Carpenters were borrowed to assist those of the abbey of Ferrières in building a better boat than could be bought.[43]

The construction of larger vessels depended on economic and military necessity, the skill of the builders and sailors, and the availability of materials. The Mediterranean area is an outstanding example of the destructive effects of man on his environment. This is particularly evident in the growing scarcity of satisfactory timber for shipbuilding. Areas such as Cyprus and Italy, which had furnished great fleets in antiquity, became largely denuded of large trees. Strabo described the forests of Cyprus as being so thick that they impeded agriculture. Even though they were used to build fleets of ships, and for the smelting of ores, they grew faster than they were consumed until a law was passed giving legal title to the land to those who cleared the forests.[44] In Ostrogothic Italy, Theodoric was still able to construct 1,000 *dromons* (large rowing vessels) at Ravenna, from cypress and pine timbers which were floated down the rivers.[45] Venice constructed a large fleet for the transport of the Fourth Crusaders.[46] Dalmatia was stripped of timber which was traded to the Moslems for the construction of their fleets. Later Venice had to range far and wide to produce adequate materials for her own fleets.[47]

Northwestern Europe furnished a contrast. The reduction in population and economic activity after the decline of Rome's authority furnished an opportunity for revitalisation of the land and regrowth of the forests. In areas which had remained outside Roman control, the availability of materials suitable for shipbuilding was in excess of the demand. It required only the development of skills and techniques to ensure fuller use of timber resources.

Increases in the size of ships necessitated changes in the methods of propulsion. The current could carry rafts and boats downstream. Only the occasional use of a pole was required for guidance. In shallow water a pole, or lance-butt, could be used to push against the stream-bottom. Merovingian Gaul provides an example of progressive desperation in boat propulsion. Twenty men and their spoils from a pillaged monastery tried to cross a river in a boat. The boat was probably overloaded and they lacked the necessary skill to handle it. The boat became unstable and they lost their oars. They attempted to use the butt-ends of their spears as poles against the river bed and the boat came apart. The misadventure came to a moral conclusion when all the thieves but one were transfixed on their own spear points and killed.[48]

In deeper waters, where the bottom was out of reach, other techniques were needed. Small boats could be paddled while the crewmen faced forward. Little force could be exerted in this manner, since one hand had to play the part of a fulcrum and paddles had to remain small to be usable. More power could be applied by rowing. The oar was a lever, balanced at the oar-lock, which acted as a fulcrum. By counterweighting the handle the blade could be made of considerable length. As men could pull more effectively than they could push, rowers faced the stern. Consequently, an additional man was needed in the stern to steer and give guidance to the oarsmen. With rowing, the power available for propulsion increased faster than the size of the vessel until certain limits were reached, which were dictated by the materials used and the size of the oars that could be manipulated by individuals or groups. Until this limit was reached, larger oared-vessels were faster and more manoeuvrable than small ones. Advantage naturally fell to the people whose rowers had the greatest strength, endurance, health, and morale. Much discipline and training were required to make an effective crew which rowed as one man and reacted swiftly to commands. The Vikings were the outstanding oarsman of the early Middle Ages and were well fitted for the task by heredity and experience.

Northern ships, which had a flexible, limber construction, and a single bank of oars, may have reached their effective limit in size quite early. King Alfred in 897 tried to counter the Vikings by making ships twice as long as theirs.[49] His sailors had difficulty in catching the Vikings, whose ships had a shallower draught and were more manoeuvrable. Attempts to increase the size of Viking ships raised problems with the keel, rigging, rowing, and steering. The great Viking ships around 1000 such as Olaf Trygvason's Long Serpent with its seventy-eight oars and King Cnut's great ship with 120 oars were clearly more for display purposes than use.[50] Mediterranean rowing ships were able to reach a greater size. Their construction was more rigid, and as they often had more than one bank of oars, they were able to build more power into a ship of given size. In addition, Mediterranean weather was not so violent as that of the Atlantic and the North Sea, so larger ships were not subjected to such great strains.[51]

The warships with their oars had sufficient manpower to navigate without the wind and even against the wind. Nevertheless, a favourable breeze was an opportune auxiliary and sails could lighten the efforts of the rowers. Many materials could be used for sails, such as skins and leather, but specially woven sail-cloth was more satisfactory. The incentive for the development of sailing came not from the warships, which with their large crews and oars were quite independent of the weather, but from the trading vessels. For the merchants each added crew member meant so much less space for valuable cargo and another partner to share in the profits of the voyage. Economic reasons dictated the use of small crews and the employment of nature whenever possible. Limiting the crews, while it encouraged ingenuity and the development of sailing techniques, did make the merchants more dependent on the vagaries of wind and weather for the transport of their goods.[52]

SOME DIFFICULTIES AND LIMITATIONS

Water transport, particularly that on the open sea, is subject to obstruction and limitation from both natural causes, such as climate and geography, and human interference, such as piracy and tolls. The weather is more severe in the northern seas than in the Mediterranean, but the capability and daring of the sailors seems to have been greater (see above, p 132).

Geographic obstacles are more forbidding to water transport than climatic phenomena. It was not the weather that caused shipwrecks as often as the rocky shore on to which the ships were driven. The Vikings lost a fleet containing badly needed reinforcements in a storm off Swanage in 877.[53] The loss seriously hampered their campaign and kept their army on the defensive in Wessex.

Land obstacles could sometimes be surmounted. The *nautae* in Roman Gaul probably handled the transport of goods overland from one river to another.[54] The Greeks even managed to haul ships over the Isthmus of Corinth by means of the *diolkos* (see above p 130). The Viking ships were often taken overland.[55] During the First Crusade, boats were dragged by oxen over the mountains and through the woods from Kivotos to the lake at Nicea.[56]

Interference from other men was often as serious as that from nature. River traffic was interrupted for tolls (see above p 94). It was checked to prevent the export of critical goods to adversaries. Merchants were not allowed to bring weapons and coats of mail to the Slavs.[57] Toll stations were established along the Danube, specifying in minute detail the charges for different types of goods.[58] Liutprand of Cremona was not allowed to bring purple cloaks from Constantinople.[59]

Those who wished to use the rivers for their own purposes interfered with transport. Fishermen constructed weirs and kiddles to channel and trap the fish, even though the rivers were supposed to be 'open for the passage of ships and boats for the common profit of the people'.[60] Millers constructed dams and erected water-wheels which hindered transport.

Saracen and Norse piracy made the open seas unsafe for shipping in the ninth century. The rising Italian cities warred on each other's ships from the eleventh century. The goods of shipwrecked vessels belonged to the owner of the shore. Some lords made it a practice to lure ships with false lights.

A rare and possibly unique hindrance to Byzantine shipping was encountered in the time of Justinian. A wandering whale named Porphyrius found its way into the Bosporus and annoyed Byzantine water transport for fifty years. It sank some boats, drove others off course, and terrified the passengers. Finally, its career was ended when it ran aground and became stuck in the mud. It was dragged ashore with ropes. Its body, forty-five feet long and fifteen feet thick, was cut up and hauled away on wagons.[61]

THE VESSELS—TECHNOLOGY OF WATER TRANSPORT

In contrast with Roman land transport, it is possible to identify many of the Roman ship types mentioned in the literature with their pictured representations found on mosaics, wall-paintings, and bas-reliefs. A mosaic found in Africa associates the names and representations of twenty-five types of ship. A further contrast with Roman vehicles is that few of the names of ships are derived from the Celtic language.[62] The ship types which the Romans used throughout the empire were of

Mediterranean origin stemming from Phoenicia and Greece by way of the Carthaginians and Etruscans.

Much light has been shed on the techniques of building and sailing ancient ships by the pioneering studies of Professor Lionel Casson.[63] Roman hulls were always carvel built, that is with the planks placed edge to edge and carefully mortised together to make a snug-fitting, rigid, and strong shell. What is new is Casson's revelation that, contrary to modern practice and the ideas of earlier scholars, the frames of Roman ships were inserted after the shell was complete.[64] Ships of such construction—large and small, warships and merchantmen—plied the Mediterranean for centuries. The end of the empire in the west may have meant a reduced volume in traffic, but it did not mean an immediate regression in the techniques of shipbuilding. The Vandals became quickly seaborne after their conquest of North Africa in the early fifth century, but they merely appropriated Roman ships and shipbuilding methods since they had no precedents of their own to follow. Similarly, the Ostrogothic kingdom in Italy continued the construction of ships on the Roman model (see above, p 135). Such large-scale construction probably dealt a severe blow to the forests of the region. The Romans tried unsuccessfully to prevent the barbarians from acquiring plans from Roman shipbuilders (Codex Theodosianus, IX, 40.24).

The Byzantine empire continued the practices of antiquity with little change, at least until the seventh century. Most of the Byzantine ships have disappeared without trace. It is only recently that the techniques of underwater archaeology have been sufficiently developed to make possible the study *in situ* of Byzantine ships which have been wrecked.[65] The results of such pioneering work amplify (and greatly modify) our knowledge of Byzantine marine technology. In general, Mediterranean ships were larger than those of the northern seas. The cataphracts of Mark Antony at Actium in 31 BC measured about 200 feet at the keel.[66] The Moslems took to seafaring with enthusiasm when their conquests reached the Mediterranean and some of the largest early medieval ships were

Moslem. One which was beached during the conquest of Egypt in 969 measured 275 feet in length.[67] Byzantine ships were not only large and numerous, but were built in many specialised varieties. An expedition sent to Crete in 960 had 2,000 warships, some of them with 250 rowers and four banks of oars, as well as 1,360 supply ships, and some landing-craft with ramps by which the heavy cavalry could disembark directly on the beach.[68] William of Tyre (Book 20.13) describes a Byzantine fleet of 1169 as having 150 galleys with beaks and double tiers of oars, 60 larger well-armoured horse transports with openings in the stern to load and unload and also bridges to embark and land men and horses, and 10 or 20 huge *dromones* carrying supplies, arms, and engines and machines of war including, doubtless, the famous Greek fire.

In the matter of sails and rigging, the researches of Lionel Casson have pushed the frontiers of knowledge back many hundreds of years, showing that not only multi-masted ships but some varieties of fore-and-aft rig were known and used by the Greeks and Romans. By convincing evidence he has shown that lateen and sprit sails were known to them and that only the gaff sail seems not to have been used.[69] A rather convincing representation of the gaff sail is to be seen on a sarcophagus from Ostia from the second or third century AD in the Ny Carlsberg Glyptotek in Copenhagen, thereby indicating that the ancients knew all types of fore-and-aft rig.[70]

Navigation, particularly in the Mediterranean, was aided by the presence of lighthouses. Elaborate harbours and numerous guiding beacons had been provided by the Romans and were continued in use, particularly by the Byzantines and Moslems. Atlantic Europe was less well-equipped and less able to maintain such installations. The chief examples to survive into the Middle Ages were the Roman lighthouses at Boulogne and Dover, placed to assist navigation in the Channel and that at La Coruña in northwest Spain. Although available as landmarks, it is doubtful whether they were used on a regular basis after the breakdown of Roman authority. The building of permanent stone lighthouses came again with the upsurge

in economic activity and the reacquired mastery of building
in stone soon after the year 1000. The Italian port cities, such
as Genoa, had stone lighthouses in the early twelfth century.[71]
In the Mediterranean, large fleets of war-vessels were controlled and manoeuvred by the use of flags and light-signals.[72]
An example of the discipline achieved in this way is the defeat
of the Russian fleet attacking Constantinople during the reign
of Constantine IX Monomachus (1042-55) by a well-controlled
Byzantine fleet using Greek fire (Michael Psellus, *Chrono-
graphia,* Book VI, Ch. 94-5). Analogues to such methods of
maritime communication were the beacon systems maintained
by both the Saracens and the Byzantines. A chain of mountain-
top beacon stations across Asia Minor was able to give warning to Constantinople within one hour whenever the Moslems
crossed the Cilician frontier.[73] In the tenth century the Arabs
were able to communicate by beacon fires across North Africa
from Alexandria to Ceuta in one day.[74]

Conditions in northern seas were much more rudimentary.
An early description of ships from the northern seas is found
in Caesar (*Bell. Gall.* 3.13). The *Veneti* of Brittany had ships
whose keels were flatter than those of the Romans. They were
'double-ended', ie both prow and stern were high and pointed.
The sides were built of oak planks held by iron spikes. Iron
was also used for anchor chains. The sails were made of skins
and thin leather. Strabo (*Geography* 4.4.1) gives a similar description and adds that the gaps in the planks were stuffed with
sea-weed to keep the wood moist when the ships were hauled
out. With few modifications, these descriptions could apply to
later Viking ships. The fact that they were hauled out of the
water during the winter season indicates that the ships of the
Veneti were not large.

Despite the similarity of appearance, it is not likely that
the vessels of the *Veneti* had much influence on the development of the Scandinavian ships. Because of the fortunate
preservation of a few northern vessels in ship burials, it is
possible to trace their evolution over a period of several centuries. Many of the characteristics of the Viking ships were in

existence before the time of the *Veneti*. A boat found at Hjort-
spring near Als, Denmark, dates from *c* 350 BC. It is about
forty feet long and the planks overlap each other (clinker-
built). The planks are lashed together rather than nailed. This
gives a flexibility which is characteristic of northern ships.
They tend to give slightly and adapt themselves to the waves
rather than rigidly oppose them as the stiff Mediterranean
vessels did. The Als boat had no mast for sails but was propelled by paddlers who faced forward.[75]

An additional step is seen in the Nydam ship, from Schles-
wig in the third century AD. The Nydam vessel is longer, about
seventy-seven feet, and twenty-eight oars were used. The
switch from paddles to oars represents an increase in power
because the oar is a lever pivoted on a firm fulcrum, the oar-
lock, while the paddler has to provide his own support. The
hull of the Nydam vessel is built up of long planks which are
both lashed and nailed, combining flexibility and durability.[76]
A literary mention from the sixth century AD (Procopius,
History of the Wars, VIII, xx. 28-31) confirms the archaeological discoveries by indicating that English ships of that
period had no sails but were propelled solely by oars.[77]

The Sutton Hoo ship, from *c* AD 650, shows several interesting tendencies, which are not necessarily progressive. The
length is about 80 feet, only slightly longer than that of the
Nydam ship, but the sides are composed of short planks riveted
together to make long strakes. This may indicate a growing
shortage, in England, of large trees from which to make long
planks. It is also peculiar that the Sutton Hoo ship has thirty-
eight oars compared to the twenty-eight of the Nydam vessel.
This necessitates placing the oarlocks closer together and may
mean that the English rowers were smaller and had shorter
arms than the northeners. Neither the Sutton Hoo nor Nydam
ships had a mast for a sail. The lack of an effective keel also
made them longitudinally weak.[78]

It is only with such vessels as that of Gokstad, Norway,
c 800, that the Viking ship becomes truly effective. The Gokstad ship, while it was nearly the same size as those of Nydam

and Sutton Hoo, had important differences. It had a keel nearly eighty feet long made from a single straight oak. In addition to its thirty-two oars, it had a mast for a single square sail.[79] It was only at this point in their development that the Viking ships became capable of long ocean voyages. The long keel gave a strength to the structure which made it truly seaworthy and also provided a firm anchorage for the keelson, the large timber which provided the socket for the mast and prevented it from smashing the ship's bottom. The addition of the sail made constant rowing unnecessary. With favourable winds the ship could continue through the night on the open seas. It was no longer necessary to hug the coast and heave-to every night to rest the rowers. These developments add a technical explanation to the reasons for the outburst of Viking activity beginning in the late eighth century. The raids were not possible before the keel and the sail were added to the oared longboat.[80]

The technological innovations which led to the unusual effectiveness of the Viking ships during the ninth century invasions also limited their future development. In the hands of their highly trained crews they were able to sail the high seas and descend without warning on their victims. Their successful navigation of violent waters was due more to cooperation with the winds, waves, and currents than to their opposing these elements. The culmination of long experience and many experiments was a ship which had the proper combination of flexibility and firmness for the northern waters. Because of its lightness it sailed over, rather than through, the waves. The lightness, small size, and shallow draught also made possible the deep penetration of hinterlands by ascending even small rivers. When need arose the ships could even be carried or dragged overland.

Despite their small size, the Vikings' ships required at least one large timber. The necessary combination of strength and flexibility was only achieved by making the keel in one piece. Such timbers as that of the Gokstad ship must always have been hard to come by. The fitting out of the numerous Viking fleets must have stripped the Scandinavian forests of suitable trees.[81] When a replica of the Gokstad ship was built in 1893, the makers were unable to find a proper tree for the keel in all the forests of Norway.[82]

While the Viking ships were extremely effective, their evolution was really towards a *cul-de-sac*. They could not be made larger without sacrificing some of their merits. Even for the smaller ships, the size of the keel taxed the capabilities of the forests. A longer keel formed by joining pieces was too weak to function properly. Increasing the size of the vessel increased its draught and limited its use in small streams and shallow waters. The heavier ships required proportionately greater strength because they sailed through, rather than over, the water. As we have seen, (above p 137), it is doubtful if King Alfred's ships, made larger than those of the Vikings, were really very successful.[83] The kings in the north sometimes had larger ships, but they were more effective for display than in war. None of these large ships has survived. The literary descriptions of their size may be exaggerated. Olaf Trygvason's Long Serpent, *c* 1000, was supposed to have been the largest and finest ever constructed, with its seventy-eight oars.[84] King Cnut is credited with a long-ship of 120 oars which would have necessitated a length of 250 to 300 feet, far too large for efficiency.[85]

It has been thought that the Viking ships, with their single square sail, could only run directly before the wind and that they could not tack, or even sail close to the wind. This view has recently been challenged.[86] While the single yard arm was attached by its centre to the top of the mast, there was nothing that required it to maintain a permanent right angle with the axis of the vessel. The mast was small enough to be stepped and unstepped easily and was so braced that no shrouds or stays seem to have been necessary.[87] The connection to the mast was flexible and the sail could be shifted to take advantage of the wind direction by adjusting the lengths of the sheets. If need be, the sail could even be swung to a fore-and-aft position by attaching the sheets to the bow and stern rather than the sides

(see Life, *Barbarian Europe*, 128). This flexibility in the use
of the sail may go far towards explaining some of the tremendous voyages made by the Northmen.

The overlapping plank method of construction (clinker-
building) resulted in a strong but light boat. In such construction the hull covering, or skin, is so bent, stressed, and nailed
at the overlapping seams that it constitutes the main element
of strength. The frame and ribs are added after the fully
formed skin is built.[88] Clinker construction is best suited for
the building of small boats which can ride lightly on the water.
It is not well suited for the construction of large ships, or
those which carry heavy cargoes. Clinker-building was another
blind-alley for the Viking ship. It was very efficient for small
ships but it limited further development.

In discussing northern ships, the caution should be added
that we have neither the great longships of the sagas nor the
more seaworthy merchantmen which the Vikings themselves
insisted on using for long ocean voyages. The Oseberg find,
in particular, is more of a royal pleasure-barge than a seafaring long-ship. The sagas note that longships could not go to
Iceland or the Faeroes (*Heimskringla*, ed. F. Jonsson, 1936,
128 and *Faereyinga Saga*, ed Rafn, 1832, 100). The usual ship
for long ocean voyages, such as that to America, was the
knörr, a type of *hafskip*, which was broader and shorter than
the longship, and had a deeper draught and higher freeboard.[89]

The Irish were unique in water transport as well as in land
transport. Like the Vikings, they achieved great results with
a type of boat whose development could only go so far (see
above, p 134).

The central stern-post rudder was not known in early
medieval times. The Greeks and Romans, as well as the later
Norsemen, had all used large steering oars attached to the side
of the ship close to the stern. This was not an inefficient
arrangement. It did not interfere with the clean hydrodynamic
lines of the ship. It could be raised and lowered easily, extended beneath the keel in deep water, and brought higher in
shallow.[90] Antique and early medieval ships were very nearly

double-ended. Both prow and stern were pointed. The ships were very manoeuvrable and could reverse direction easily. The modern Vikings who sailed a replica of the Gokstad ship across the Atlantic in 1893 were amazed at the responsiveness and sure control they obtained from their steering-oar rudder.[91] When the central stern rudder was introduced, it was necessary to redesign the ship hull in order to accommodate it. The stern had to be flattened to evade hull turbulence before the central stern rudder could be effective.[92] The origins of the stern-post rudder, like those of so many other medieval inventions, can be traced to China where it was known in the eighth century AD.[93]

The European introduction or invention of the stern-post rudder probably occurred in the late twelfth century, although the evidence is not conclusive. The ship on the font in Winchester Cathedral is usually dated to about 1180, but there is doubt as to whether it really represents a centralised stern-post rudder. Similarly, the Ipswich seal may be almost as old as the Winchester font, or it may be a forgery, but in any case, it has not been found in use on any document dating before 1349. Clear evidence of the stern rudder is found in the seals of the Baltic towns of Elbing (1242) and Wismar (1256).[94] The changeover to the stern-post rudder was not necessarily rapid. Representations of the old steering-oar continue for centuries, particularly in the Mediterranean. The Scandinavians lagged in converting to the new type of hull, and Holland and England became leaders in shipbuilding in the fourteenth century.[95]

The future did not lie with the Viking longships, which reached the peak of their development in the ninth century. It did not lie with the Irish leather-covered wickerwork boats. Both of these types made remarkable voyages but they were incapable of further development. If ships of greater capacity were to be built, they had to be made in another style. The ordinary, small, tub-like trading ship (variously called round ship, cog, or kogge) did have possibilities for evolution. It was constructed with a rigid frame. Its size could be increased without lessening its capabilities. Less skill was needed in the construction and smaller pieces of timber could be used. Carvel-building, with the planks laid edge-to-edge, was adopted from the Mediterranean. From the twelfth century shipping turned to the round ship. By the fourteenth century the round ship had evolved considerably. It was larger, had more masts and sails, had a stern-post rudder, and was carvel-built.[96] The new ships may not have been as handy in the water as the Viking longships, but they did have a greater capacity. The increase in the number of sails (and eventually the introduction of the lateen sail from the Mediterranean) made them more controllable and resulted in a saving in the use of manpower.

NAVIGATION

Little can be said of navigation techniques in the early medieval period. They were probably based on long experience and great familiarity with nature. The Vikings used a technique similar to that of the Roman voyagers to India. From about 800 to 850 they came directly across the North Sea to England with the east winds of the spring and returned by the westerly gales of the autumn.[97] This technique enabled them to surprise the English. Their accurate landfalls are still unexplained. They seem to have come directly to predetermined targets. Celestial observations without instruments are not likely to yield such results. It has been seriously proposed that the Vikings may even have known the use of the magnetic compass.[98]

In high latitudes where magnetic declinations are so great and where many of the Viking voyages were made, the mariner's compass even if known would have been of little use. It has been observed that many of the voyages were made by following parallels of latitude, eg from Hernum in Norway to Hvarf in Greenland, and this could not have been done by use of a magnetic compass because of variation. It is just possible that the Vikings may have possessed something better than the compass.

Page 149 (*above*) A monument at Igel showing a Roman two-wheeled vehicle drawn by two mules; (below) Roman two-wheeled vehicle drawn by a single horse in shafts (Provincial Museum, Trier)

Page 150 (*above*) Typical Roman four-wheeled vehicle; (*below*) Roman child's chariot drawn by a single ass in shafts (Louvre, Paris)

They needed methods of latitude estimation as well as directivity determination. Oddi Helgason, usually called 'Star Oddi', living in the early eleventh century, not only studied the stars but made a table of sun azimuths.[99] Since voyages in high latitudes were made in summer months when stars are invisible, solar observation would seem the more likely method. The problem of fog and cloud raises difficulties here. There is mention in the Saga of St Olaf of a sun stone (*Solarstein* or *Sonnenstein*) which showed the position of the sun when it was invisible because of clouds. Dr Heinrich Winter was unable to discover any mineral with such a quality.[100] The account sounds like legend, but, in a daring hypothesis, Dr Thorkild Ramskou of the Danish National Museum has suggested that materials do exist in Scandinavia and Iceland which have such properties. Crystals, such as cordierite, have natural polarising characteristics and react like modern sky compasses with their polarising lenses. In tests a crystal located the sun within $2\frac{1}{2}°$ and even tracked it 7° below the horizon.[101] While this is theoretical, it does provide a plausible explanation of the sun stone.

Simpler methods, of course, such as boards to measure the sun's shadow could be used when the sun was visible.[102] In some cases, conjectures can be made as to other methods used. The annual migration of geese from Ireland to Iceland also coincides with the season of favourable winds. It is possible that the Irish may have found their way to Iceland by following the geese.[103] Tame, or captive, birds could be released at sea to find the nearest land. The Norse found Iceland in the late ninth century by this method. Floki took three ravens to sea—the first released returned to Norway, the second stayed with the ship, and the last he followed towards Iceland.[104]

In the rest of Europe the introduction of instruments for navigation occurred only in the late Middle Ages. Astrolabes to find the latitude were known in the Mediterranean from the sixth century, but there is no record of their use for navigation. They were instruments for the land-based astrologer and astronomer. The directive properties of the lodestone had long

K

been known to the Chinese. By the fifth century AD they had learned to magnetise a steel needle by stroking its point with a lodestone, and by the tenth century they were using it for navigation. The earliest clearly attested mention of the magnetic compass in the west is in 1190 by Alexander Neckham (*De naturis rerum*, II, cap 98; ed T. Wright, p 183) in which sailors wishing to find their way touch a lodestone with a needle which whirls in a circle and then settles down to point north. This tells little of the way in which the needle may have been suspended and probably indicates a poor quality of steel which had to be magnetised for each use.[105] Maps for the use of navigators and accurate sailing charts (*portolani*) for the Mediterranean area only appear in the late thirteenth century.[106] The achievements of the Irish and Norse navigators are the more remarkable because they were accomplished with only crude sighting devices, giving merely an approximation of the latitude and no information on the longitude. The Icelandic sagas, especially in their earlier oral versions, were also useful as sailing directions.[107] Leif Ericson had no difficulty in following Bjarni Herjulfson's directions to reach Vinland.

Notes to this chapter are on pp 206-13.

Some social and economic
considerations

THE RELATIONSHIP OF LAND AND WATER TRANSPORT

LONG-DISTANCE TRANSPORT can scarcely ever confine itself exclusively to either land or water. It is more often necessary for both methods to be used to link the places of production and consumption. Land and water ways may act to reinforce each other. Roads may be built linking the head of navigation of one river with that of another. The ways may also interfere with each other. A bridge or ford may be a connecting link in a road network but at the same time an interruption to river navigation, necessitating the transhipment of cargoes.

Inscriptions have been found relating to organisations responsible for water transport in Roman Gaul but there are, as yet, no corresponding inscriptions concerning land transport corporations. From this it is possible to infer that the boatmen on lakes and rivers (*nautae*) also handled transport between bodies of water.[1] If such was the case, there still remained the problems of initial delivery to the waterhead and final transport from the nearest convenient point on the water to the destination or place of consumption. As groups like the *nautae* were merely transporters, it is unlikely that they handled initial collection and final delivery; probably these were matters for the producers and the consumers. Similarly, the *navicularii,* who handled shipping on the seas and great rivers, would only deliver at the ports. The proprietors of *villae,* or estates, must

153

have made their own arrangements—usually with their own slaves or draught animals—for receipt from and delivery to the organisation of water transporters.

Evidence for organisations of transport workers in early medieval times is rare. There were such associations in seventh-century Rome.[2] Land and water transport were associated in late Merovingian Gaul. Transport by carts as well as boats is mentioned in 716 (*constituta evectio tam carralis quam navalis*).[3] The officials at the Fos toll were required to furnish goods to the monastery. They also had to provide transport for the goods to the emissaries of the monastery. Unfree *fiscalini* (serfs belonging to the government) were organised for transport work in royal charters at Worms in 897 and 904.[4]

Land and water transport assisted each other under the Huns with their portable bridges carried on wagons.[5] Charlemagne, also, had a bridge, set up on river boats, which could be put together and taken apart, presumably for ease in transporting (*Annales Regni Francorum,* under year 792). The early Viking raiders travelled light, bringing only themselves and their weapons to East Anglia. There they seized horses for use in land transport.[6] Within a few years they were transporting not only their wives and children but even horses on their ships.[7] The method was little, if any, improved by the Normans who also brought horses to England by ship for their invasion.[8] As mentioned above (p 141), horse transport was better handled in the Mediterranean, especially by the Byzantines. By the time of the Fourth Crusade horse transport was managed in specially built boats (*vuissiers*) by the Venetians.[9]

Land and water transport are most likely to complement and assist each other at the head of navigation on a river. Here water-borne goods must be shifted to land transport to reach the interior and goods headed downstream or overseas find it advantageous to switch to water transport. The head of navigation is also likely to mark the lowest fordable or bridgeable point on the stream. If such is the case, land and water transport have little cause for conflict and such a location may be advantageous for the growth of a trading settlement.

Land transport often conflicts with water transport when there is still navigable water above the crossing-point. Fords which are shallow enough for safe crossing by pedestrians and pack-animals are not deep enough for much shipping. The design of bridges is controversial. Water transport prefers no bridges, but requires them to be high enough above the water surface for the passage of boats. Single-span Roman bridges with their semi-circular arches tended to be of this type. Land transport requires bridges for the safe and dry crossing of men and goods and prefers a flat, rather than an arched, surface for the roadway as it crosses the bridge. Piers channel the river, create currents, and obstruct navigation. Bridges and fords by interfering with navigation often made it necessary to tranship goods from one vessel to another.

Bridging points are often the best locations for interrupting water-borne invasions. The Ostrogothic leader Totila attempted to block the approach of Belisarius up the Tiber to Rome. He spanned the river with very long timbers and built wooden towers on the ends of this bridge to block boats coming up from Portus (next to Ostia). In addition, he stretched an iron chain across the river below the bridge. Nevertheless, Belisarius was able to remove the chain, burn the towers, and destroy the bridge.[10]

It is not likely that the precedent of Totila influenced the Parisians in their efforts to protect their city against the Vikings. The city had been sacked several times and it was not until 885 that the inhabitants were ready to obstruct the passage of the Norsemen by means of fortified bridges. The bridges were substantial enough to support powerful catapults.[11] The bridges withstood furious assaults. Finally, it was not the action of the Vikings but the pressure of the river Seine that broke the bridge from the Isle of the City to the left bank, isolating the tower there and enabling the Norsemen to burn it and force the defenders to surrender.[12] Charles the Bald had made many attempts to forbid river passage to the Vikings. In 862 he stationed troops on both banks of the Oise, Marne, and Seine to prevent pillage by the Norsemen. When they destroyed the bridges and seized all available boats, Charles repaired a bridge to prevent their coming back down the river (*Annales Bertiniani,* under year 862). His most extensive work of this type was near Pistre on the Seine where he marched with labourers and carts to construct works (probably a forti- fied bridge) to stop the Vikings from reascending the river (*Annales Bertiniani,* under year 866).

That the Vikings learned to handle the problem of fortified bridges is seen in the Saga of St Olaf, *c* 1009. According to the account, a bridge broad enough for two wagons side-by-side crossed the Thames connecting London with Southwark. The bridge had parapets and towers and was supported by piles driven into the bed of the river. Troops stood all over the bridge and prevented the ships of Olaf and King Ethelred from ascending the river. Olaf roofed his ships with wood from old houses to protect them from the stones, arrows, and spears cast down from the bridge. With such protection, his ships were able to row under the bridge, attach cables to the supporting piles, and pull the piles loose by rowing back downstream as hard as possible. The bridge collapsed and many of the de- fenders fell into the river.[13]

Another fundamental cause of conflict between land and water transport occurred when routes of both types connected two localities. Traffic was confronted with a choice. Such factors as economy, speed, and safety often influenced the decision. Justinian seems only to have been swayed by economy in his modifications of the *cursus publicus*. By making the couriers use boats between Byzantium and Helenopolis in Bithynia he was able to eliminate several stations, with their stables of post-horses, along the route. His act resulted in a less dependable public post. The sea route was slower and more dangerous. The couriers were unskilled sailors and re- sented being unseated from their mounts. Justinian's reforms of the public post resulted in a deterioration of morale and efficiency.[14]

In the Middle Ages, wars, political instability, brigandage, piracy, and the multiplication of tolls often made a change of routes advisable for travellers and merchants. The application of tolls was often very selective. In the later Middle Ages tolls forced the transporters of grain away from the Rhine river route. Grain was moved by land transport at the same time that lumber, intended for the same destination, was floated down the Rhine.[15]

Competition between types of transport led to improvements in routes. Tolls might be reduced to retain traffic. Transport altered its route accordingly. Usually water transport remained cheaper per unit of distance than land transport, but often the water route was so much longer that total transport costs were nearly equal and traffic would be influenced by minor changes in routes and charges. In a very rare case in 1318 land transport was cheaper than sea transport for a comparable distance. The Del Bene company of Florence paid lower transport charges per mile overland from Paris to Marseille than from Marseille to Pisa by water.[16]

THE COST OF TRANSPORT

Late Roman. Costs of transport seldom concerned classical writers. When Rome was in the ascendancy and manpower was abundant there was no need to consider economy. In earlier times, during the Republic, at least one writer did focus his attention on the expenses of transport. Cato the Elder, 234-149 BC, considered the problem of moving a large oil-crusher or mill. Nearly five hundred years later, in AD 301, Diocletian attempted to control prices in an economy where costs had again become of extreme importance.

Cato the Elder needed an oil-crusher for his farm at Venafrum in central Italy. He knew he could buy one at Suessa, twenty-five miles away, for 400 sesterces and fifty pounds of oil, or at Pompeii, a distance of seventy-five miles, for 384 sesterces. Such a mill was too large to be shipped complete. To transport it disassembled would require the services of six men, including drivers of oxen. The ox teams would require six days to make the trip from Suessa. (An average of scarcely four miles per day says little for the speed of the oxen or the condition of the roads.) The expense of transport would be seventy-two sesterces, the wages of six men for six days.

Daily wages would then be two sesterces per man, or the mill could be moved for about three sesterces per mile. Less information is given about the mill at Pompeii, but the total freight charge to Venafrum would be 280 sesterces. This probably refers to land transport, as the Via Latina would have been available for much of the distance between the two points. Movement by water along the coast and up the river Volturnus would have been longer and would have necessitated several transhipments. Transport of the mill from Pompeii would then have been at a rate of nearly four sesterces per mile. The data indicate that transport by land increased total costs very quickly. A movement of one hundred miles would nearly double the price of the mill.[17]

By the time of Diocletian, the Roman Empire had lost much of its prosperity and the currency was severely inflated. Concern for costs was again necessary. In AD 301, Diocletian issued an Edict concerning prices, wages, and transport costs. Although there is reason to doubt whether the price regulations prescribed by Diocletian were adhered to, the Edict on Prices does contain a mass of economic and social information. From the prescriptions given it is possible to calculate the proportion transport costs bear to the total price of a product. Most of the Edict's material on transport is concerned with land transport. Only recently-discovered fragments give information on sea transport.

As envisaged by the Edict, the selling price of an item was to be determined by a computation including the original price, the weight, the distance transported, and the time involved in transit.[18] No allowance seems to have been made for profit, which doubtless helps to explain the unpopularity and lack of success of the Edict. Since freight charges were based on weight and not on the value of the cargo, the cheaper heavy articles suffered a steeper proportional rise in price as a result of transport charges.

Difficulties arise in interpreting the Edict because many items are measured in units of volume while wagon-loads are measured by weight. In making computations it is necessary to estimate the weight of a camp-measure (*castrensis modius*) of certain commodities. Authorities are in agreement that a *castrensis modius* equals about two pecks of English measure. A *castrensis modius* of wheat, for example, should weigh about thirty pounds, and about forty of them should fit into the normal wagon-bed of the time. Draught animals for wagons are not specified in the Edict, but were probably oxen. The daily distance travelled by an ox team was probably six or seven miles.[19]

By applying these estimates to the data given in the Edict, the cost of land transport can be calculated. The price of wheat was 100 *denarii* per *castrensis modius*.[20] A wagon-load cost about 4,000 *den*. The freight charge was 20 *den*. per mile,[21] but this was increased by the driver's wages, 25 *den*. per day, plus maintenance.[22] Fodder for the animals came at the rate of 4lb of hay for 2 *den*.,[23] and there may have been other charges. A fair estimate for a day's journey (seven miles by ox-team) would probably be about 200 *den*. Two weeks' time and nearly 3,000 *den*. (75 per cent of the purchase price) would have to be allowed to move the wheat for a journey of one hundred miles. In certain areas and seasons it might be appropriate to use other means of transport, such as pack-animals. Camels could carry 600 lb for 8 *den*. per mile and an ass-load (probably of 300lb) travelled a mile for only 4 *den*.[24]

Pack-animals are thus more economical than wagons, according to the Edict's tariffs (1 1/3 *den*. per 100lb per mile compared with 1 2/3 *den*. per 100lb per mile for wagons). In actuality, the differential was greater because several pack-animals can be linked together or driven in a group by one man, whereas each wagon requires a driver. Such other factors as the amount of fodder consumed and the ability to negotiate rough terrain also favoured the use of pack-animals. Consequently, under the conditions of the Edict, loads which could be broken into smaller units could be more economically borne by pack-animals than drawn by oxen, even though a load could be left on a wagon, whereas pack-animals must be unloaded every night.

The enormous cost of land transport was even more apparent in the case of articles which were heavy but comparatively cheap. The price for a 1,200lb wagon-load of wood was set at 150 *den.*[25] It is not likely that this price was in force for choice timbers, such as those used for ship and wagon-building, but for scraps useful for burning. This was not a negligible item of commerce. The 800-900 public baths of the city of Rome consumed tremendous quantities of wood for heating water. The bulky nature of wood made it more unwieldy for pack-animals. Camels could carry 400lb and asses 200.[26] The most extraordinary characteristic of such an article as wood was the rapidity with which transport charges mounted. After scarcely seven miles, the freight charge was equal to the original cost.[27] Under such conditions, wood could scarcely be transported far, either by wagon or pack-animal.

Major factors affecting the cost of ancient land transport were the lack of carrying capacity and the lack of speed. The pack-animals seem to cut a better figure here than the wheeled vehicles. The loads carried by camels, mules, and asses seem reasonable, while those of the wagons seem to be extremely light. Camels in their proper environment, and asses under nearly any conditions, can cover many miles daily, but the four miles per day of Cato the Elder's ox teams, or even the six to seven miles a day attained by the ox-drawn wagons of the public post (*cursus publicus*) during the later Empire, are unimpressive. Nevertheless, heavy goods had to be transported by ox power. Because of inefficient harness, the speedier horses and mules could only perform light, fast, and ostentatious services such as the transport of high government officials.

Information was lacking concerning the cost of water transport in the late Roman Empire until the discovery of additional fragments of the Edict of Diocletian. From these it seems that sea transport was extremely cheap. The largest charge given is 26 *den.* to transport a *castrensis modius* of wheat (cost 100 *den.*) from the Diocese of Oriens, at the eastern end of the Mediterranean, to the province of Lusitania on the western shore of the Iberian peninsula. Other tariffs are correspondingly low: Alexandria to Rome, 16 *den.*, and Africa to the Gauls, 4 *den.*[28] It is probable that the cost of river transport was equally low. The fragments have incomplete items referring to river traffic. But representations of river barges carrying goods are numerous in Roman funerary bas-reliefs from Gaul and Germania.[29] In contrast with land transport, then, ancient water transport was economical. It was possible to ship heavy goods thousands of miles for a fraction of their original cost.

It was an outstanding failure of Rome that she was unable to bring land transport charges into a reasonable relationship with the costs of water transport. The Rome roads, solid, substantial, and expensive to build, were primarily military in purpose and did not provide surfaces or gradients congenial to land transport. They certainly did not succeed in making land transport cheap. Vehicles which could move rapidly were either not allowed, or not able, to carry heavy loads. Vehicles which could carry heavy materials moved at the speed of the ox, and this was a constant not likely to be much affected by changes in road surface or in organisation of transport. As we have seen above (p 158), oxen in the time of Cato the Elder (200 BC) moved about four miles per day, while oxen in the freight service of the carefully organised *cursus publicus* operating over the best Roman roads more than 500 years later could still only attain six to seven miles per day (see above, p 159). There may have been slight increases in carrying capacity. The standard 1,200lb wagon-load of the Edict of Diocletian becomes the 1,500lb cargo of the post-wagon (*angaria*) of the Theodosian Code in a little over a hundred years. The slow speed of the ox meant proportionately greater expense in wages and keep of the drivers and in fodder for the animals.

Tremendous amounts of heavy building materials were

moved for the purposes of the state, but the construction of great public works, magnificent and ostentatious as well as utilitarian, was not characterised by economy or rapidity. The ox was the standard heavy draught animal. The conservative Roman mind could not make the bold leap to a faster animal for heavy pulling. The Romans felt no need to develop a more rational horse harness. The rapid movement of heavy loads was beyond their mental horizon. Their approach was to increase capacity slightly and to organise the transport service by providing stations along the roads with fresh animals for relief purposes.

Early medieval. The early medieval evidence for the costs of transport consists of the toll charges levied at various stations by the authorities for the passage of goods. Nothing is said of the expense of the transport itself. This was a matter of individual, rather than state concern. There was little organisation of transport. If an individual transported his own goods, he was not likely to make a computation of transport costs. If the transport was accomplished by unfree personnel for their owners, it was a duty or service which they owed and not computable in money.

As mentioned above (p 154) the toll house at Fos near Marseille in 716 was required to furnish transport by which emissaries from the abbey of Corbie in northern France could convey their annual allowance of goods back to the monastery. The transport, consisting of boats, wagons, and pack-horses, was to be made available to the representatives of the monastery from the resources available to the toll house. It is possible that this was an alternating arrangement and that the transport made available in one year would return in the next for another load. It is more likely that the transport which reached Corbie replenished the monastery's stocks and was available for its local needs.[30]

Long lists of the types of tolls levied and enumerations of the amounts to be paid for varying types of transport give the impression that tolls were a main constituent of early medieval transport costs. The immunities granted to monasteries furnish a clear idea of the charges to which other transporters were subject. In the immunity granted to St Germain des Près by Charlemagne in 779, the monastery is exempted from ship toll, wagon toll, pack-animal toll, foot toll, safe-conduct toll, and road-repair toll.[31]

Charges are given for salt transported from the Cheshire salt works. At the time of Domesday Book the toll for a cartload of salt drawn by four oxen was four pennies, for a packhorse load two pennies, and for four men's loads one penny. Local residents paid reduced tolls.[32] Although the basic price of the salt is not given, it is probable that the tolls added significantly to the total price paid by the buyer.

Merely to enter the Lombard kingdom in the tenth century it was necessary to pay one-tenth of the value of the goods which were brought in. Entry from beyond the mountains was channelled by the passes and the existing roads and was easily controlled by the establishment of toll-stations. Pilgrims were exempt and the Anglo-Saxons paid only a fixed tribute every three years rather than one-tenth of their goods.[33] A toll rate of ten per cent at a single stop confirms the impression that toll charges must have made up most of the sale price of an article.

It is only in the later Middle Ages that true charges, i.e. payments for the movement of goods or for the hiring of vehicles and draught or pack-animals, begin to make their reappearance for the first time since the days of the Roman Empire. The return of transport charges can probably be attributed to a decline in forced services, increased specialisation in the handling of goods, the revival of transport as a means of livelihood, and the formation of organisations to handle it. In the fourteenth century it was considered possible for a merchant with an interpreter and two servants to transport goods worth 25,000 gold florins from Azov in the Crimea to Cathay for the equivalent of 300 to 400 gold florins.[34] This remarkably low figure for transport costs could not have been matched in Europe and can undoubtedly be attributed to the good order maintained by the Mongols along the route.

In fourteenth-century Flanders a hoisting fee of one *gros tournois* of silver was charged for each tun, or barrel, unloaded at Sluis, regardless of the contents or size of the cask. A transport charge in the form of passage money was levied by professional transporters for bringing goods from Sluis to Bruges. One *sterling* of silver (one third of a *gros tournois*) was charged for each bale of merchandise and four *gros tournois* for each tun. This system was obviously inequitable, not being based on either the value or the weight of the merchandise. The carriers were responsible for safe delivery to the cellar of the consignee and had to make reparation for damages suffered in transit and delivery.[35]

In fourteenth-century England bulk goods could be moved for relatively small charges. A standard rate of one penny per ton per mile was charged for the use of peasant carts. Wool could be transported fifty miles for one and a half per cent of its value.[36] Grain, being heavier in relation to its volume, increased more rapidly in price as it was moved, that rate of increase being fifteen per cent every fifty miles.[37] Modern transport can handle bulk materials more economically. Wheat can often be shipped by rail from Kansas City to Chicago (500 miles) for about three per cent of its value.

Despite the artificial impediments of tolls and other restrictions, land transport was relatively more economical in the Middle Ages than in Roman times. The increased number of horses, along with such technological developments as better harnessing methods, horse-collars, and iron horseshoes, made it possible to move larger loads at a faster rate, so making transport economies possible.

Medieval sea transport could be considered economical even by modern standards. In the fourteenth century wine could be shipped from Bordeaux to Ireland for ten per cent of its cost.[38] River transport was hampered by the lack of effective political jurisdiction over large areas. Despite the multiplicity of tolls, it was generally more economical than land transport.

Medieval water transport was as cheap comparatively as that of the Roman Empire. What it lacked in international organisation in early medieval times was made up by competition between merchants, and in later medieval times by the use of improved vessels and navigational techniques. The medieval performance in land transport was superior to that of the Romans with respect to costs. Cheap, heavy goods could be transported economically by land in medieval times. The medieval vehicles and the routes over which they passed were better adapted to each other than the Roman vehicles and roads had been.

PLAY AND DISPLAY

The spirit of play manifests itself in transport by means of contests. Not all competition in transport has an economic base. There is an inborn desire to outdo one's fellow. Local fame attends the man whose means of transport is faster or has a greater weight-carrying capacity than his neighbour's. Competition can encourage improvements in both the vehicle or vessel and its method of propulsion.

The Romans both fostered and discouraged competition in transport. The chariot races in the Circus encouraged the breeding and importing of the fastest horses, although little was done to improve the racing chariot. The Edict of Prices of Diocletian and the Theodosian Code with their standardisation of vehicles and their limitation of loads discouraged improvements in wagons and increases in their capacity. It was characteristic of Rome to attempt to standardise and control an existing situation rather than to encourage innovation and improvement.

A more uncontrolled and spontaneous play-element is seen in Anglo-Saxon England. Even the young men accompanying a bishop want to race their horses when they come to an inviting stretch of ground. This was no prepared course but a natural plain with holes and concealed rocks. To point the moral, one who raced without the bishop's permission took a fall when his horse leaped over a hole and struck his head on a hidden stone.[39] His insecure seat may be blamed on his youth and inexperience or, possibly, on a lack of stirrups.

Hunting and coursing on horseback served more than one purpose. It was a source of food for the aristocracy, but it was also a form of play. It was a type of physical exercise and also a school for training in horsemanship and the use of weapons. Preparation for war by engaging in the chase is certainly play. The main element in the hunt was not the obtaining of food or the acquisition of skills for the future but the pleasure of the moment. William the Conqueror 'loved the tall deer as if he were their father'.[40]

The most indefatigable players of the Middle Ages were the Vikings, and many of their games were related to transport. They competed in swimming and running. The sight of a precipitous cliff was enough to inspire a race to its top. They competed on skis and snowshoes. Some of their games required amazing agility. Olaf Trygvason was able to run on the shafts of the oars while the ship was being rowed. While others could perform this feat to some extent, he was the only one credited with being able to run completely round the ship, leaping from one bank of oars to the other across the bow and stern when the oars were at their fullest extent.[41]

Improvements in techniques and equipment may result from competition and play. Changes may be incorporated directly on the vehicle or vessel being used, but it is often more convenient and inexpensive to use models. A child's toy may point the way to an innovation in transport. The effect of an idea may be tested conveniently by constructing a small wagon or boat.[42] It is often difficult to determine the purpose of small objects of this nature found in burials. They may have been votive objects, children's toys, or even representations of actual vehicles.

Play and display are often closely related in transport. The chariot races in the Circus Maximus at Rome or the Hippodrome at Constantinople put on a fine show for the population. Elephants and exotic beasts were used to draw chariots

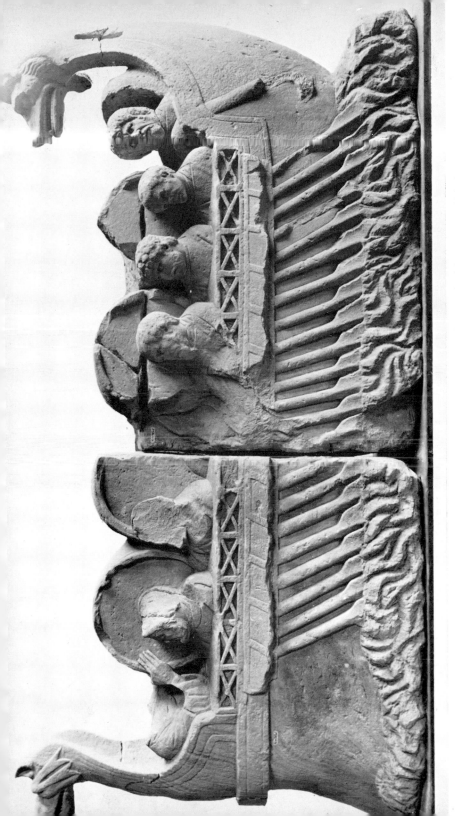

Page 167 Roman wine transport on the Moselle, showing barrels (Provincial Museum. Trier)

carrying religious figures and statues of the emperors.[43] Mules and horses had gilded hooves and richly ornamented harness.[44] Whatever the inefficiencies of ancient horse-harness may have been, the horse was required to hold his head high and made a fine appearance, which was more important to the driver than pulling a few more pounds.[45] The charioteer who handled a four-horse team demonstrated his dexterity and was proud of his skills in much the same way that English lords in the nineteenth century liked to replace a low-born coachman in order to demonstrate their handling abilities.

Ostentation rather than practicality was the keynote for the transport used by most rich Romans of the Empire. Fortunes were lavished on the decoration of vehicles. Some luxurious conveyances were covered with silver. They were customarily drawn by more animals than were necessary, in order to impress the populace. The impression was heightened by the use of precious metals and jewels as harness ornaments.[46]

While the emperors attempted to discourage ostentatious display, particularly among the newly wealthy, it is doubtful if they were very successful. The builders, rather than the possessors, of oversize vehicles were severely punished.[47] Ancient republican virtues were praised, especially for the lower classes. Self-transport was encouraged for the legions. Even as late as the time of Theodosius II (408-50), a legion on the march was allotted only two vehicles, and these were only for the sick.[48]

Display did not cease with the Romans. The Visigothic princess Galswintha was seen rolling luxuriously along in a silver tower on wheels.[49] Great care was taken over display. When a Merovingian princess set out to be married, the furnishings for the horses and carriages were carried in separate wagons in the rear so that they could be put on at the last moment to make a fine appearance before the bridegroom.[50]

The ships and vehicles of the Norsemen were richly carved and decorated. Gilded dragons were used as figureheads. Sails were colourful and sewn with designs. The wagon found with the ninth-century Oseberg ship in Norway is of simple design

L

with particularly heavy-seeming wheels, but the body is covered with wood carving of very fine workmanship. Sleds were also found at Oseberg which, from their ornamentation, can have had little use except as vehicles for display. They are ancestors of the *Prunkschlitten*—highly decorated sleighs which became popular among the rich of Germany during the Renaissance.[51]

Display could have other forms than the visual. The Irish kings of the sixth century were distinguished by the great noise their vehicles made.[52] Lubrication, although known, may have been dispensed with to help achieve this announcement of their coming. Combined with the noises to be expected from unsprung wheels with metal tyres bouncing over stony roads, the result must have been impressive.

Display could be for purposes of mockery or ridicule as well as ostentation. In Merovinginian Gaul a priest was placed on a wagon filled with thorns and driven into exile by King Charibert.[53] Mummolus was tortured and then sent by cart to his native city of Bordeaux. The indignity was considered as bad as death.[54] The old Queen Brunehilde was paraded before the army on a camel before being dragged to her death by wild horses in 614.[55] Knights in disgrace and criminals on their way to be hanged were displayed in carts. Serfs were shipped in wagons (*in plaustris*).[56] The famous oxcart of the last Merovingian kings seems to have been a subject for satire rather than a long-surviving luxury vehicle, or a reminder of the cow-drawn cart of the goddess Nerthus described by Tacitus.[57] The Merovingians were constrained to use such transport by poverty and weakness rather than choice. It made them such figures of ridicule that their removal from office was made easier.

CUSTOM AND HABIT

Not only do different societies have varying attitudes towards transport, but ideas change within the same society. In the time of the Roman Republic only priests and women were allowed to use wheeled vehicles; in the Empire men of rank customarily did so.[58] Increasing wealth and contact with other societies may have influenced the Romans. The Celts in Gaul and Britain were not prejudiced against wheeled transport. Their leaders used horse-drawn chariots in both war and peace. Cicero was so impressed that he requested a British chariot. The combination of Roman roads and light Celtic vehicles made possible fast and relatively comfortable transport. Julius Caesar covered surprising distances whenever necessary,[59] often sleeping in the wagon.[60]

Vehicles were put to uses that would have seemed strange to their originators. The elder Pliny dictated to his secretary while his chariot was in motion.[61] Such an achievement would hardly have been possible without smooth roads. It indicates also the possession of a shorthand system, probably the Tironian method introduced by a freedman of Cicero's.

As Ireland was never conquered by the Romans, it developed in relative isolation and provides insights into the Celtic civilisation which prevailed in most of western Europe until the coming of the Romans. In war the Irish continued the old Celtic custom of fighting from chariots until at least the seventh century. Riding on horseback seems to have been little practised. The kings and wealthy customarily travelled in horse-drawn chariots. Ireland was well supplied with horses but perhaps they were of too small a breed to be useful as mounts. Horse-drawn transport was probably an aristocratic monopoly at least until the coming of Christianity in the fifth century.

St Columba, St Columban, and other Irish missionaries, while they may have been of aristocratic lineage, lived simply and humbly. In one respect at least, they may have initiated a social change in the status of the horse. Horses are mentioned in connection with the Irish missionaries and they were sometimes used for tasks other than carrying aristocracy. It was a two-horse chariot he had brought from Ireland which St Samson of Dol used in Cornwall in the early sixth century.[62] A horse on the island of Iona at the time of the death of St Columba in 595 assisted the brethren in carrying their burdens. The horse probably was used as a pack-animal but may have drawn loads in the same wagon in which St Columba was pulled to the small western plain of the island during the summer in which he died.[63] The use of a horse-drawn wagon for the transport of goods is more clearly attested at about the same time on the Continent. While St Columban was starving at Anegray *c* 575, food was brought to him in a horse-drawn wagon.[64] This is a unique case. Horse-drawn vehicles are seldom encountered in the early Middle Ages outside Ireland, and horses being used for vehicular goods transport are rarer still. The horse's humbler cousin, the mule, was more likely to be used for drawing vehicles. In Merovingian Gaul, St Ouen (*c* 680) as an old man rode in a carriage drawn by mules because he was no longer able to go on horseback.[65]

In western Europe, except for Ireland, custom was quite clear and uniform with respect to transport during the early Middle Ages. The mass of the people walked. Goods moved on pack-asses, or mules, and ox-drawn carts. Priests walked or rode asses. Kings, nobles, bishops, and abbots rode horseback. To travel in a vehicle was considered unmanly, and only those who could not avoid it travelled in this manner. Usually only the criminal, the aged, the sick, and women were transported by wagon.

A cart made an admirable adjunct for a hangman. It was much simpler to stand the victim on a cart, attach the noose tightly, and then drive out from under him than it was to construct a trap. This custom may help explain the aversion of knights to non-equine transport. Riding in a cart was *prima facie* evidence of wrong-doing. Only as forceful a character as Sir Lancelot could break the pattern. He commandeered a cart and carter to carry him when his horse was shot from ambush, but a lady observing his approach thought he was a poor knight being taken to be hanged.[66]

Nevertheless, warriors had not always been too proud to use vehicles. The Homeric Greeks had ridden their chariots to the battlefield and then dismounted to fight. The various Celtic people had driven and fought from war chariots. The importation and development of larger horses made riding possible as a replacement for driving. Scattered illustrations of armoured figures in vehicles are found in medieval manuscripts but not frequently enough to indicate any reversal of the chivalric attitude, despite the obvious advantage to be derived from arriving fresh at the battle site rather than fatigued after a hard ride in heavy armour. Armed warriors being transported in vehicles are seen in the Hortus Deliciarum of Herrad of Landsberg.[67] An illuminated manuscript[68] shows three knights seated in a two-wheeled cart drawn by a single horse in shafts, guided by a rider carrying a whip. It is doubtful whether these illustrations represent a type of transport considered honourable by those who rode.

There is also a statement in de Vaublanc's work that knights were even carried on litters. As authority he selects a line from Jean Bodel's *Chanson des Saxons* which says that more than a hundred were carried on litters.[69] This seems clear enough until the passage is carefully examined. Other manuscripts give different endings to the line. One version is 'en charteres mener', another 'an charrete mener'. The method of transport may therefore have been by cart rather than litter. The contention is completely destroyed when it is observed that it was not the knights but the old men who were transported.[70] This is consistent with the usual medieval view that only the women, the old, and the wounded or sick should be transported.

The speed of transport helps to explain custom. There was little advantage in riding an ox-drawn cart. It was uncomfortable and slower than a normal man's walk. Horse-drawn wagons for carrying groups of people had been known in Roman Gaul. St Martin of Tours encountered a horse-drawn vehicle loaded with soldiers in the fourth century.[71] The use of such vehicles probably ceased with the invasions of the fifth century. The Germanic invaders undoubtedly frowned upon their use and horses may have become too rare for such employment.

Many poor but devout persons who later became saints walked from choice as well as necessity. They wished to identify themselves with the humblest, and walking was an

effective way to establish such an equality. St Martin was walking when he met the wagon-load of soldiers.[72] St Willibald of
Eichstätt, in the eighth century, set out with his father and
brother from England to Rome and continued to the Holy
Land and back, walking much of the way.[73] In the eleventh
century, St Godric of Finchale made many pilgrimages on
foot, even though he had become wealthy through trading.
Asceticism was carried even further by his mother, when
she accompanied him barefoot on his last pilgrimage to Rome
(p 61, above). Godric assisted her zealous project by often carrying her on his shoulders across fords and rivers. While not a
large man, Godric was broad-shouldered and deep-chested and
developed great endurance as a wandering merchant carry-
carrying his own goods, as a sailor on many strenuous voyages,
and as a frequent pilgrim.[74]

The ass was a humble beast, long-lived, with great endurance. Its qualities and its Biblical associations made it a very
appropriate beast for the use of the lower clergy. It provided
neither great speed nor comfort. Riding it was a form of
penance. The use of the ass was a badge of asceticism. It was
a poor man's substitute for a rich man's pleasures, like eating
barley instead of wheat, or drinking water in place of wine.[75]
The geographic range of the ass was probably extended by
Christian missionary activity. As seen above (p 63), in the
middle of the eighth century St Sturm rode an ass as he set
out from Hersfeld in search of a site for the monastery that
became Fulda. The dangerous beasts of the northern forest
necessitated certain precautions. Each night St Sturm had to
cut trees and make a circular fence to protect his ass.[76] Sturm's
ass is found beyond the borders of what is usually considered
his normal area. Victor Hehn believed that the ass accompanied the expansion of the vine and olive oil culture north
from the Mediterranean into France but not beyond.[77]

Popular prejudice required that men ride only stallions. A
strong taboo forbade heathen Anglo-Saxon priests the perquisites of the normal male warrior, such as carrying weapons
or riding a male horse.[78] The heathen high-priest Coifi, in

seventh-century Northumbria, indicated the depth of his conversion to Christianity by publicly breaking the taboo. He seized arms, bestrode one of the king's stallions, and rode off to destroy a heathen temple.[79] The temper and spirit of the stallion, contrasted with the comparative docility of the gelding or mare, made him the choice for the masculine pursuit of war. The preference for stallions is graphically shown in the Bayeux Tapestry. Duke William's knights rode only stallions.[80] Shakespeare was aware of the prejudice and transferred it back to Roman times (incidentally giving a reason for the practice). *Antony and Cleopatra*, Enobarbus says, 'If we should serve with horse and mares together, the horse were merely lost; the mares would bear a soldier and his horse.'[81]

Notes to this chapter are on pp 213-16.

5

Conclusion - continuity or independent development?

ANY ASSESSMENT OF transport and communication should consider such factors as speed and capacity. The speed at which humans and animals can travel could have been increased by selective breeding and training, as is witnessed by the continuous improvement in athletic records, but it did remain relatively constant through the ages until modern times. Men, horses, and oxen all had their normal rates of progress, but these could be modified by conditions. They could travel faster and go farther when they had good roads and good weather. Careful organisation, the provision of stopping-places along the route and of spare animals increased the average distance covered. While the Romans were probably not physically superior to medieval men, they did consistently travel greater distances in less time.

It is possible to make some direct comparisons. In the first century BC, Cicero mentions four letters which came to him at Rome from Britain.[1] This was a time when Gaul had hardly been conquered and Britain was visited for the first time by the Romans. There had been no time for road-building and little time in which to organise a messenger service. Nevertheless, three of the letters reached Cicero in twenty-seven days and the fourth in thirty-four days from the time of sending. It is probable that these letters were carried by a single messenger on foot without relays.[2] The route is unknown, but the consistency in times argues against using the sea route from Marseille to Rome, and in favour of a land route from Vienne through the Graian Alps to Milan and then by the Aemilian and Flaminian Ways to Rome. Such a route totals nearly 1,000 miles, indicating that the messenger averaged more than 36 miles per day.

In the twelfth century, notice of an excommunication was brought from the Lateran to Canterbury in twenty-nine days.[3] The messenger was presumably mounted and he travelled as rapidly as possible. The route is almost identical with that of the bearer of Cicero's letters, but no improvement in speed is apparent. A factor which may have been influential is the season in which the events took place. Cicero's letters were carried between August and October, perhaps the best time of year for travelling in western Europe, while the messenger from the Vatican travelled in March and April, and may have been delayed by mud from spring thaws.

These were express couriers. Normal travellers took much longer. The average time from Rome to Canterbury was closer to fifty days, or approximately seven weeks.[4] Such a journey meant that a normal day's travel was about twenty miles. This is a reasonable figure for pedestrian travel. Those who travelled on horseback could travel somewhat farther, in greater comfort, and with less exertion, particularly after the introduction of the stirrup in about the eighth century. Frederick Barbarossa, after his election at Frankfurt, travelled to Aachen (about 150 miles) in three days.[5] However, he travelled by ship down the Main and the Rhine, from Frankfurt to Sinzig, about ninety miles. As he was going with the current, he may have covered this stretch in one to one and a half days. The sixty miles from Sinzig to Aachen must have been covered in between one and a half and two days, an average of thirty to forty miles per day.

In one aspect of transport, the early Middle Ages have no comparisons to offer. This is in the field of long-distance, horse-drawn travelling wagons. Caesar had no prejudices against riding in a wagon. He was reported to have covered 120 miles in a day,[6] and even to have been able to sleep while travelling.[7] The precedents set by Caesar were followed by the carefully organised *cursus publicus*. Medieval men would not have ridden such wagons even if they had been available.

The Roman land transport system was characterised by the low capacity of its vehicles. Its pack-animals were much more sensibly loaded. Nothing happened during the early Middle Ages to increase the capacity of pack-animals. Similarly, ox harness remained little changed during the same period. Ox-drawn vehicles carried no greater loads than they had during the Roman period and earlier. It is only in horse-drawn transport that there is a notable change. The Romans had used horses only for light and rapid transport. The popularisation of the horse-collar, the introduction of tandem harnessing, the common use of iron horseshoes, and the increase in the number of horses in the eleventh century made possible the widespread application of horses to heavy transport duties. The Middle Ages proved that heavy materials did not have to be transported slowly.

There was continuity in land transport, but it was through the Celts rather than the Romans. The Celts had horse-drawn vehicles before the Romans came. They gave to the Latins the vehicles and their names. In Roman Gaul, horses and mules were common and were used for light, fast transport of goods, as well as of people. The coming of the Germans disrupted horse-breeding and interrupted the use of horse-drawn vehicles. Mules and low-grade horses were still used as pack-animals. Custom disapproved of able-bodied men riding in wagons. In Ireland, the use of horse-drawn chariots was continued until the seventh century. In western Europe, generally, the horse became rarer after the fifth century invasions and remained in short supply until the beginning of the eleventh century. The complex of inventions—the horse-collar, iron horseshoes, and tandem harnessing—which adapted the horse to agricultural work and heavy transport also encouraged an increase in the number of horses. Simultaneously, the horse lost prestige and was no longer an exclusive attribute of the aristocracy.

The Romans had administered a large empire by carefully organising land communications. They did not attempt to improve the speed and capacity of their land transport. Roman land transport was really keyed to the needs of a small city state. It was inadequate for a large empire. The continuing high expense of land transport throughout Roman history bears out this contention.

In the eleventh century, the last century of the early Middle Ages, technology was successfully applied to land transport. The adaptation of the horse to heavy transport meant that more goods could be transported more economically for a greater distance in a shorter time. Cities could become larger because they could draw their supplies from a larger hinterland. Better transport and communication meant an increase in the size of the state that could be effectively governed. This tendency contributed to the rise of royal power and the decline in local feudal authority. The improvement in land transport technology owed little to the Romans. Even though the essential inventions may have originated elsewhere, it was in western Europe that they were most effectively utilised on a large scale.

In sea transport, the development of the northern ships can be traced and approximately dated through the ship burials. The evidence of the ship-finds leads to the conclusion that the Viking raids only became technologically possible towards the end of the eighth century. Despite their excellent sailing qualities, the Viking ships were incapable of further development. They were efficient only within a narrow size-range. When they were made larger, they lost their effectiveness. The Viking ships were developed independently. They bear little resemblance to Roman vessels. Whatever their merits may have been as raiding vessels, they were not well-adapted to cargo carrying.

There was a type of ship in northern waters to which technology could be applied. This was the round-ship which had been used for centuries by peoples bordering on the North Sea. Beginning in the twelfth century, changes were made in the old round-ship, or *kogge*. It was made larger, with greater capacity. More masts and sails were added, making it more controllable, and even a bit faster. By the fourteenth century, the stern-post rudder was widely used, and sterns were flattened to make it effective. This change in the shape of the hull also increased the ship's capacity.

Medieval transport thus owed little to Roman precedent. Roman vehicles and roads were not well suited to each other. The Romans never solved the problem of rapid, heavy transport on land. What success they achieved was due to administrative skill rather than technology. In the comparatively protected waters of the Mediterranean, and on the rivers of Gaul, the Romans did achieve economical water transport. Their ships were not well adapted to the more violent waters of the northern seas. In the eleventh century, by efficiently harnessing the horse, medieval men achieved more rapid and economical land transport than the Romans had known. In the twelfth century, improvements began to appear in the old round-ship, fitting it for a more effective role in sea transport. Europe entered the late Middle Ages on an encouraging note. Both land and sea transport had made a beginning in applying technology to transport. The way had been opened to further improvement.

Notes to this chapter are on p 216.

Notes and References

Notes and references

Chapter 1

1 The *Hodopoericon of St Willibald*, Monumenta Germaniac Historica (cited hereafter as MGH) *Scriptores*, Vol XV, I, 80-117. English translations exist in the *Palestine Pilgrims Text Society* and in C. H. Talbot, *The Anglo-Saxon Missionaries in Germany* (London and New York, 1954) pp 152-77, which will be cited for convenience

2 'Wer ist die Nonne von Heidenheim?' (*Studien und Mitteilungen zur Geschichte des Benediktiner-Ordens*, xlix, 1931, pp 387-8). For the convenience of readers with an interest, here is the cryptogram with its interpretation. Secdgquar . quin . npri . sprixquar . nter . epri . nquar . mter . nsecun . hquin . gsecdbquinc . qarr . dinando . hsecdc . scrter . bsecd . bprim. Only the vowels of the original message have been enciphered. Abbreviations for the ordinal numbers were substituted for the vowels: primo for A, secundo for E, etc. Secdgquar then becomes EGO, and the complete interpretation is 'Ego una Saxonica nomine Hugeburc ordinando hec scribebam'. For this, and other examples of a similar nature see Wilhelm Levison, *England and the Continent in the Eighth Century* (Oxford, 1946), Appendix VIII, St Boniface and Cryptography, pp 290-4

3 Benjamin Thorpe (ed), *Ancient Laws and Institutes of England* (London, 1840), 411-12. Quoted more recently in W. O. Hassall, *How They Lived* (Oxford, 1962), 72-3

4   Nothing comparable to these distances was achieved in Western Europe in Medieval and Renaissance times. See my 'A Papal Cipher and the Polish Election of 1573', *Jahrbücher für Geschichte Osteuropas,* Band 17, Heft 1 (March 1969), pp 27-8, for a late Renaissance example. It is only in more open country such as that occupied by the Islamic and Mongol empires that organisations comparable to the *cursus publicus* were maintained. The Islamic governmental post, the *barid,* is well-known (*Encyclopedia of Islam,* 2nd ed, article 'Barid'), but a previously unknown system intended for use of merchants and other private individuals has recently been revealed in the *Geniza* documents (S. D. Goitein, *A Mediterranean Society. The Jewish Communities of the Arab World as Portrayed in the Documents of the Cairo Geniza,* Volume I, *Economic Foundations,* Berkeley, 1967, pp 281-95). This commercial mail service, well organised but lacking the relay stations of the government posts, usually travelled overland and could operate when the seas were closed, as for the winter season. In addition to the regular service, normally accompanying caravans, there were express couriers and special messengers. Since this system did not carry goods or money it was safe from bandits. It is even possible that pigeons were sometimes employed in this system. The *yamb* (horse-post) of Kublai Khan is described by Marco Polo as having luxurious hostelries every 25 or 30 miles on all the main highways, each furnished with 300 to 400 horses. The total number of hostelries is given as 10,000, with more than 200,000 horses available. The messengers, tightly belted and bandaged, could cover 300 miles in a day. The Great Khan also had a parallel system of foot runners who covered 3-mile legs at full speed and so could bring messages and light articles like fresh fruit a ten days' journey in one day. (*The Travels of Marco Polo,* trans Ronald Latham, Penguin Books, 1958, pp 150-5.) The American Pony Express in 1860-1 was comparable in speed, distance, and organisation but not in scale. The 1,975 miles from St Joseph, Missouri, to Sacramento, California, was covered in as little as seven days, seventeen hours (for the transmittal of Lincoln's First Inaugural Address). Forty riders were constantly going west and another forty east with only 400 to 500 horses required for

the whole system. See the spirited description in Chapter VIII of Mark Twain's *Roughing It*.

5   For a sympathetic view of the much-maligned mule see my 'The Mule as a Cultural Invention', *Technology and Culture,* VIII, 1 (Jan 1967), pp 45-52

6   Gregory of Tours, *History of the Franks,* IX, 9

7   Ibid, VI, 22

8   Ibid, VII, 30

9   Ibid, IX, 28

10 On this subject see my 'Secret Communication among the Greeks and Romans', *Technology and Culture,* X, 2 (April 1969), pp 139-54. Secrets could also be concealed even from most of the literate by the use of shorthand. The system devised by Cicero's freedman, Tiro, was in use for hundreds of years. Apollinaris Sidonius (*Epistolae,* ix. 9), Cassiodorus (Thomas Hodgkin, *The Letters of Cassiodorus,* 110), and even Gregory of Tours, (*Miracula S Martini,* iv, 10) all have references to the use of the Tironian system. In the field of visual communication this age was singularly inept. Setting fire to a village on a hill as a signal that troops were coming can serve as an example of their concept of optical signalling (Gregory of Tours, Hist X, 3)

11 Robert James Forbes, *Studies in Ancient Technology,* Vol II (Leiden, 1955), 157

12 General Capitulary for the Missi, 802. Univ of Pennsylvania, *Translations & Reprints,* VI, 5, pp 16-27. Cf V. Krause, 'Geschichte des Instituts der Missi Dominici', *Mitteilungen des Instituts für österreichische Geschichtsforschung,* XI, 1890. See Theodulf of Orleans, 'Against Judges' in MGH, Poet, i, 498f for a picture of a *missus* at work.

13 See James Westfall Thompson, *The decline of the missi dominici in Frankish Gaul,* Chicago, 1903 (Decennial publications of the University of Chicago, first series, no 4)

14 See definitions in Du Cange or J. F. Niermeyer, *Mediae Latinitatis Lexicon Minus*

15 MGH, *Leges I,* Capit Karisiac Art 25, 540

16 *Cartularium Saxonicum,* ed W. Birch, no 1136

17 *Rectitudines Singularum Personarum,* in *English Historical Documents,* ed D. C. Douglas, II, 813

18 See Josef Kulischer, *Allgemeine Wirtschaftsgeschichte des*

M

Mittelalters und der Neuzeit, I, 85-7 for a statement of the evidence

19 MGH, Diplom Karol, No 6, 6-10. The Charter of Dagobert often cited as founding the Fair of St Denis *c* 630 (See *Cambridge Economic History*, Vol II, 168 and 264) is branded as a tenth-century forgery based on some authentic material in Lopez and Raymond, *Medieval Trade in the Mediterranean World*, 80

20 MGH, *Epist Karol Aevi*, II, No 100, 144-6

21 MGH, *Legum, sectio* II, 1, No 44, 122-3

22 Ibid, No 72, 163

23 *Medieval Cities*, 80-1

24 MGH, *Legum, sectio II*, 1, No 75, 168

25 Alfons Dopsch, *The Economic and Social Foundations of European Civilization* (London, 1957), 109

26 MGH, *Legum, sectio* II, 1, Capitulare de villis, art 44

27 Wulf Schadendorf, *Zu Pferde, im Wagen, zu Fuss. Tausend Jahre Reisen* (Munich, 1961), 10

28 Walter Map, *De Nugis Curialium*, ed M. R. James (Anecdota Oxoniensia, Oxford, 1914), V, v, 219

29 *Dialogus de Scaccario*, ed C. Johnson (Nelson's Medieval Classics, London, 1950), 129-35

30 *The Great Roll of the Pipe for the Eighth Year of the Reign of King John*, ed Doris M. Stenton, *Pipe Roll Society, Vol 58* (London, 1942), 55. 'Et pro uno (pari) Paneriorum ad capellam R . . .'

31 MGH, *Formulae*, 309-10

32 Henri Pirenne, *Economic and Social History of Medieval Europe* (New York, 1937), 93

33 P. Boissonnade, *Life and Work in Medieval Europe*, trans Eileen Power (New York, 1927), 109

34 See Sir Samuel Dill, *Roman Society in the last century of the western empire*, Book IV, Ch 1, 'The General Character of the Invasions', 285-302

35 Ekkehard of Aura, *Hierosolymita*, chapters VII-XI, and Guibert of Nogent, *Historia Hierosolymitana*, give a good impression of the popular aspect of the Crusade

36 See Sir Steven Runciman, *A History of the Crusades*, Vol I, for a fine account of the preparations and march

37 See the lively account, drawn from the sources, of how the

Romans accomplished these feats in Daniel P. Mannix, *Those About to Die* (New York, 1958), ch 13

38 Gino Gentili, *La Villa Erculia di Piazza Armerina. I Mosaici Figurati* (Rome, 1959)

39 Symmachus, *Epistolae*, V, 56

40 Ibid, VII, 121; IX, 132, 135, 137, 142

41 Ibid, VI, 43; IX, 141, 151

42 Ibid, IV, 46

43 Gentili, *La Villa Erculia di Piazza Armerina*, Appendice, fig 5

44 P. Armandi, *Histoire militaire des Éléphants* (Paris, 1843), 422-3

45 *Annales Regni Francorum (Annales Einhardi)* under 801 and 802

46 Armandi, *Histoire militaire des Éléphants*, 528

47 Ibid, 529. A contemporary portrait of this elephant is seen in *Matthew Paris*, MS 16, Cambridge, Corpus Christi College, f. iv a. All these elephants were only curiosities. Laverne Gay in her novel *Wine of Satan* (New York, 1949), 39 and 47, has elephants being used as work animals in the eleventh century to carry the bronze doors of the cathedral of Amalfi. I know of no warrant for this.

48 R. W. Hutchinson, *Prehistoric Crete* (Harmondsworth, 1968), 118

49 *Anglo-Saxon Chronicle*, anno 866

50 Ibid, anno 892

51 Sir Frank M. Stenton, *The Bayeux Tapestry* (London, 1957), plates 42-3

52 Fulcher of Chartres, *Chronicle of the First Crusade*, VIII, 1-4

53 Geoffroy de Villehardouin, *Chronicle of the Fourth Crusade and the Conquest of Constantinople, Memoirs of the Crusades*, trans Sir Frank Marzials (London and New York, 1908), 37-8

54 Jean, Sire de Joinville, *Chronicle of the Crusade of St Lewis, Memoirs of the Crusades*, trans Sir Frank Marzials (London and New York, 1908), 167

55 Lambert of Hersfeld, *Annales*, (Band XIII, 'Ausgewählte Quellen zur Deutschen Geschichte des Mittelalters', Berlin (1956)) anno 1077, 397-9

56 Transhumance is well described in *Cambridge Economic*

History, 2nd ed, Vol 1 (1966), Chap III, Charles Parain, 'The Evolution of Agricultural Technique', 132-3.

57 See J. Klein, *The Mesta: A Study in Spanish Economic History*, 1273-1836 (Harvard Economic Studies, xxi, 1920).

58 Paul-Marie Duval, *La vie quotidienne en Gaule* (Paris, 1952), 187-8

59 A. H. M. Jones, *The Later Roman Empire* (Norman, Okla, 1964), II, 829

60 Procopius *History of the Wars* v. xxvi. 9-13

61 MGH, *Scriptores 13*, Annales Nordhumbrani, anno 795

62 For the widespread economic and cultural effects of Charlemagne's liberal dissemination of accumulated treasures see E. Patzelt, *Karolingische Renaissance* (Vienna, 1924), 111 and H. Fichtenau, *The Carolingian Empire* (New York, 1964) trans Peter Munz, 79-86

63 See A. Burford, 'Heavy transport in classical Antiquity', *Economic History Review*, 2nd series, XIII, 1960, 1-18, and R. F. Heizer, 'Ancient Heavy Transport, Methods and Achievements', *Science,* CLIII (19 Aug 1966), 821-30

64 *Scriptores Historiae Augustae* Aelius Spartianus—*Vita Hadriani* 19

65 F. M. Feldhaus, 'Die Ingenieure des Theoderich: die Hebeösen am Grabmal des Theoderich', *Umschau,* XXXVIII, 1934, 596-8. See Lynn White, jr, 'Technology and Invention in the Middle Ages', *Speculum,* XV (April 1940), 150 and Giuseppe Bovini, *Das Grambal Theoderichs* (Ravenna, 1959)

66 *Bibliotheca Rerum Germanicorum* ed P. Jaffe (Berlin, 1867), IV, 268, Codex Carolinus, Epistolae, 89. 'Hadrianus I papa Carolo regi musiva et marmora palatii Ravennatii concedit.'

67 Leo of Ostia, *The Chronicle of Monte Cassino, III, 26,* trans Dr Herbert Bloch in *A Documentary History of Art,* ed Elizabeth G. Holt (New York, 1957), Vol I, 10-11

68 Suger, *The Other Little Book on the Consecration of the Church of St-Denis II,* trans Erwin Panofsky in *A Documentary History of Art,* Vol I, 38-9

69 Haimon, *Abbott Haimon to his Brothers at Tutbury,* trans Henry Adams and Charles P. Parkhurst, jr in *A Documentary History of Art,* Vol I, 49-50

70 T. K. Derry and Trevor I. Williams, *A Short History of Technology* (Oxford, 1961), 174-5

71 *The Cambridge Economic History of Europe, Vol II*, eds M. Postan and E. E. Rich (Cambridge, 1952), 500

72 Albert Grenier, *Manuel d'archéologie gallo-romaine, tome II, Les routes* (Paris, 1931), 950

73 Derry and Williams, *A Short History of Technology*, 177

74 *The Cambridge Economic History of Europe*, Vol I, eds J. H. Clapham and Eileen Power (Cambridge, 1941), 391

75 Ellsworth Huntington, *Mainsprings of Civilization* (New York, 1945), 598-9

76 Robert Latouche, *The birth of Western economy; economic aspects of the Dark Ages*, trans E. M. Wilkinson (London, 1961), 94

77 Emile Esperandieu, *Recueil général des bas-reliefs de la Gaule romaine* (Paris, 1907-38), vol V, nos 4072, 4080; vol VI, nos 5148, 5184, 5193, and 5198

78 Goitein, *A Mediterranean Society*, Vol I, 334

79 Gregory of Tours, VII, 46

80 MGH, *Diplom Karol*, I, No 6, 6-10

81 Henri Pirenne, *Annales d'histoire économique et sociale*, vol V, 1933, 230-1

82 *Medieval England*, ed A. L. Poole (Oxford, 1958), Vol 1, 206

83 Karl Jordan, *Friedrich Barbarossa* (Göttingen, 1959) (Persönlichkeit und Geschichte, Band 13), 79-80. Sir Steven Runciman, *A History of the Crusades*, Vol III, 16-17

84 Charles Singer et al *A History of Technology*, Vol II, (Oxford, 1956), R. J. Forbes. 'Hydraulic Engineering and Sanitation', 683

85 *The Domesday Survey of Cheshire*, ed J. Tait, Chetham Society, New Series, Vol 75, 217-25

86 MGH, *Capitularia Regum Francorum, I*, No 44, 123, 'Capitulary of Thionville'

87 Ibid, II, no 253, 250, 'Raffelstetten Tolls'

88 MGH, *Epist Karol Aevi, II*, no 100, 144-6, 'Charlemagne to King Offa'

89 Grenier, *Manuel d'archéologie gallo-romaine*, Vol I, 155

90 Schadendorf, *Zu Pferde, im Wagen, zu Fuss*, 10

91 *The Letters of St Boniface*, trans Ephraim Emerton (Vol

XXXI, *Records of Civilization*, New York, 1940), Letter XXII, 61
92   Ibid, Letter XXV, 64
93   Ibid, Letter XXVI, 65
94   Ibid, Letter LI, 116
95   Einhard, *The History of the Translation of the Blessed Martyrs of Christ Marcellinus and Peter*, trans Barrett Wendell (Cambridge, Mass, 1926), 12-26
96   Leopold Delisle, *Rouleaux des Morts du IXe au XVe Siècle* (Paris, 1866), XIX, Rouleau de Guifred, comte de Cerdagne, 49-124. See account of the journeys of this and other rolls in R. W. Southern, *The Making of the Middle Ages* (New Haven, 1952), 21-4
97   See Charles Homer Haskins, 'The Spread of Ideas in the Middle Ages', *Speculum, I*, (1926), 19-30 and *The Renaissance of the 12th Century* (Cambridge, 1927) Ch. II, 'Intellectual Centres', 32-69
98   Gregory of Tours, IX, 22
99   Wilfrid Bonser, 'Epidemics during the Anglo-Saxon Period', *The Journal of the British Archaeological Association*, Third Series, IX (1944), 49
100   Ibid, 50
101   Ibid, 59
102   Gregory of Tours, VI, 31 (44). See Robert A. M. Conley, 'Locusts "Teeth of the Wind" ', *National Geographic Magazine*, Vol 136, No 2 (Aug 1969), 202-27 for explanation of the mechanism of locust plagues
103   Hans Zinnser, *Rats, Lice and History* (Boston, 1940), 197

Chapter 2

1   Vaillé, *Histoire générale des postes françaises*, Vol I, 349
2   An unusual example of a Roman timber road from the North Sea frontier area is illustrated in Albert Neuburger, *The Technical Arts and Sciences of the Ancients* (New York, 1930), 453, fig 614, which shows a road made up of wedge-shaped planks laid like clapboards (similar to the clinker-built ships of the north) over swampy ground
3   See Victor W. von Hagen, *The Roads that led to Rome*

(Cleveland, 1967), a detailed text with excellent illustrations
4 Vitruvius, *De Architectura*, vii, 1
5 Grenier, *Manuel d'archéologie gallo-romaine*, Vol I, 325
6 L. A. G. Strong, *The Rolling Road* (London, 1956), 27-8
7 Dopsch, *The Economic and Social Foundations of European Civilization*, 63
8 Forbes, *Studies in Ancient Technology*, Vol II, 159
9 Ibid, 149
10 'Technology in the Middle Ages' in *Technology in Western Civilization* (New York, 1967) eds Melvin Kranzberg and Carroll W. Pursell, jr, I, 66-7
11 Sir Steven Runciman, 'Byzantine Trade and Industry', in *Cam Econ Hist* II, 87
12 Robert S. Lopez, Chapter V, 'The Trade of Medieval Europe: The South', in *Cambridge Economic History*, Vol II (1952), 284-5
13 Desmond Stewart, *Early Islam* (New York, 1967), 56
14 Lynn White, jr, 'Technology and Invention in the Middle Ages', *Speculum*, XV (1940), 150-1
15 Albert Chatellier Rose, 'Via Appia in the days when all roads led to Rome', *Smithsonian Report for 1934*, 366
16 Forbes, *Studies in Ancient Technology*, Vol II, 157
17 Hermann Schreiber, *Merchants, Pilgrims and Highwaymen. A History of Roads through the Ages* (New York, 1962), 156-7
18 Rose, *Via Appia*, 366
19 Grenier, *Manuel d'archéologie gallo-romaine*, Vol I, 170
20 See 'The Treaty between Alfred and Guthrum' in F. L. Attenborough, *The Laws of the Earliest English Kings* (Cambridge, 1922), 99-101
21 Marc Bloch, *Les caractères originaux de l'histoire rurale française* (Paris, 1952), Vol II, 27
22 Rose, *Via Appia*, 366
23 Henry St L. B. Moss, *The Birth of the Middle Ages*, (Oxford, 1935), 243
24 Schadendorf, *Zu Pferde, im Wagen, zu Fuss*, 10
25 Pirenne, *Economic and Social History of Medieval Europe*, 86
26 Dopsch, *The Economic and Social Foundations of European Civilization*, 349

27   Schadendorf, op cit, 10

28   Sir Frank M. Stenton, *Anglo-Saxon England* (Oxford, 1947), 265

29   Octave Uzanne, *La locomotion à travers l'histoire et les moeurs* (Paris, 1900), 50

30   MGH, *Poetarum latinorum medii aevii*, II, (1884), 429. 'Brunni-secunda mali Zezabel cognominis-hilda Cuius ad omne malum rumor per saecula durat'

31   Schreiber, *Merchants, Pilgrims and Highwaymen*, 159

32   Jules Vannerus, 'La Reine Brunehaut dans la Toponymie et dans la Légende', *Académie royale de Belgique. Bulletins de la classe des Lettres*, 5e Serie, Vol XXIV (1938), 301-420

33   Ibid, 307

34   Ibid, 396-8

35   Ibid, 341-2. Vannerus quotes lines 2086-8 of *Auberon*
     'Sa mere et il font les cemins feres
     Parmi les regnes par lors soushais faes;
     Encor i sont, bien savoir le poes.'

36   'in calciata Brunicheld' (*c* 1070) in the *Cartulaire de Gellone* (the monastery of St (Count) William Courtnez of Toulouse), cited in *Revue Internationale d'Onomastique* (Paris), XIII 1961) No 4, p 259. 'viam que dicitur Brunehildis', (*c* 1090) in the *Recueil des chartes de l'abbaye de Cluny*, eds Bernard and Bruel (Paris, 1876-1903), Vol IV, Charter 3302 (Also cited in *Annales de Bourgogne* (Dijon), X, 1938, fascicule IV, 297-8). There is additional information on *chaussées Brunehaut* in *Annales de Bourgogne*, XI, 1939, 121-31

37   Strong, *The Rolling Road*, 40

38   Orderic Vitalis, *Historia Ecclesiastica*, Book VI, Ch III

39   Grenier, *Manuel d'archéologie gallo-romaine*, Vol I, 164

40   R. S. Lopez in *Cambridge Economic History*, Vol II (1952), 279

41   Johannes Brøndsted, *The Vikings* (Harmondsworth, 1965), 147-8

42   James Westfall Thompson, *An Economic and Social History of the Middle Ages* (New York, 1928), 279

43   *Gesta Francorum*, ed Rosalind Hill (Nelson's Medieval Texts, London, 1962), II, 7, p 14

44   Robert S. Lopez, 'Les Influences Orientales et l'Eveil

économique de l'Occident', *Journal of World History*, Vol I, No 3 (Jan 1954), 601
45 Forbes, *Studies in Ancient Technology*, Vol II, 159
46 Rose, *Via Appia*, 365
47 *Cambridge Economic History*, Vol II, 147-8.
48 Gregory of Tours, II, 27 (37), and IV, 30 (44)
49 Grenier, *Manuel d'archéologie gallo-romaine*, Vol I, 185-6
50 Ibid, 190
51 A. Neuburger, *The Technical Arts and Sciences of the Ancients* (New York, 1930), 468
52 Gregory of Tours, V, 11 (17)
53 Ibid, VI, 23 (32)
54 Ibid, X, 9
55 Einhard, *Vita Caroli*, c. 17
56 Gregory of Tours, MGH, *Scriptores Rerum Merovingicarum I, pars II, Miracula et Opera Minora, Liber de Virtutibus S. Iuliani*, c 23, p 574
57 M. Postan in *Cambridge Economic History*, Vol II (1952), 162
58 Robert James Forbes, 'Land transport and road-building (1000-1900)', *Janus*, XLVI, 1957, 108
59 Esperandieu, *Recueil général des bas-reliefs de la Gaule romaine*, Vol VI, Nos 5148 and 6268; Vol IX, No 6699
60 *Libellus de Vita et Miraculis S. Godrici, Heremitae de Finchale* (The Surtees Society, Vol 20, London, 1845), cap VII, p 38
61 R. Cagnat and V. Chapot, *Manuel d'archéologie romaine* (Paris, 1920), Vol II, 377-81
62 Eduard Wagner, *Medieval Costume, Armour and Weapons* (London, nd), Part I, plate 87. Cf Notker, *Gesta Karoli*, I. 34 for description of cross-lacing
63 Paul B. du Chaillu, *The Viking Age* (New York, 1890), Vol II, 371 (running on ice, Njala Saga, c 92) and 388 (running on snowshoes, Flateyjarbok, iii). See, in this connection, D. S. Davidson, *Snowshoes* (Memoirs of the American Philosophical Society), Philadelphia, 1937 and L. J. Dresbeck, 'The Ski: Its History and Historiography', *Technology and Culture*, Vol 8, No 4 (1967), 467-79
64 J. J. Jusserand, *English Wayfaring Life* (London, 1909), 224-30. See illustration of messenger on page 224 (from British

Museum MS, Royal 10 Edward IV), carrying his spear like a badge of office and displaying his lord's seal on the missive.

65 Baudry de Saunier, *Histoire de la locomotion terrestre* (Paris, 1936), 6. Has reproduction of illustration from thirteenth century MS, from Bibliothèque Nationale showing man on stilts and anecdotes concerning use of stilts. In Namur, Belgium, in the sixteenth century a unit of stilt-walkers manoeuvred and fought with great spirit in the presence of the Archduke Albert. In 1808, stilt-walkers from the Landes easily kept up with the fast horses of the Empress Josephine. Speed and endurance runs on stilts were popular in the 1890s for a time

66 Ludwig Croon, 'Aus der Geschichte des Fahrrades', *Beiträge zur Geschichte der Technik*, XXIII (1934), 63-5

67 The Christopher story first appears in the *Golden Legend* of Jacobus de Voragine, d 1298

68 For this and other similar incidents see Lynn White, jr, 'Eilmer of Malmesbury, an Eleventh-Century Aviator: a Case Study of Technological Innovation, its Context and Tradition', *Technology and Culture*, Vol. 2, 1961, 97-111

69 Gregory of Tours, X, 8

70 Talbot, *The Anglo-Saxon Missionaries in Germany*, 'Life of St Sturm', 186. See the article by Willi Görich, 'Ortesweg, Antsanvia und Fulda in neuer Sicht', *Germania*, Vol 33, 1955, 70, for an analysis of St Sturm's routes by water and land in 743. This passage marks the western limit of Slavic expansion.

71 Victor Hehn, *Kulturpflanzen und Haustiere*, (Berlin, 1911), 8th ed, 133

72 Norman Cohn, *The Pursuit of the Millennium* (Oxford, 1957), 40-52, gives a sympathetic account of the poor and their participation in the Crusade.

73 On the mule see my 'The Mule as a Cultural Invention', *Technology and Culture*, Vol 8, No 1, (1967), 45-52, and Frederick E. Zeuner, *A History of Domesticated Animals* (New York, 1963), 382-3.

74 Horace, *Satire*, v

75 Pliny, *Natural History*, xxiii

76 Clive Day, *A History of Commerce* (New York, 1922), 35

77 *Gesta Francorum*. 23. Fulcher of Chartres I, xiii, 3

78 See, in this context, Henri Polge, 'L'Amélioration de l'Attelage: a-t-Elle Réellement fait reculer le Servage?' *Journal
des Savants* (Jan-March, 1967), 13. 'Depuis la préhistoire, le
cheval est traditionnellement considéré comme l'animal noble;
c'est l'auxiliaire du guerrier, du chasseur, du chevalier, du
sportif ou de l'amazone', and again on 25-6: 'Ainsi replace
dans la perspective de ses emplois usuels chez les anciens, le
cheval apparait comme un animal de trait singulier, apte à la
guerre, à la course, aux honneurs et au service des dieux.
De lui on attend des performances de vitesse et des prouesses
sportives plus souvent que des tâches serviles'.

79 Duval, *La vie quotidienne en Gaule,* 177

80 *The Letters of St Boniface.* Letter XX

81 Gregory of Tours, III, 24. '. . . quod regem habere decet.'

82 See comment in Fredegar, II, 58. Compare Pierre Megnin,
Le Cheval et ses Races (Vincennes, 1895), 183.

83 MGH, *Scriptores I,* 140. *Annales Regni Francorum* under
758

84 *Annales Laurissenses vel Einhardi,* anno 791 '. . . tanta
equorum lues exorta est, ut vix decima pars de tot millibus
equorum remansisse dicatur.'

85 *Monk of St Gall,* II, 9

86 Megnin, *Le Cheval et ses Races,* 189

87 Lopez, *Les Influences Orientales et l'Eveil économique de
l'Occident,* 599. The rapid fall in the price of mules is also
noted by Lopez in 'The Evolution of Land Transport in the
Middle Ages', *Past and Present,* IX (1956), p 24

88 Lynn White, jr, *Medieval Technology and Social Change,*
73-4

89 *Economic and Social History of Medieval Europe* (New York,
1937), 89

90 Robert Latouche, *The Birth of Western Economy* (New York,
1966), 271

91 Stenton, *The Bayeux Tapestry,* plate 12

92 Ordericus Vitalis, *Historia Ecclesiastica,* IX. 3. '. . . et boves
et equi arantes et homines carrucas ducentes et hereatores et
equi de quibus herceant, et homines ad carrucas fugientes
. . . perpetua sint in pace.'

93 Kreisel, *Prunkwagen und Schlitten,* 10

94 Gregory of Tours, VII, 35

95 MGH, *Scriptores rerum merovingicarum*, IV, p 702

96 St Columban (by the Monk Jonas), trans and ed Dana C. Munro (University of Pennsylvania Translations and Reprints), Vol II, No 7, ch 58

97 MGH, *Scriptores rerum merovingicarum*, V, p 525

98 Zeuner, *A History of Domesticated Animals*, 358

99 Fulcher of Chartres, *Chronicle of the First Crusade*, I, xii

100 *Scriptores Historiae Augustae*: Aelius Spartianus, *Vita Hadriani*. 19

101 Armandi, *Histoire militaire des Éléphants*, 385-6

102 Zeuner, op cit 112 and 428-9

103 Paul-Marie Duval, *La vie quotidienne en Gaule* (Paris, 1952), 247

104 Johann Christian Ginzrot, *Die Wagen und Fahrwerke der Griechen und Römer und anderer alten Völker; nebst der Bespannung, Zäumung und Verzierung ihrer Zug- Reit- und Last-Thiere* (Munich, 1817), two vols, and *Die Wagen und Fahrwerke der verschiedenen Völker des Mittelalters und der Kutschenbau neuester Zeiten* (Munich, 1830), two vols. As examples of many such reproductions see *Harper's Dictionary of Classical Literature and Antiquities* (New York, 1897) ed Harry Thurston Peck, articles: 'Arcera', 'Basterna', 'Currus', 'Funalis Equus', 'Lectica', 'Reda', and 'Plaustrum'.

105 Albert Chatellier Rose, 'Via Appia in the days when all roads led to Rome', *Smithsonian Report for 1934* (Washington, 1935), 347-70

106 Joseph Needham, *Science and Civilisation in China*, Vol 4, Part II, 75 note j, 'a work of technological history quite extraordinary for the time it was written (1817)', Jürgen Smolian in 'Vorgänger und Nachfolger des gefederten Wagens', *Technikgeschichte* Vol 34 (1967) No 2, 151, calls him 'Der berühmte alte Wagenforscher und Wagenkonstrukteur J. Ch. Ginzrot . . .'

107 Richard Lefebvre des Noëttes, *La Force motrice animale à travers les âges* (Paris, 1924), 1

108 *Daremberg—Saglio, Dictionnaire des Antiquités grecques et romaines*, art 'Lectica'

109 Charles Singer, E. J. Holmyard, A. R. Hall, and Trevor I. Williams, *A History of Technology* (Oxford, 1956), Vol. II,

540 and *Histoire Générale des Techniques,* ed Maurice Daumas (Paris, 1962), Vol I, 232

110 Bonjour, Offler, and Potter, *A Short History of Switzerland* (Oxford, 1955), 32

111 Edmund Virieux, *Aventicum die Römerstadt. Schweizer Heimatbücher,* 10/10A, German trans (from French) Dr G. Theodor Schwarz (Bern, 1961), 8

112 *Codex Theodosianus,* trans Clyde Pharr (Princeton, 1952) 8.5.2

113 Ibid, 8.5.8.1

114 Ibid, 8.5.8.2

115 Ibid, 8.5.11

116 Ibid, 8.5.17 and 8.5.47. 60lb is allowed for the saddle and bridle, 35lb for the saddlebag.

117 Ibid, 8.5.17

118 Ibid, 8.5.18 and 8.5.20

119 Ibid, 8.5.28 and 8.5.30

120 A. Burford, 'Heavy transport in classical Antiquity', *Economic History Review,* 2nd Series, XIII, 1960, 1-18

121 *Edict of Diocletian on Prices,* XV, *Wood for vehicles*

122 H. Kreisel, *Prunkwagen und Schlitten* (Leipzig, 1927), 9

123 *Edict of Diocletian on Prices,* XV, 31a, 32, 34, and 35

124 Ibid, XV, 36

125 James Curle, *A Roman Frontier Post and its People. The Fort of Newstead* (Glasgow, 1911), 292-4

126 One is reminded of 'The Deacon's Masterpiece' (The Wonderful One-Hoss Shay) by Oliver Wendell Holmes, sr, where by logical means every part was made as strong as the rest so that it could not break down. This goal still eludes manufacturers

127 *Edict of Diocletian on Prices,* XIV

128 Roux, *Herculaneum et Pompei,* Vol III, plate 126

129 Gell and Gandy, *Pompeii,* Description of Engraving—Waggon and Horses

130 Roux, *Herculaneum et Pompei,* Vol V, plates 38 and 39

131 Ibid, plate 40

132 Ibid, plate 46

133 Marcel E. Marien, *Les monuments funéraires de l'Arlon Romain* (Arlon, 1945), 91 and fig 37

134 Ibid, 137 and fig 52

135 Richard Lefebvre des Noëttes, *L'Attelage et le cheval de selle à travers les ages* (Paris, 1931); Vol II, fig 85

136 Dragendorff—Krüger, *Das Grabmal von Igel* (Römische Grabmäler des Mosellandes, Vol I; Berlin and Leipzig, 1924), 79-80

137 Daremberg—Saglio, art *Cisium*

138 Wilhelm von Massow, *Die Grabmäler von Neumagen* (Römische Grabmäler des Mosellandes; Berlin and Leipzig, 1932), 2:1, 141-2

139 Ibid, 2:1, 217 and 2:2, plate 60

140 Duval, *La vie quotidienne en Gaule*, 177

141 Renard, 'Technique et agriculture en pays trevire et remois', *Latomus*, XVIII, 1959, 91, fig 7

142 Emile Esperandieu, *Recueil général des bas-reliefs, statues et bustes de la Germania romaine* (Paris and Brussels, 1931), no 258

143 Ibid, nos 297-8

144 Esperandieu, *Recueil général des bas-reliefs de la Gaule romaine*, Vol IV, No 3245

145 E. M. Jope, 'Vehicles and Harness', in *A History of Technology*, ed Singer et al Vol II (Oxford, 1956), 551

146 Needham, *Science and Civilisation in China*, Vol 4, Part II, 93-4

147 Ole Klindt-Jensen, *Denmark before the Vikings*, trans Eva and David Wilson (Ancient Peoples and Places, Vol 4: London, 1957), 88-9

148 *Acta Archaeologica*, XX (1949), 95; Singer, *A History of Technology*, Vol II, 545

149 Otto Mahr, 'Zur Geschichte des Wagenrades', *Beiträge zur Geschichte der Technik*, XXIII (1934), 59; Marjorie Nice Boyer, 'Medieval pivoted axles', *Technology and Culture*, I (1960), 131; Kreisel, *Prunkwagen und Schlitten*, 14

150 Giraldus Cambrensis, *Topography of Ireland*, I, iv

151 Patrick W. Joyce, *Social History of Ireland* (London, 1903), Vol II, 393

152 Ibid, 402

153 J. O'Beirne Crowe, 'Siabur-Charpat con Culaind', *Journal of the Royal Historical and Archaeological Association of Ireland*, Vol I, 4th Series (1870-1), 415

154 Ibid, 421-2

155 Joyce, *Social History of Ireland*, Vol II, 408
156 Ibid, 410
157 *Columba* (by Adomnan), trans and ed Alan Orr Anderson and Marjorie Ogilvie Anderson (London, 1961), 290
158 Ibid, 440
159 Ibid, 388-90
160 *St Columban*, ch 14
161 Gregory of Tours, III, 26
162 Ibid, II, 16
163 Ibid, II, 24
164 Ibid, VII, 35
165 MGH, Legum sectio II, Vol I, *Capitularia Regum Francorum, Capitulare Bononsiense*. Oct 811, ch 8
166 Ibid, Capitulare Aquisgranense, 801-13, ch 10
167 Ibid, Capitulare de villis, 800, ch 64
168 Ibid, Letter of Charles to Abbot Fulrad, 804-11
169 MGH, *Scriptores*, XIII, p 155. Ex vetustis Annalibus Nordhumbranis. anno 795 '. . . sublatis inde 15 plaustris auro argentoque palliisque olosericis pretiosis repletis, quorum quodque quattuor trahebant boves . . .'
170 D. M. Wilson, *The Anglo-Saxons* (New York, 1960), 89
171 See illustration from Prudentius MS, reproduced in Thomas Wright, *A History of Domestic Manners and Sentiments in England During the Middle Ages* (London, 1862), 73
172 Ralph Straus, *Carriages and Coaches* (London, 1912), 46 J. H. Markland, 'Early Use of Carriages in England', *Archaeologia*, XX, 1824, 451. See Neil R. Ker, *Catalogue of Manuscripts containing Anglo-Saxon* (Oxford, 1957), 178, for the date.
173 I. Venedikov, *Trakijslata Kolesnica* (Bulgar. Akademie der Wissenschaft, Sofia, 1960).
174 Georg Jacob, *Arabische Berichte von Gesandten an germanische Fürstenhöfe* (Berlin-Leipzig, 1927), 18
175 *Libellus de Vita et Miraculis S Godrici, CCXXIV*, s 613 p 480
176 Stenton, *The Bayeux Tapestry*, plate 41
177 Simeon of Durham, *Gesta Regum*, anno 1093, 'Corpus regis . . . duo ex indigenis carro impositum in Tynemuthe sepelierunt.'
178 *Recueil des chartes de l'abbaye de Cluny*, Charter 3, 302, '. . . plaustrum quod habebant illi de Beresi in Peronna.'

179 William of Malmesbury, *History of the Kings of England*, IV, 333, 'Pauci rusticanorum cadaver, in rheda caballaria compositum, Wintoniam in episcopatum devexere, cruore undatim per totam viam stillante'.

180 Procopius, *History of the Wars*, VI, vii, 2-5

181 Ammianus Marcellinus XXXI.xii.11. Other references XXXI.xv.5, XXXI.vii.5, and among the Alans (Halani) XXXI.ii.18. Other descriptions are in Claudian, *In Rufin ii* 127ff, Vegetius, iii. 10 and earlier in Caesar, *Bell Gall* i 26 and i 51

182 The invention of this strange machine is attributed to Heribert, Archbishop of Milan, who needed a visible symbol for the newly organised commune. It was first used in 1038. There is a fine description of the Florentine *carroccio* in Villani's *Cronica* VI, 76.

183 At least in western Europe, but Needham has shown in *Science and Civilisation in China*, Vol 4, Part II, 258-74, that the Chinese were familiar with many types of wheelbarrow, particularly the form with the load above, or balanced on, a centre wheel, at least from the second century AD

184 *Codex Theodosianus* 6.29.2 and 8.5.9

185 Duval, *La vie quotidienne en Gaule*, 178

186 See illustration of early wheelbarrow in Matthew Paris, *The Lives of the Two Offas* (British Museum MS Nero D 1). Cf Bibliothèque Nationale, Paris, lat 6769, for a similar wheelbarrow

187 Robert Capot-Rey, *Geographie de la circulation sur les continents* (Paris, 1946), 83, note 1

188 See reproduction from St Bertin Bible in Baudry de Saunier, *Histoire de la locomotion terrestre*, Vol II, 70

189 Needham, *Science and Civilisation in China*, Vol 4, Part II, 271

190 Gösta Berg, *Sledges and Wheeled Vehicles* (Nordiska Museets Handlingar 4, 1935), 64

191 Ibid, 79-80

192 Franz Maria Feldhaus, *Die Technik der Vorzeit, der geschichtlichen Zeit und der Naturvölker* (Leipzig and Berlin, 1914), col 977

193 Gregory of Tours, *History*, X, 19

194 Schreiber, *Merchants, Pilgrims and Highwaymen*, 174

195   Gregory of Tours, III, 37
196   Huntington, *Mainsprings of Civilization,* 610. The only accounts of the freezing of the Kattegat which can be authenticated are in the years 1296, 1306, 1323 and 1408
197   Wilhelm Levison, *England and the Continent in the Eighth Century* (Oxford, 1946), 12
198   *Cambridge Economic History,* Vol II, 147-8
199   Priscus, *fragment* 8
200   Day, *A History of Commerce,* 57
201   Thompson, *An Economic and Social History of the Middle Ages,* 573-4
202   Josef Kulischer, *Allgemeine Wirtschaftsgeschichte des Mittelalters und der Neuzeit* (Munich and Berlin, 1928), II, 300-1
203   Kulischer, op cit, 302 and 309
204   Day, *A History of Commerce,* 60-1
205   MGH *Diplomata Karolinorum,* I, No 122, pp 170-1
206   Ibid, No 6, pp 6-10
207   See the grant by Chilperic II to the abbey of Corbie in Leon Levillain in 'Examen critique des chartes merovingiennes et carolingiennes de l'Abbaye de Corbie' in *Mémoires et documents publiés par la Societé de l'École des Chartes* (Paris, 1902) V, No 15, pp 235-7
208   Thompson, *An Economic and Social History of the Middle Ages,* 634-5
209   C. W. Previté-Orton, *The Shorter Cambridge Medieval History* (Cambridge, 1952), Vol I, 370-1
210   Lynn White, jr, *Medieval Technology and Social Change* (Oxford, 1962), 66, note 4. (His fig 3 reproduces the vehicle from the Trier Apocalypse)
211   Reproduced in Guy Metraux and François Crouzet, *The Evolution of Science* (New York, 1963), fig 3, p 170. Commented on on p 187, by Bertrand Gille
212   See reproduction in André Haudricourt *L'Homme et la Charrue à travers le monde* (Paris, 1955), 163, and comment in Berg, *Sledges and Wheeled Vehicles,* 100
213   Will Cuppy, *The Decline and Fall of Practically Everybody* (New York, 1950), 159
214   Stenton, *The Bayeux Tapestry,* plate 41
215   Lynn White, jr, *Medieval Technology and Social Change,* 24
216   For example, the contention of Lynn White, jr, *Medieval*

N

Technology and Social Change, 61, that metal objects found in ninth-century Swedish graves are mountings for horse-collars is disputed by Joseph Needham, *Science and Civilisation*, Vol 4, Part II, 316, who finds the same objects to be only ornamental

217 *Cambridge Economic History*, Vol I, 134

218 *Miniature sacre e profane dell'anno 1023, illustranti l'enciclopedia medioevale di Rabano Mauro*, ed A. M. Amelli (Montecassino, 1896). The illustration is reproduced in Carl Stephenson, 'In Praise of Medieval Tinkers', *The Journal of Economic History*, VIII, No 1 (May 1948), 33

219 See statement of the evidence in Lynn White, jr, *Medieval Technology and Social Change*, 45-6

220 Claudian, *Carmina minora, de mulabus Gallicis*

221 Ginzrot, *Die Wagen und Fahrwerke der Griechen und Römer*, Vol I, 71

222 See *The Bayeux Tapestry* (London, 1965, 2nd ed), Sir Frank M. Stenton, ed, plate 53

223 Feldhaus, *Die Technik der Vorzeit, der geschichtlichen Zeit und der Naturvölker*, col 897

224 L. Sprague de Camp, 'Before stirrups', *Isis*, LII, Part 2, No 164 (June 1960), 160

225 Lynn White, jr, in chapter I of *Medieval Technology and Social Change* ably summarises and develops the subject.

226 Lynn White, jr op cit, 26-7

227 Simple 'snaffle' bits acting on the horse's mouth were in use from the fourteenth century BC in Egypt. 'Curb' bits, much more severe in action, which also had a rod passing under the horse's lower jaw when the reins were pulled, were known to the Celts from the third century BC. John K. Anderson, *Ancient Greek Horsemanship* (Berkeley, 1961), 47 and 53

228 Apparently the Greeks were the first to use spurs (Anderson, op cit, 205) but these were of the simple 'prick' variety. 'Rowel' spurs terminating in a small rotatable wheel with projecting points were a later medieval development, not found, for example, in the Bayeux Tapestry but seen on the first seal of Henry III of England

229 Talbot, *The Anglo-Saxon Missionaries in Germany*, 'The Life of St Sturm', 187

230 MGH, *Leges*. iii, 317

231 Day, *A History of Commerce*, 293
232 Esperandieu, *Recueil général des bas-reliefs de la Gaule romaine*, Vol VI, Nos 5148, 5268; Vol VII, No 5499; Vol X, No 7556; Vol XI, Nos 7685, 7725, *et al*
233 Megnin, *Le Cheval et ses Races*, 180
234 *St Columban*, ch 14
235 Comptes rendus de la XIVᵉ session du Congrès international d'anthropologie of d'archéologie prehistorique, Geneva, 1912, 593-627
236 *Wirtschaftsgeschichte des Altertums*, Leiden, 1938, 2 vols, I, 572, with numerous references to the archaeological reports in II, 1159
237 'Weitere keltische Hufeisen aus Salzburg und Umgebung', *Archaeologica austriaca*, xii (1953), 44-9
238 *The Ancient World*, Boston, 1969, 269
239 R. E. M. and T. V. Wheeler, *Verulamium*, 220 and plate LXIII b
240 R. E. M. Wheeler, *Maiden Castle, Dorset*, 77, 120, 290-1 and C. F. C. Hawkes and M. R. Hull, *Camulodonum*, 342
241 See accounts in the *Saalburg Jahrbuch*, I (1910), 52; II (1911), 41; III (1912), 51; VI (1927), 57; and XV (1956), 29-37. Also Carl Blümlein, *Bilder aus dem Römisch-Germanischen Kulturleben* (Munich and Berlin, 1919), who shows illustrations of *hipposandales* (Abb 192 c, d) and horseshoes (Abb 193)
242 Lynn White, jr, 'The Life of the Silent Majority', in Robert S. Hoyt, *Life and Thought in the Early Middle Ages* (Minneapolis, 1967), 94
243 *Die Wagen und Fahrwerke der Griechen und Römer*, II, 470, fig 1
244 See illustrations in Singer, *History of Technology*, II, 76-7
245 Guibert of Nogent, *Historia Hierosolymitana*, quoted in Regine Pernoud, *The Crusades*, 28
246 See *The Annotated Sherlock Holmes* by Sir Arthur Conan Doyle (edited by W. S. Baring-Gould), II, 629
247 Summarised in Lynn White, jr, *Medieval Technology and Social Change*, 61, where an illumination in the Trier *Apocalypse c* 800, is claimed as the earliest European picture of the modern horse-collar. Needham, op cit 317, g, disagrees and prefers the early tenth century for the introduction of the collar harness to the west

248 Reproduced in Stephenson, 'In Praise of Medieval Tinkers', *The Journal of Economic History*, VIII, No 1 (May 1948), 34

249 MGH, *Capit* I, 132, *c* 7 (781?) and II, 321, *c* 25 (864)

250 *Ruodlieb*, V, 468-9; Stenton, *The Bayeux Tapestry*, plate 12; *The Russian Primary Chronicle, Laurentian Text*, trans S. H. Cross and O. P. Sherbowitz-Wetzor (Cambridge, Mass, 1953), 200; Orderic Vitalis, *Historia Ecclesiastica*, IX, 3. Joseph Needham, op cit 317, registers his dissent once more and regards even the Bayeux Tapestry example as breast-strap harness

251 *Encyclopaedia Britannica*, 11th ed, Vol 13, 718

252 William Fitzstephen, *Descriptio noilissimae civitatis Londoniae*

253 Needham, op cit, 308-19

254 See Esperandieu, *Recueil général des bas-reliefs de la Gaule romaine*, Vol V, No 4031, Vol XI, Nos 7685, 7725; Dragendorff and Krüger, *Das Grabmal von Igel*, pl 12, i

255 A. G. Haudricourt and M. J. B. Delamarre, *L'Homme et la charrue à travers le monde* (Paris, 1955), 178. See table in Needham, op cit, 327

256 W. Holmquist, 'Germanic art during the first millennium AD', *Kungl Vitterhets, Historie och Antikvitets Akademiens Handlingar*, XC (1955), fig 134

257 John Philipson, *Harness: as it has been, as it is, and as it should be* (London, 1882)

258 Joseph Needham, 'Central Asia and the history of science and technology', *Journal of the Royal Central Asian Society* (1950), 139-41

259 See the impassioned attacks on restrictive harnessing in Anna Sewell, *Black Beauty* (numerous editions) *passim*, eg, Ch 44, where it is likened to having a horse's head and tail fastened together at the saddle

260 G. Calza and G. Beccati, *Ostia* (Rome, 1957), 65, fig 5; Esperandieu, *Recueil général des bas-reliefs de la Gaule romaine*, Vol XI, Nos 7685, 7725

261 Lefebvre des Noëttes, *l'Attelage et le cheval de selle à travers les ages* (Paris, 1931), Vol I, 159

262 Pliny, *Natural History*, xviii. xlvii. '. . . in Italia octoni boves ad singulos vomeres anhelent.'

263 *Codex Theodosianus*, 8.5.8.2

264 MGH, *Scriptores, XIII*, p 155. Ex vetustis Annalibus Nord-humbranis. anno. 795

265 *Codex Theodosianus*, 8.5.8.2

266 See example reproduced in *Les routes de France depuis les Origines jusqu'à nos jours*, 38-9

267 Singer, *A History of Technology*, II, 84 (fig 46) and 91

268 *Documents relating to the Colonial History of the State of New York. Holland Documents*. Vol I (Albany, 1856), 368, 'Information respecting Land in New Netherland' (4 March 1650)

269 Lynn White, jr, in 'The Life of the Silent Majority', *Life and Thought in the Early Middle Ages*, ed Robert S. Hoyt, Minneapolis, 1967), 96

270 A Goldschmidt, *Die Bronzetüren von Novgorod und Gnesen*, (Marburg, 1932), 8, plate 26

271 See reproductions in Schadendorf, *Zu Pferde, im Wagen, zu Fuss*, plate 1, or Wilfred Owen and Ezra Bowen in *Wheels* (Life Science Library), New York, 1967, 22-3

272 Berg, *Sledges and Wheeled Vehicles*, 163

273 André G. Haudricourt, 'Contribution à la Géographie et à l'Ethnologie de la voiture', *La Revue de Géographie humaine et d'Ethnologie*, Vol. 1, No. 1 (Jan-Mar 1948), 57

274 Boyer, *Medieval pivoted axles*, 131

275 Ibid, 128-9

276 Ibid, 128, 'It is well established that the Romans knew and used the pivoted front-axle'; Kreisel, *Prunkwagen und Schlitten*, 5, 'According to all sources the pivoted front-axle was an invention of Rome'. Lynn White, jr, 'The Life of the Silent Majority' in *Life and Thought in the Early Middle Ages* ed Robert S. Hoyt (Minneapolis, 1967), 96, 'The pivoted front axle for wagons was known to the Romans and continued in use . . .' See also Hugo Mötefindt, 'Die Erfindung des Drehschemels am Vierrädrigen Wagen', *Geschichtsblätter für Technik und Industrie*, (6/1919), 30-41, who reproduces Ginzrot's drawing, Abb 6 on p 35

277 Ginzrot, *Die Wagen und Fahrwerke der Griechen und Römer*, Vol I, 112-16

278 *Oxford Classical Dictionary*, s.v. Pollux

279 Julius Pollux, *Onomasticon* I, x. *Military*, 10. *Of the parts of the chariot*

280 Du Cange, *Glossarium Mediae et Infimae Latinitatis*, s.v. *Estor*, 2. 'Clavus quo temoni aptatur jugum', and Daremberg-Saglio, *Dictionnaire des Antiquités* I, 1638 b, article: Currus.
281 As examples of this continuing trend see above, p 71
282 Pliny the Younger, *Epistolae*, iii, v
283 Kreisel, *Prunkwagen und Schlitten*, 10
284 See articles by Jürgen Smolian, 'Zur Frage der Entwicklung der Wagenfederung' and 'Vorgänger und Nachfolger des gefederten Wagens' for illustrations, schematic diagrams, and comment
285 Jacob, *Arabische Berichte von Gesandten an germanische Fürstenhöfe*, 18
286 Boyer, *Medieval Suspended Carriages*, 359-66
287 Cato, *de re rustica* cap. 97
288 Pliny, *Natural History*, xxviii, xxxvii, 141
289 *Prince Igor*, trans Norma Lorre Goodrich, in *The Medieval Myths* (New York, 1961), 160
290 Oskar Gromodka and Rudolf Müller, 'Über Wagen und Wagenbau', *Technikgeschichte*, 1934, Vol 23, p 73

Chapter 3

1 Day, *A History of Commerce*, 55
2 *The Life of St Sturm* in Talbot, *The Anglo-Saxon Missionaries in Germany*, 184-7
3 Blaise Pascal, *Pensées. Préface Générale. Les règles du langage*, 45 (439) 'Les rivières sont des chemins qui marchent, et qui portent ou l'on veut aller' (17). *Oeuvres complètes* (Paris, 1954), p 1099
4 Albert S. Cook, 'Augustine's Journey from Rome to Richborough', *Speculum*, I (1926), 386
5 Constantine Porphyrogenitus, *De Administrando Imperio*, trans R. J. H. Jenkins (Budapest, 1949), 57-63
6 J. E. Eubanks, 'Navigation on the Tiber', *Classical Journal*, June 1930, 684-90
7 Procopius, *History of the Wars*, V, xxvi, 9-13
8 Ibid, VI, vii, 6-12
9 Gregory of Tours, VIII, 12; Fortunatus, *Carm* x, 10, xi, 27-28, vi 10

10 *The Life of St Sturm* in Talbot, *The Anglo-Saxon Missionaries in Germany*, 193-4. Willi Görich in 'Ortesweg, Antsanvia und Fulda in neuer Sicht', *Germania*, Vol 33, 1955, 68-88, analyses routes in the Fulda area in the mid-eighth century and gives on the rear side of enclosure 2 (between 80 and 81) a map showing possible routes for the return of Boniface's body from Mainz to Fulda

11 *Annales Regni Francorum* (Ausgewählte Quellen zur Deutschen Geschichte des Mittelalters, Band V, Berlin), Anno 793

12 Liutprand, *Antapodosis*, IV. See also *Cambridge Economic History*, Vol II, 265

13 *Medieval England*, Vol I, 205

14 Thompson, *An Economic and Social History of the Middle Ages*, 444-5. The air, the sea, the seashore, and the flowing rivers are common to all. *Corpus Iuris Civilis, Digesta* 1, 8; *Institutiones* 2, 1, pr 2

15 Horace, *Satires* V, 1-24

16 Tacitus, *Annales* II, viii

17 Pliny the Younger, *Epistolae* X, Letters xli and xlii

18 Suetonius, *Nero* 16 and 19

19 See George H. Allen, 'A Problem of Inland Navigation in Roman Gaul', *Classical Weekly* XXVII, 9 (11 Dec 1933), 65-9, for a discussion of this and other canal projects. He supposes that the Romans must have known the hydraulic chamber-lock system even to have entertained the scheme

20 *Annales Regni Francorum*, Anno 793

21 For a fine description of the newly-uncovered *diolkos* see the article by the discoverer, Nicholas M. Verdelis, 'How the Ancient Greeks transported Ships over the Isthmus of Corinth: Uncovering the 2550-year-old *Diolkos* of Periander', *Illustrated London News* (19 Oct 1957), vol 231, 649-51. The older views, based on the literary sources, believed that the *Diolkos* was a grooved wooden roadway along which the ships themselves were dragged. See the article *Isthmos* by Fimmen in *Pauly-Wissowa* 9.2256-65 and William Linn Westermann, 'On inland transportation and communication in antiquity', *Classical Journal*, April 1929, 494. A possible echo of the *diolkos* is seen in the feat of the First Crusaders in 1097 in bringing ships overland to Lake Isnik in the siege

of Nicaea. The most complete description is that of William of Tyre (Ch LIX) who says some ships were set whole on four or five carts coupled together and pulled by many men with ropes, others were broken down into two or three pieces and put on chariots. The largest carried 100 people; the smallest twenty. A similar method was used in 1453 by Sultan Mohammed II at the conquest of Constantinople to transport vessels overland to surprise the defenders. There are modern paintings of this event in the Dolmabace Palace in Istanbul and in the National Geographic Society. See Irving and Electa Johnson, 'Yankee Sails Turkey's History-Haunted Coast', *National Geographic,* Vol 136, No 6, 840-3

22 Pirenne, *Histoire économique de l'Occident mediéval,* 543-4

23 Roger of Hoveden, *Annals,* Anno 1121

24 L. F. Salzman, *English Trade in the Middle Ages* (London, 1964), 253

25 Vegetius IV, 39. See William W. Mooney, *Travel among the Ancient Romans* (Boston, 1920), 118. Compare *Codex Theodosianus* XIII, IX, 3, 380, which gives the open season as 1 April to 15 October

26 Goitein, *A Mediterranean Society,* Vol I, p 316

27 Harlan W. Gilmore, *Transportation and the Growth of Cities* (Glencoe, III, 1953), 9. Detailed routes are given in Pliny, *Natural History* VI, 26

28 *The Hodopoericon of St Willibald* in Talbot, *The Anglo-Saxon Missionaries in Germany,* 171

29 *Orkneyingers' Saga* (Rolls Series), p 220. The curious word *viking* whose etymology is much disputed began as a verb rather than as a noun. See Howard La Fay, 'The Vikings', *National Geographic Magazine,* Vol 137, No 4 (April 1970) p 495

30 Joseph Kulischer, *Allgemeine Wirtschaftsgeschichte des Mittelalters und der Neuzeit* (Munich and Berlin, 1928), I, 305

31 Procopius, *History of the Wars* V, i, 19-23. The normal tide in this part of the Adriatic is about 18 inches. In 467, Sidonius saw food supplies being brought in to Ravenna in this way (Epistles, I, v 6). In the same citation he gives an early description of environmental pollution. 'The whole situation is most favourable to trade, and in particular we saw large

food-supplies coming in. But there was one drawback: on one side the briny sea-water rushed up to the gates, and elsewhere the sewer-like filth of the channels was churned up by the boat traffic, and the bargemen's poles, boring into the glue at the bottom, helped to befoul the current, slow and sluggish at the best: the result was that we went thirsty though surrounded by water, finding nowhere pure water from aqueducts, nowhere a filthproof reservoir, nowhere a bubbling spring or mud-free well.'

32 Beowulf, VIII, Einhard, *Vita Karoli*, c 22. See also numerous swimming exploits in Grettissaga

33 Camille Jullian, *Histoire de la Gaule* (Paris, 1908-26), Vol IV, 401. In another sense of the word, *utricularii* were also bagpipers.

34 Priscus, *fragment* 8

35 Gregory of Tours, III, 15

36 *Histoire Générale des Techniques*, Vol I, 445

37 Marc Bloch, 'Un Episode de l'histoire humaine des rivières', *Annales d'histoire économique et sociale*, VI, 184-5

38 *Cambridge Economic History*, Vol II, 149-50

39 Constantine Porphyrogenitus, *De Administrando Imperio*, 57-63

40 Joyce, *Social History of Ireland*, Vol II, 422-5

41 *Columba*, 440-4

42 Translation Sir R. C. Hoare, 1806, 332-33. Quoted in W. O. Hassall, *How they lived*, 52

43 Loup de Ferrières, *Correspondance*, ed Levillain (Paris, 1927), Vol II, epistle 105, pp 134-5

44 Ellen C. Semple, *Geography of the Mediterranean Region* (New York, 1931), 272

45 Cassiodorus, *Variae Epistolae* V. Letters 16-20

46 Villehardouin, *Chronicle of the Fourth Crusade*, 6

47 Frederick C. Lane, *Venetian Ships and Shipbuilding in the Renaissance* (Baltimore, 1934), 232-3

48 Gregory of Tours, IV, 33 (48)

49 *Anglo-Saxon Chronicle*, Anno 897

50 A. W. Brøgger and H. Shetelig, *The Viking Ships* (Oslo, 1951), 191. Cf *Medieval England*, Vol I, 171-4

51 *Histoire Générale des Techniques*, Vol I, 381-2

52 Singer, *History of Technology*, Vol II, 567

53 *Anglo-Saxon Chronicle*, Anno 877
54 Duval, *La vie quotidienne en Gaule*, 188
55 Peter H. Sawyer, *The Age of the Vikings* (London, 1962), 82
56 *Gesta Francorum*, 16
57 MGH, *Capitularia Regum Francorum*, I, No 44, Capitulary of Thionville, AD 805
58 Ibid, II, No 253, *The Raffelstetten Tolls*, AD 903-6
59 *Relatio de legatione Constantinoplitana*, Chs LIV, LV
60 James F. Willard, 'Inland transportation in England during the 14th Century', *Speculum*, I (1926), 369
61 Procopius, *History of the Wars* VII, xxix, 9-16
62 Duval, *La vie quotidienne en Gaule*, 249
63 See such works as his 'Notes: The River Boats of Meso-potamia', *Mariner's Mirror*, V. 53 (1967) 286-8
    'Ancient Shipbuilding: New Light on an Old Source', *American Philological Association* 94 (1963) 28-33
    'Odysseus' Boat (Od V, 244-257)', *American Journal of Philology* 85 (1964) 61-4
    'New Light on Ancient Rigging and Boatbuilding', *American Neptune*, Vol 24 (1964), 81-94
    'The Sails of the Ancient Mariner', *Archaeology* 7 (1954), 214-19
    'Fore-and-aft Sails in the Ancient World', *Mariner's Mirror*, 42 (1956), 3-5
    'Speed under Sail of Ancient Ships', *Transactions of the Am. Philological Assoc.* LXXXII, 1951, 136-48
64 Lionel Casson, 'New Light on Ancient Rigging and Boatbuilding', *American Neptune* 24 (1964), 88
65 For fine accounts of the development of undersea archaeo-logical technology see articles by George F. Bass, 'Underwater Archaeology: Key to History's Warehouse', and 'New Tools for Undersea Archaeology', *National Geographic*, Vol 124 (1963) 138-56 and Vol 134 (1968), 403-23, and Peter Throckmorton, 'Ancient Shipwreck Yields New Facts—and a Strange Cargo', *National Geographic*, Vol 135 (1969), 282-300. Prof Bass' earlier opinion that the seventh-century Byzantine ship discussed in 'Underwater Archaeology: Key to History's Warehouse', (p 156) was the earliest evidence for frame-first construction has since been modified. (See Casson

'Ancient Shipbuilding: New Light on an Old Source', *Transactions and Proceedings of the American Philological Association*, 94 (1963), p 32.) One must still look for evidence for the beginning of the frame-first technique. That the change-over was not universal is indicated by the fact that the *Grace Dieu* built in England in 1418 still had its frame inserted after the completion of the shell (Singer, *History of Technology*, Vol II, 588).

66   Warships of this size were not common in the Atlantic until the time of Nelson in the early nineteenth century. Singer, *A History of Technology*, Vol II, 573

67   A. R. Lewis, *Naval Power and Trade in the Mediterranean*, 191

68   Ibid, 184

69   Casson, 'The Sails of the Ancient Mariner', *Archaeology*, Vol 7 (1954), 214-19

70   See reproduction: Life's *Great Ages of Man*, 'Imperial Rome' by Moses Hadas, 154-5

71   Singer, *History of Technology*, Vol II, 516-23

72   *Histoire Générale des Techniques*, Vol I, 381-2

73   Constantine VII Porphyrogenitus, *De Cerimoniis aula byzantinae* (Migne, P.G. 112. I, Append, 14, 932-3). The system is well described in Louis Brehier, *Le Monde Byzantin*, II, *Les Institutions de l'Empire Byzantin*, 331-3

74   A. R. Lewis, *Naval Power and Trade in the Mediterranean*, 165. This has sometimes been described as a heliograph system complete with reflecting mirrors (*Encyclopaedia Britannica*, 11th ed, Article, 'Bougie') which seems very doubtful at this date. The true heliograph only makes its appearance in the nineteenth century. The Jewish merchants in Egypt had many observation points on the coast west from Alexandria to beyond Tobruk to relay information quickly about ship positions. Goitein, *A Mediterranean Society*, Vol I, 319-20

75   *Medieval England*, Vol I, 171

76   Ibid, 171-4

77   See A. R. Burn, 'Procopius and the Island of Ghosts', *English Historical Review* 70 (1955), 259

78   *Medieval England*, Vol I, 171-4

79   Singer, *A History of Technology*, Vol II, 578-81

80 Peter H. Sawyer, *The Age of the Vikings* (London, 1962), 76. See reconstructions of the northern ships in Björn Landström, *Das Schiff, vom Einbaum zum Atomboot* (Gütersloh, 1961)

81 A. W. Brøgger and H. Shetelig, *The Viking Ships, their Ancestry and Evolution* (Oslo, 1953), 212

82 Ibid, 141; Thorleif Sjøvold, *The Oseberg Find* (Oslo, 1957), 58

83 *Anglo-Saxon Chronicle*, Anno 897

84 *Olaf Trygvason's Saga, c* 95

85 Du Chaillu, *The Viking Age*, Vol II, 169

86 Sawyer, *The Age of the Vikings*, 74

87 R. and R. C. Anderson, *The Sailing Ship*, p 71

88 Brøgger and Shetelig, *The Viking Ships*, 109

89 See G. J. Marcus, 'The Norse Emigration to the Faeroe Islands', *English Historical Review*, 71 (1956), pp 56-61, and 'The Evolution of the Knörr', *Mariner's Mirror* XLI, 115-22

90 Brøgger and Shetelig, *The Viking Ships*, 130

91 Ibid, 143

92 *Histoire Générale des Techniques*, Vol I, 451

93 Singer, *History of Technology*, II, 771. Needham, *Science and Civilisation in China*, Vol 4, Part 3, Section 29, Nautical Technology, 1971

94 See discussion in Bertrand Gille, 'Technological Developments in Europe: 1100 to 1400', *The Evolution of Science*, eds Metraux and Crouzet, 187-9, and in R. and R. C. Anderson, *The Sailing Ship*, 86-90 and plate III

95 Brøgger and Shetelig, *The Viking Ships*, 239

96 R. J. Forbes and E. J. Dijksterhuis, *A History of Science and Technology* (Baltimore, 1963), Vol 1, 136

97 Peter Hunter Blair, *An Introduction to Anglo-Saxon England* (Cambridge, 1959), 62-3

98 A. R. Lewis, *The Northern Seas*, p 316. Heinrich Winter, 'Die Nautik der Wikinger', *Hansische Geschichtsblätter*, XLII (1937), 173-84 and 'Who Invented the Compass?' *Mariner's Mirror* 23 (1937), 95. This has been refuted by G. J. Marcus, 'The Navigation of the Norsemen', *Mariner's Mirror* 39 (1953), 112, and 'The Early Norse Traffic to Iceland', *Mariner's Mirror*, 46 (1960), 179, on the basis that there are late interpolations in the texts

99 Marcus, 'The Navigation of the Norsemen', *Mariner's Mirror*, XXXIX, p 121
100 Winter, 'Die Nautik der Wikinger', *Hansische Geschichtsblätter* 62 (1937), p 175
101 Howard La Fay, 'The Vikings', *National Geographic Magazine*, Vol 137, No 4, 526-30
102 Marcus, 'The Navigation of the Norsemen', *Mariner's Mirror*, XXXIX, 126
103 E. G. R. Taylor, *The Haven-Finding Art* (New York, 1957), 76-7
104 Ibid, 72; *Landnamabok,* trans T. Elwood (Kendal, 1898), Part I, Ch 2, p 4
105 See accounts of the early history of the compass in Lynn White, jr, *Medieval Technology and Social Change*, p 132, and Joseph Needham, *Science and Civilisation in China*, Vol 4, Part 1, Section 26, pp 229-314
106 Bertrand Gille, 'Technological Developments in Europe; 1100 to 1400', *The Evolution of Science,* ed Guy S. Metraux and François Crouzet (New York, 1963), 190
107 See, for example, *Landnamabok* in *Thule*, XXIII, p 62, and the instances cited by G. J. Marcus, 'The Navigation of the Norsemen', *Mariner's Mirror*, XXXIX, 112-31

Chapter 4

1 Duval, *La vie quotidienne en Gaule*, 188
2 Dopsch, *The Economic and Social Foundations of European Civilization*, 339; *Lex Visigot*, V, 4.19
3 'Grant by Chilperic II to the Abbey of Corbie, April 29, AD 716', *Mémoires et documents publiés par la Societé de l'École des Chartes*, V, No 15, pp 235-7
4 Alfons Dopsch, *Die Wirtschaftsentwicklung der Karolinger Zeit* (Weimar, 1922) Vol II, 178
5 Priscus, *fragment* 8
6 *Anglo-Saxon Chronicle*, Anno 866
7 Ibid, Anno 892
8 Sir Frank M. Stenton, *The Bayeux Tapestry*, plates 42-3
9 Villehardouin, *Chronicle of the Fourth Crusade and the Conquest of Constantinople*, 6
10 Procopius, *History of the Wars VII*, xviii-xix

11 Abbo, *Bella Parisiacae Urbis* I, 236
12 Ibid, I, 504-64
13 *Heimskringla, St Olaf's Saga*, chs XI-XII
14 Procopius, *Anecdota* XXX, 1-17
15 *Cambridge Economic History*, Vol II, 135
16 Ibid, 333
17 Cato, *De agri cultura* XXII, 3-4
18 Diocletian, *Edict on Prices*, preamble
19 *Cambridge Economic History*, Vol II, 65
20 *Edict on Prices* I, 1
21 Ibid, XVII, 3
22 Ibid, VII, 17-19
23 Ibid, XVII, 7
24 Ibid, XVII, 4-5
25 Ibid, XIV, 8
26 Ibid, XIV, 9-11
27 Ibid, XIV, 8, and XVII, 3
28 Elsa Rose Graser, 'The Significance of Two New Fragments of the Edict of Diocletian', *Transactions and Proceedings of the American Philological Society*, LXXI (1940), 166
29 Esperandieu, *Recueil général des bas-reliefs de la Gaule romaine*, Vol VI, Nos 5148, 5184, 5193, 5198, 5268 *et al*
30 Grant by Chilperic II to the Abbey of Corbie, April 29, AD 716', *Mémoires et documents publiés par la Societé de l'École des Chartes* V, No 15, pp 235-7
31 MGH, *Diplomata Karolinorum*, I, No 122, pp 170-1
32 James Tait, *The Domesday Survey of Cheshire* (Manchester, 1916), 221-3
33 MGH, *Scriptores*, XXX, part 2, pp 1451-54, 'Honorantia civitatis Papiae'.
34 Pegolotti, *La Pratica della Mearcatura*, ed Allen Evans (Cambridge, Mass, 1936), 21-2
35 Ibid, 240-2
36 *Cambridge Economic History*, Vol II, 152
37 Forbes, *Land transport and road building*, 109
38 *Cambridge Economic History*, Vol II, 152
39 Bede, *Ecclesiastical History*, V, vi
40 *Anglo-Saxon Chronicle*, Anno 1087
41 Du Chaillu, *The Viking Age*, Vol II, 383; Olaf Trygvason's Saga, *c* 92

42 Lewis Mumford, *Technics and Civilization* (New York, 1934), 101

43 Armandi, *Histoire militaire des Éléphants*, 385-6

44 Pliny, *Natural History* XXXIII, xlix

45 Burford, *Heavy transport in classical Antiquity*, 9

46 Strong, *The Rolling Road*, 24

47 *Codex Theodosianus* 8.5.17

48 Ibid, 8.5.11

49 Fortunatus, *Carmina*, VI, 5, line 224 (*molliter argenti turre rotante vehi*: drawn smoothly in a rolling silver tower)

50 Gregory of Tours, VII, 9

51 Kreisel, *Prunkwagen und Schlitten*, 132

52 Joyce, *The Social History of Ireland*, Vol II, 406

53 Gregory of Tours, IV, 19 (26)

54 Ibid, VI, 25 (35)

55 *St Columban*, ch 58

56 Gregory of Tours, VI, 45

57 See Einhard, *Vita Karoli*, 1. Henri Pirenne, *Histoire économique de l'Occident mediéval* (Bruges, 1951), 114-15

58 Kreisel, *Prunkwagen und Schlitten*, 7

59 Suetonius, *Julius Caesar c* 57

60 Plutarch, *Caesar c* 17

61 Pliny the Younger, *Epistolae* III, v

62 *Life of St. Samson of Dol* (ed and trans Taylor) Part I, XXVI, pp 48-9

63 *Columba*, 388-90

64 *St Columban*, ch 14

65 Duckett, *The Wandering Saints of the Early Middle Ages*, p 149

66 Sir Thomas Malory, *Le Morte d'Arthur*, (New York, 1962), a new rendition by Keith Baines, *The Book of Sir Lancelot and Queen Gwynevere*, 'The Knight of the Cart', 461

67 Reproduced in *Les routes de France depuis les Origines jusqu'à nos jours*, Association pour la Diffusion de la Pensée Française, Colloques (Cahiers de Civilisation, Paris, 1959), 38-9

68 Reproduced in de Vaublanc, *La France au Temps des Croisades*, Vol IV, 84

69 F. Menzel and E. Stengel, *Jean Bodels Saxonlied* ('Ausgaben und Abhandlungen aus dem Gebiete der romanischen Philo-

logie', Vol 99, Marburg, 1906-9), 59, line 808, 'Plus de C. s'an i firent an litiere porter'.

70 Ibid, line 807, 'Li vieil home d'aage n'en fistrent a blamer'.
71 Sulpicius Severus, *Life of St Martin* II, 4
72 Ibid
73 Talbot, *The Anglo-Saxon Missionaries in Germany*, 158-72
74 *Libellus de Vita et Miraculis S. Godrici, Heremitae de Finchale*, cap VII, p 38
75 Gregory of Tours, X, 8
76 Talbot, *The Anglo-Saxon Missionaries in Germany*, 'Life of St Sturm', 186
77 Victor Hehn, *Kulturpflanzen und Haustiere* (8th ed) p 133. 'Mit der Wein- und Ölkultur—die Grenze derselben nicht überschreitend—ging auch der Esel weiter nach Norden . . . In Deutschland war es ihm schon zu kalt.'
78 Thomas Wright, *A History of Domestic Manners and Sentiments in England During the Middle Ages* (London, 1862), 317
79 Bede, *Ecclesiastical History* II, xiii
80 Sir Frank M. Stenton, *The Bayeux Tapestry, passim*
81 Shakespeare, *Antony and Cleopatra*, Act III, scene vii

Chapter 5

1 Cicero, *Epistolae ad Quintum fratrem* 3.1.13, 3.1.17, 3.1.25; *ad Atticum* 4.17.3
2 Wolfgang Riepl, *Das Nachrichtenwesen des Altertums* (Leipzig and Berlin, 1913), 204
3 *Chronicles and memorials of the reign of Richard I*, ed William Stubbs, Bishop of Oxford (London, 1864-5), Vol II, *Epistolae Cantuarienses*, ccxiii, ccxix
4 Ibid, clxv, ccv, cccclxxxix ccccxcii
5 Otto of Freising, *Gesta Friderici I imperatoris*, II, 1.3
6 Suetonius, *Julius Caesar c 57*
7 Plutarch, *Caesar c 17*

Works consulted and further reading

I. PRIMARY SOURCES

NO ATTEMPT IS made to enumerate the many volumes of the *Monumenta Germaniae Historica,* containing much of the source material for the early medieval period, which were examined. Specific volumes are listed in the text footnotes. Other sources which were particularly useful are listed below, although the listing is by no means exhaustive. Editions are not specified except when necessary to prevent confusion. The latest available editions have normally been used.

Abbo. *Bella Parisiacae Urbis,* ed and trans Henri Waquet, (Paris, 1942)

A Documentary History of Art, Vol I, ed Elizabeth G. Holt, (New York, 1957)

Al-Sabbagh, Mikhail. *La colombe messagère,* trans Arabic to French by A. I. Silvestre de Sacy, (Paris, 1805)

Anglo-Saxon Chronicle

Annales Bertiniani

Bede. *Ecclesiastical History*

Beowulf

Bernard, Auguste, and Bruel, Alexandre. *Recueil des Chartes de l'abbaye de Cluny.* (Documents inédits sur l'histoire de France). Première Serie, Histoire Politique, Vol 4, (Paris, 1888)

Bibliotheca Rerum Germanicorum, ed P. Jaffe, (Berlin, 1867)

Boniface, St *The Letters of St Boniface,* trans Ephraim Emerton (No XXXI of Records of Civilization), (New York, 1940)

Caesar. *De Bello Gallico*

Cartularium Saxonicum, ed Birch, (London, 1885-93)

Cassiodorus. *Variae Epistolae*

Cato. *de re rustica (de agri cultura)*

Chronicles and memorials of the reign of Richard I. Ed William Stubbs, Bishop of Oxford. Vol II, *Epistolae cantuarienses,* (London, 1864-65)

Cicero. *Epistolae*

Claudian. *Carmina minora*

Codex Theodosianus, trans Clyde Pharr, (Princeton, 1952)

Columba, Adomnan's Life of, ed and trans Alan Orr Anderson and Marjorie Ogilvie Anderson, (London, 1961)

Columban, St, by the Monk Jonas, ed and trans Dana C. Munro (Translations and Reprints, Vol II, No 7, Univ of Penn)

Columella

Constantine Porphyrogenitus. *De Administrando Imperio,* trans R. J. H. Jenkins, (Budapest, 1949)

Corpus Iuris Civilis

Delisle, Leopold. *Rouleaux des Morts du IXe au XVe Siècle,* (Paris, 1866)

Dialogus de Scaccaria, ed C. Johnson (Nelson's Medieval Classics), (London, 1950)

Edict of Diocletian on Prices

Einhard. *The History of the Translation of the Blessed Martyrs of Christ Marcellinus and Peter,* trans Barrett Wendell, (Cambridge, Mass, 1926)

Einhard. *Vita Karoli*

Ekkehard of Aura. *Hierosolymita*

English Historical Documents, ed D. C. Douglas, Vols I and II, (New York, 1953)

Flateyjarbok
Flodoard. *Historia ecclesiae Remensis*
Fortunatus. *Carmina*
Fredegar
Fulcher of Chartres. *Chronicle of the First Crusade*

Geoffroy de Villehardouin. *Chronicle of the Fourth Crusade and the Conquest of Constantinople. Memoirs of the Crusades,* trans Sir Frank Marzials, (London and New York, 1908)
Gesta Francorum, ed Rosalind Hill, (Nelson's Medieval Texts), (London, 1962)
Giraldus Cambrensis. *Topography of Ireland*
Gregorius, St, Bishop of Tours. *Libri historiarum X. (MGH Scriptores rerum merovingicarum,* Vol I, part 1), (Hanover, 1951)
Guibert of Nogent. *Historia Hierosolymitana*

Hassall, W. O. *How They Lived. An Anthology of original accounts written before 1485,* (Oxford, 1962)
Heimskringla
Horace. Satires

Ibn Khordadhbeh. *Bibliotheca Geographicorum Arabicorum,* vol 6, ed M. J. de Goeje, (Lugduni-Batavorum, 1889)

Jacob, Georg. *Arabische Berichte von Gesandten an germanische Fürstenhöfe,* (Berlin-Leipzig, 1927)
Jacobus de Voragine. *The Golden Legend*
Jean Bodels Saxenlied, ed F. Menzel and E. Stengel (Ausgaben und Abhandlungen aus dem Gebiete der romanischen Philologie, Vols 99-100), (Marburg, 1906-9)

Jean, Sire de Joinville. *Chronicle of the Crusade of St Lewis. Memoirs of the Crusades,* trans Sir Frank Marzials, (London and New York, 1908)
Julius Pollux. *Onomasticon*

Lambert of Hersfeld. *Annales*
Landnamabok. The Book of the Settlement of Iceland, trans Rev T. Ellwood, (Kendal, 1898)
Libellus de Vita et Miraculis S. Godrici. Heremitae de Finchale (The Surtees Society, Vol 20), (London, 1845)
Liebermann, F., *Die Gesetze der Angelsachsen,* (Halle, 1903-16)
Liutprand. *Antapodosis*
———. *Relatio de legatione Constantinopolitana*
Loup de Ferrières. *Correspondance,* ed Levillain, (Paris, 1927)

Malory, Sir Thomas. *Le Morte d'Arthur*
Marco Polo. *The Travels of Marco Polo,* trans Ronald Latham, (Penguin Books, 1958)
Marculf, *Formulae*
Medieval Myths, trans Norma Lorre Goodrich, (New York, 1961)
Melrose, The Chronicle of (facsimile edition) (Studies in Economics and Political Science, London School of Economics and Political Science, No 100), (London, 1936)
Mémoires et documents publiés par la Societé de l'école des Chartes, (Paris)
Monk of St Gall (Monachus Sangallensis)

Neckham, Alexander. *De naturis rerum*
Njala Saga

Ordericus Vitalis. *Historia Ecclesiastica*
Orkneyingers' Saga, trans Sir G. W. Dasent (Rerum britannicarum medii aevi scriptores, v 88), (London, 1887-94)
Orosius, King Alfred's
Otto of Freising. *Gesta Friderici I imperatoris*

Palestine Pilgrims' Text Translations, 13 vols, (London, 1896-7)

Paulus Diaconus *History of the Lombards*

Pegolotti, Francesco Balducci. *La Pratica della Mercatura,* ed Allen Evans, (Cambridge, Mass, 1936)

Pliny. *Natural History*

Pliny the Younger. *Epistolae*

Plutarch. *Caesar*

————. *C. Gracchus*

Priscus. *Fragmenta*

Procopius. *Anecdota*

————. *History of the Wars*

Richer. *Historiarum libri IV*

Roger of Hoveden. *Annals*

Ruodlieb

Russian Primary Chronicle, Laurentian Text, trans S. H. Cross and O. P. Sherbowitz-Wetzor, (Cambridge, Mass, 1953)

St Samson of Dol. *Vita*

Scriptores Historiae Augustae

Sidonius, Apollinaris. *Epistolae*

Simeon of Durham. *Historia regum*

Statius. *Silvae*

Strabo. *Geographica*

Suetonius. *Lives of the Twelve Caesars*

Sulpicius Severus. *Life of St Martin*

Symmachus. *Epistolae*

Tacitus. *Annales*

Tait, James. *The Domesday Survey of Cheshire* (Chetham Society, Vol 75, New Series), (Manchester, 1916)

Talbot, C. H. *The Anglo-Saxon Misisonaries in Germany,* (New York, 1954)

The Great Roll of the Pipe for the Eighth Year of the Reign of King John, ed Doris M. Stenton (Pipe Roll Society, Vol 58)

The Laws of the Earliest English Kings, ed F. L. Attenborough, (Cambridge, 1922)

The Laws of the Kings of England from Edmund to Henry I ed A. J. Robertson, (Cambridge, 1925)

Thorpe, Benjamin. *Ancient Laws and Institutes of England,* (London, 1840)

Vegetius. *De Re Militari*

Villani. *Cronica.*

Vitruvius. *De Architectura*

Walter Map. *De Nugis Curialium,* ed M. R. James (Anecdota Oxoniensia), (Oxford, 1914)

William Fitzstephen. *Descriptio nobilissimae civitatis Londoniae*

William of Malmesbury. *History of the Kings of England*

William of Tyre. *History of Deeds done beyond the Seas*

Xenophon. *Anabasis*

————. *On Equitation*

II. GENERAL REFERENCE WORKS

Daremberg—Saglio. *Dictionnaire des Antiquités grecques et romaines*

Du Cange. *Glossarium Mediae et Infimae Latinitatis*

Harper's Dictionary of Classical Literature and Antiquities

Niermeyer. *Mediae Latinitatis Lexicon minus*

Oxford Classical Dictionary

Pauly-Wissowa. *Real-Encyclopädie der classischen Altertumswissenschaft*

III. ARTISTIC AND ARCHAEOLOGICAL SOURCES

Brøndsted, J. T. *The Sutton Hoo Ship Burial*, (London, 1947)

Calza, G., and Beccati, G., *Ostia*, (Rome, 1957)

Cichorius, Conrad. *Die Reliefs der Traianssäule*, (Berlin, 1896-1900)

Cockerell, S. C., James, M. R., and Ffoulkes, C. J., *A Book of Old Testament Illustrations of the Middle of the Thirteenth-Century sent by Cardinal Bernard Maciejowski to Shah Abbas the Great, King of Persia, now in the Pierpont Morgan Library*, (Cambridge, 1927)

Curle, James. *A Roman Frontier Post and its people, The Fort of Newstead*, (Glasgow, 1911)

Dragendorff-Krüger. *Das Grabmal von Igel* (Römische Grabmäler des Mosellandes. I), (Berlin and Leipzig, 1924)

Drögereit, Richard, 'Bemerkungen zum Bayeux-Teppich', *Mitteilungen des Instituts für österreichische Geschichtsforschung*, Vol 70, 257-93, (1962)

Esperandieu, Émile. *Recueil général des bas-reliefs, statues et bustes de la Gaule romaine*, (Paris, 1907-38)

———. *Recueil général des bas-reliefs, statues et bustes de la Germania romaine*. Paris and Bruxelles, (1931)

Evans, Sir Arthur. *The Palace of Minos*, Vol II, part 1, (London, 1928)

Gell, Sir William, and Gandy, J. P. *Pompeii*, (New York, 1880)

Gentili, Gino. *La Villa Erculia di Piazza Armerina. I Mosaici Figurati*, (Rome, 1960)

Goldschmidt, A. *Die Bronzetüren von Nowgorod und Gnesen*, (Marburg, 1932)

Heinsius, Dr. Elisabeth. *Der Bildteppich von Bayeux als Quelle für die Seemannschaft der Wikingerzeit,* Vorzeit am Bodensee, 15th year, Nos 1-4, (1966) 19-28
Herrad von Landsberg. *Hortus deliciarum*

Klindt-Jensen, Ole. 'Foreign Influences in Denmark's early Iron Age', *Acta Archaeologica,* XX, (1949) 1-229
Kroon, H. M. 'Hoefijzers uit de vroege Middeleeuwen', *Tijdschrift Diergeneeskunde,* Vol 53, (1926) 579-86

Lehner, H. 'Ein gallo-römischer Wagen aus Frenz an der Inde im Kreis Düren', *Bonner Jahrbücher,* 128, 28-62

Marien, Marcel Édouard. *Les monuments funéraires de l'Arlon Romain,* (Arlon, 1945)
Massow, Wilhelm von. *Die Grabmäler von Neumagen* (Römische Grabmäler des Mosellandes), (Berlin and Leipzig, 1932)
Matthew Paris. *The Lives of the Two Offas* (British Museum MS, Nero D 1)
Mau, August. *Pompeii in Leben und Kunst,* 2nd ed (Leipzig, 1908)
Miniature sacre e profane dell'anno 1023, illustranti l'enciclopedia medioevale di Rabano Mauro, ed A. M. Amelli, (Montecassino, 1896)
Moll, F. *Das Schiff in der bildenden Kunst,* (Bonn, 1929)

Pace, B. *I mosaici di Piazza Armerina,* (Rome, 1955)

Roux, Henri. *Herculaneum et Pompei,* (Paris, 1840)

Saalburger Jahrbücher (Berichte des Saalburgmuseums)
Sjøvold, Thorleif. *The Oseberg Find,* (Oslo, 1957)
Stenton, Sir Frank. *The Bayeaux Tapestry,* (London, 1957)

The Illustrations of the Utrecht psalter, (Princeton, 1932)

Venedikov, Ivan. *Trakijskata Kolesnica,* (Bulgarische Akademie der Wissenschaften, Sofia, 1960)

Verdelis, Nicholas M. 'How the Ancient Greeks transported Ships over the Isthmus of Corinth: uncovering the 2550-year-old Diolcos of Periander', *Illustrated London News* (19 Oct 1957), Vol 231, 649-51

Wheeler, R. E. M. 'Maiden Castle, Dorset', *Reports of the Society of Antiquaries of London,* XII, (1943)

Zemp, Joseph. *Die schweizerischen Bilderchroniken und ihre Architektur-Darstellungen,* (Zurich, 1897)

IV. SECONDARY SOURCES

Abaecherli (Boyce), A. L. 'Fercula, Carpenta and Tensae in the Roman Procession', *Bolletino dell' Associazione Internazionale Studi Mediterranei,* VI (1935-6) 6

Abgrall, Chanoine J.-M., and Leguennec. 'Etude de la voie romaine et du chemin de pélérinage des Sept Saints de Bretagne entre Quimper et Saint-Pol-de-Leon', *Bulletin archéologique de l'Association bretonne,* 3rd series, vol 30, (1911) 202-30

―――. 'Voie romaine conduisant de Quimper à l'oppidum de Tronoen en Saint-Jean-Trolimon', *(Bulletin de la Societé archéologique de Finistère,* vol 18, (1891) 223-7

Adler, Elkan (ed.). *Jewish Travellers,* The Broadway Travellers, (London, 1930)

Africa, Thomas W. *The Ancient World,* (Boston, 1969)

Allen, G. H. 'A Problem of Inland Navigation in Roman Gaul', *Classical Weekly,* 27, (1933-4)

Anderson, John K. *Ancient Greek Horsemanship,* (Berkeley and Los Angeles, 1961)

―――. 'Early Horseshoes Again', in Notes and News, *Antiquity,* (Dec 1969), XLIII, No 172, 317-18

Anderson, Romola and Roger Charles. *The sailing ship*, (London, 1947)

Ardant, Maurice. 'Etude sur les voies gallo-romaines du Limousin et de la Marche', *Mémoires de la Societé des sciences naturelles et archéologiques de la Creuse*, (1862) 36-62

Armandi, P. *Histoire militaire des Éléphants*, (Paris, 1843)

Armstrong, C. A. J. 'Some examples of the Distribution and Speed of News in England at the Time of the Wars of the Roses', *Studies in Medieval History presented to F. M. Powicke*, (1948) 444-5

Avenel, G. d'. 'Les Moyens de transport depuis sept siècles', *Revue des Deux Mondes*, 1 Oct 1913, 615-44; 15 Dec 1913, 805-34

———. *L'evolution des moyens de transport*, (Paris, 1919)

Baker, John Norman Leonard. *Medieval Trade Routes*, Historical Association Pamphlets no III, (1938)

Baldwin, Summerfield. *Business in the Middle Ages*, Berkshire Studies in European History, (New York, 1937)

Ballen, Dorothy. *Bibliography of Road-making and Roads in the United Kingdom* (1914)

Baneat, Paul. 'Étude sur les voies romaines du departement d'Ille-et-Vilaine', *Bulletins et mémoires de la Societé archéologique du departement d'Ille-et-Vilaine*, (1927) 1-82

Barrière, P. 'A propos des voies romaines du Nontronnais', *Bulletin de la Societé historique et archéologique du Périgord*, (1937) 389-99

Bass, George F. 'Underwater Archaeology: Key to History's Warehouse', *National Geographic Magazine*, Vol 124 (1963) pp 138-56

———. 'New Tools for Undersea Archaeology', *National Geographic Magazine*, Vol 134 (1968) 403-23

Baudot, Marcel. 'Le reseau routier antique du département de l'Eure', *Normannia*, (1932) 339-63

Baudry de Saunier, Louis. *Histoire de la locomotion terrestre*, Vol II, (Paris, 1936)

Bautier, R. H. 'Les registres des foires de Champagne', *Bulletin Phil et Hist des Comité des Travaux Historiques,* (1942-3) 157-88

Beazley, C. Raymond *The Dawn of Modern Geography,* (London, 1897)

Belloc, Hilaire. *The highway and its vehicles,* (London, 1926)

———. *The Old Road,* (London, 1904)

———. *The Road,* (London, 1930)

Belloni, Luigi. *La carozza nella storia della locomozione,* (Milan, 1901)

Berg, Gösta. *Sledges and Wheeled Vehicles,* (Nordiska Museets Handlingar 4, 1935)

Birk, Alfred. *Die Strasse,* (Karlsbad, 1934)

Bischoff, Bernhard. 'Wer ist die Nonne von Heidenheim?' *Studien und Mitteilungen zur Geschichte des Benediktiner-Ordens,* XLIX, pp 387-8 (1931)

Bizeul. 'Aperçu général sur l'étude des voies romaines', *Bulletin archéologique de l'Association bretonne,* (1849) 3-8

———. 'Voies romaines du département du Finistère', Ibid (1849) 259-62

———. 'Des voies romaines sortant de Carhaix', Ibid, 9-40, (1851) 3-67

Blair, Peter Hunter. *An Introduction to Anglo-Saxon England,* (Cambridge, 1959)

Bloch, Marc (pseud M. Fougères, 1942-4). 'Problems d'histoire des techniques', Annales d'histoire économique et sociale, (1932) 482-6

———. 'Le Problème de l'Or au Moyen Âge', Ibid, (1933)

———. 'Un Episode de l'histoire humaine des rivières', Ibid, (1934) 184-5

———. 'Les inventions mediévales', Ibid, (1935) 634-44

———. *'Sur les routes mediévales',* Ibid (1936) 584.

———. *Les caractères originaux de l'histoire rurale française,* (Paris, 1952)

———. Feudal Society, (London, 1961)

———. Revue historique, Vol 184, (1938) 179

———. Rev. Synthèse histor, (1913) 1, 161

Blum, Otto. *Die Entwicklung des Verkehrs,* (Berlin, 1941)

Blümlein, Carl. *Bilder aus dem Römisch-Germanischen Kulturleben,* (Munich and Berlin, 1918)

Blümner, Hugo. *Technologie und Terminologie,* (Leipzig, 1875-87)

Boissonnade, P. *Life and Work in Medieval Europe,* trans Eileen Power, (New York, 1927)

————. 'L'ascension, le declin et la chute d'un grand État feodal du Centre-Ouest', *Bulletin et mémoires de la Societé archéologique et historique de la Charente,* (1935) 1-258, and (1943) 1-198.

Bombal, E. 'Anciens chemins et voies romaines d'Argentat et de ses environs', *Bulletin de la Societé des lettres, sciences et arts de la Corrèze,* (1909) 239-89

Bonjour, Offler, and Potter. *A Short History of Switzerland,* (Oxford, 1955)

Bonnard, Louis. *La navigation intérieure de la Gaule à l'époque gallo-romaine,* (Paris, 1913)

Bonser, Wilfred. 'Epidemics during the Anglo-Saxon Period', *The Journal of the British Archæological Association,* Third Series, Vol IX, (1944) 48-71

Boulton, W. H. *The pageant of transport through the ages,* (London, 1935)

Boumphrey, Geoffrey Maxwell. *The story of the wheel,* (London, 1932)

Bouton, Archibald Lewis. *Outline history of transportation from 1400* BC, (Detroit, 1934)

Bovini Giuseppe. *Das Grabmal Theodorichs,* (Ravenna, 1959)

Boyer, Marjorie Nice. 'A day's journey in medieval France', *Speculum,* Vol 26 (1951) 597-608

————. 'Medieval pivoted axles', *Technology and Culture,* Vol 1 (1960) 128-38

————. 'Medieval Suspended Carriages', *Speculum,* Vol 34, (1959) 359-66

————. 'Roads and Rivers: Their Use and Disuse in late Medieval France', *Medievalia et Humanistica,* Fasc XIII, (1960) 68-80

Brehier, Louis. *Le Monde Byzantin;* II. *Les Institutions de l'Empire Byzantin,* (Paris, 1949)

Brochet, Louis. 'Études sur les voies romaines en Bas-Poitou et pays circonvoisins', *Annuaire de la Société d'Émulation de la Vendée,* (1907) 101-201.

Brogan, Olwen. 'The Camel in Roman Tripolitania', *Papers British School,* (new series), (Rome, 1954), 9: 126-31

———. 'The Fortified Farms of Ghirza, Libya', *Illustrated London News,* (Jan 22 and 29, 1955) 138-42 and 182-5

———. *Roman Gaul,* (London, 1953)

———. 'Trade between the Roman Empire and free Germany', *Journal of Roman Studies,* XXVI, (1936) 195-222.

Brøgger, A. W., and Shetelig, H. *The Viking Ships, their Ancestry and Evolution,* (Oslo, 1953)

Brøndsted, Johannes. *The Vikings,* (Hardmondsworth, 1965)

Brunel, Georges. *Les Transports à travers les âges,* (Paris, 1935)

Brunot, Ferdinand. *Histoire de la langue française.* Vol VII, (Paris, 1905)

Bugge, Alexander. 'Die Nordeuropäischen Verkehrswege im Früheren Mittelalter', *Vierteljahrschrift Für Soz. und Wirtschaftsgeschichte,* IV, (1906) 227-77.

Burford, A. 'Heavy transport in classical Antiquity', *Economic History Review,* 2nd series, XIII, (1960) 1-18

Burke, Thomas. *Travel in England,* (London, 1942)

Burn, A. R. 'Procopius and the Island of Ghosts', *English Historical Review,* Vol 70, (1955), p 259

Cabanes, A. Docteur. *Moeurs intimes du Passé. neuvieme serie. Les moyens de transport intérieur,* (Paris, 1933)

Cagnat, R, and Chapot, V. *Manuel d'Archéologie romaine,* (Paris, 1920)

Cambridge Economic History of Europe, eds J. H. Clapham and Eileen Power, Vol I, (Cambridge, 1941)

———. 2nd ed, Vol I, (Cambridge, 1966)

———. Vol II, Trade and Industry in the Middle Ages, eds M. Postan and E. E. Rich, (Cambridge, 1952)

Capot-Rey, Robert. *Géographie de la circulation sur les continents*, (Paris, 1946)

Carnat, Germain. *Le Fer à cheval à travers l'histoire et l'archéologie. Contribution à l'histoire de la civilisation*, (Paris, 1951)

Carrington, R. *Elephants. A short account of their Natural History, Evolution and Influence on Mankind*, (London, 1958)

Carus-Wilson, Eleanor Mary. *Medieval Merchant Venturers*, (London, 1954)

Casson, Lionel, 'Fore-and-aft Sails in the Ancient World', *Mariner's Mirror*, 42, (1956) 3-5

———. 'Speed under Sail of Ancient Ships', *Transactions of the American Philological Association*, LXXXII (1951), 136-48

———. 'The Sails of the Ancient Mariner', *Archaeology* 7, (1954) 214-19

———. 'Notes: The River Boats of Mesopotamia'. *Mariner's Mirror*, Vol 53 (1967), 286-8

———. 'Ancient Shipbuilding; New Light on an old Source', *American Philological Association* 94, 28-33 (1963)

———. 'Odysseus' Boat (Od V, 244-257)'. *American Journal of Philology* 85 (1964), 61-4

———. 'New Light on Ancient rigging and boatbuilding', *American Neptune*, 24 (1964) 81-94

Cavailles, Henri. *La route française. Son histoire, sa fonction*, (Paris, 1946)

Cerralbo, Marquis de. 'Necropole iberiques', *Comptes rendus de la XIVᵉ session du Congrès international d'anthropologie et d'archéologie préhistorique*, (Geneva, 1912) 593-627

Charbonneau and Rouchon. 'Sur l'ancienne voie romaine de Clermont à Limoges', *Revue d'Auvergne*, (1934) 72-83

Charlesworth, M. P. *Trade routes and commerce of the Roman Empire*, (Cambridge, 1926)

Chenon, Émile. *Les voies romaines du Berry*, (Paris, 1922)

Childe, V. Gordon. 'The First Wagons and Carts—from the

Tigris to the Severn', *The Prehistoric Society,* (1951), No 8, p 177

Clagett, Marshall. *The Science of Mechanics in the Middle Ages,* (Madison, Wisconsin 1959)

Clapham, J. H. 'The Horsing of the Danes', *English Historical Review,* XXV, (1910) 287-93

Clark, Grahame. 'Horses and Battle-axes', *Antiquity,* XV (1941) 50-70

Clouet, Marcell. 'En suivant deux voies preromaines de la Saintonge', (*Revue de Saintonge et d'Aunis. Bulletin de la Societé des Archives historiques* (1928) 93-108, 177-190

————. 'Voie preromaine de Coutras à Nantes par Saintes', Ibid, (1936-40) 77-9 and 125-47

————. 'Voie neolithique de Parignac au Terrier de Toulon et à l'Ocean', Ibid, (1931-2) 240-53 and 279-94

Cochet, M. L'Abbé. *Le Tombeau de Childeric Ier,* (Paris, 1859)

Cockrill, W. Ross. 'The Water Buffalo'. *Scientific American,* Vol 217, No 6, (Dec 1967) pp 118-25

Codrington, Thomas. *Roman Roads in Britain,* (London, 1918)

Cohn, Norman. *The Pursuit of the Millennium,* (Oxford, 1957)

Collinder, Per Arne. *A History of Marine Navigation,* trans Maurice Michael, (London, 1954)

Conley, Robert A. M. 'Locusts: 'Teeth of the Wind', *National Geographic Magazine,* Vol 136, No 2, (Aug 1969) pp 202-27

Cook, Albert Stanburrough. 'Augustine's Journey from Rome to Richborough', *Speculum, I.* (1926) 375-97

Couffon, R. 'Contribution à l'étude des voies romaines des Côtes-du-Nord', *Bulletins et mémoires de la Societé d'émulation des Côtes-du-Nord',* (1943-44) 1-17

Coulton, George Gordon. *Social Life in Britain from the conquest to the reformation,* (Cambridge, 1918)

Croon, Ludwig. 'Aus der Geschichte des Fahrrades', *Beiträge zur Geschichte der Technik,* XXIII, (1934)

Crowe, J. O'Beirne. 'Siabur-Charpat con Culaind', *Journal of the Royal Historical and Archaeological Association of Ireland,* Vol I, 4th series, (1870-71) 371-448

Crump, C. G. 'The Pilgrim's Way', *History,* (June 1936) 22-3

Cuppy, Will. *The Decline and Fall of Practically Everybody,* New York, 1950)

Davidson, D. S. 'Snowshoes', *Memoirs of the American Philosophical Society,* (Philadelphia, 1937)

Day, Clive. *A History of Commerce,* (New York, 1922)

de Camp, L. Sprague. *The Ancient Engineers,* (New York, 1963)

———. 'Before Stirrups', *Isis,* LII, Part 2, No 164, (June, 1960) 159-64

———. 'Sailing Close-Hauled', *Isis,* L, Part 1, No 159. (March, 1959) 61-65

Deloche, Maximin. 'Étude historique sur les voies d'accès de Tulle', *Bulletin de la Societé des lettres, sciences et arts de la Corrèze* (1902) 141-50

Derry, T. K., and Williams, Trevor I. *A Short History of Technology,* (Oxford, 1961)

de Souza, Bernardino José. *Ciclo do Carro de Bois no Brasil,* (São Paulo, 1958)

Dewall, Dr Magdalene von. *Pferd und Wagen im frühen China,* Saarbrücker Beiträge zur Altertumskunde, 1 (Bonn, 1964)

Dill, Samuel. *Roman society in Gaul in the Merovingian Age,* (London, 1926)

———. *Roman society in the last century of the Western Empire,* (London, 1899)

Dion, R. 'Orléans et l'ancienne navigation de la Loire', *Annales de Géographie,* XLVII, (1938)

Documents relating to the Colonial History of the State of New York, Holland Documents, Vol 1 (Albany, 1856)

Domestication and Exploitation of Plants and Animals, eds Peter J. Ucko and G. W. Dimbleby, (London, 1969)

Dopsch, Alfons. *Die Wirtschaftsentwicklung der Karolinger Zeit,* (Weimar, 1922)

———. *The Economic and Social Foundations of European Civilization,* (London, 1937)

Doranlo. 'Les voies antiques du Lieuvin', *Annuaire de l'association normande,* Vol 94 (1927) 82-9

Doyle, Sir Arthur Conan. *The Annotated Sherlock Holmes,* ed W. S. Baring-Gould, 2 vols, (New York, 1967)

Dresbeck, L. J. 'The Ski: Its History and Historiography', *Technology and Culture,* Vol 8, No 4, (1967), 467-79

Dubourg. 'Les voies romaines. Leur relation avec l'industrie gauloise et gallo-romaine', *Bulletin de la Societé historique et archéologique de l'Orne,* (1924) 395-400

Duby, Georges. *Societé aux XIe et XIIe Siècles dans la region mâconnaise,* (Paris, 1953)

du Chaillu, Paul B. *The Viking Age,* 2 vols, (New York, 1890)

Duckett, Eleanor. *The Wandering Saints of the Early Middle Ages,* (New York, 1959)

Ducourtieux, Paul. 'Les voies romaines en Limousin', *Bulletin de la Societé archéologique et historique du Limousin,* (1916) 137-75, (1917) 331-69, (1919) 93-120

———. 'Les grands chemins du Limousin (la grande voirie)', Ibid, (1905) 713-50, (1906) 235-75, (1907) 501-39.

Duval, Paul-Marie. *La vie quotidienne en Gaule,* (Paris, 1952)

East, William Gordon. *An Historical Geography of Europe,* (London, 1949)

Eickhoff, E. *Seekrieg und Seepolitik zwischen Islam und Abendland 650 bis 1040,* (Berlin, 1966)

Encyclopedia of Islam (2nd ed), article 'Barid' (governmental postal system)

Encyclopedia of the Social Sciences (1st ed), article 'Roads'

Enlart, C. *Manuel d'Archéologie Française,* I (Architecture Religieuse)

Estienne, Charles. *Le Guide des chemins de France,* ed Jean Bonnerot, Bibliothèque de l'École des Hautes Études, section hist et philol, fasc 265 and 267), 2 Vols, (Paris, 1935-36)

Eubanks, J. E. 'Navigation on the Tiber', *Classical Journal,* (June, 1930) 683-95

Ewart, J. C. *The Penicuik Experiments,* (London, 1899)

Fabre, Maurice. *A History of Land Transportation* (Vol VII in *The New Illustrated Library of Science and Invention,* ed Dr Courtlandt Canby), (New York, 1963)

Feldhaus, Franz Maria. 'Die Ingenieure des Theoderich: die Hebeösen am Grabmal des Theoderich', *Umschau,* XXXVIII, (1934) 596-8

———. *Die Technik der Antike und des Mittelalters,* (Potsdam, 1931)

———. *Kulturgeschichte der Technik,* 2 vols, (Berlin, 1928)

———. *Die Technik der Vorzeit, der geschichtlichen Zeit und der Naturvölker,* (Leipzig and Berlin, 1914)

———. *Die Maschine im Leben der Völker,* (Basle, 1954)

———. *Ruhmesblätter der Technik,* (Leipzig, 1924-6)

Feuchtinger, Max Erich. *Der Verkehr im Wandel der Zeiten seit dem Jahre 1000,* (Berlin, 1935)

———. *Strassenbau,* Vol 27, (1936) 168-73

Fichtenau, H. *The Carolingian Empire,* trans Peter Munz, (New York, 1964)

Firestone, Harvey S. *Man on the Move: the Story of Transportation,* (New York, 1967)

Flower, C. T. *Public Works in Medieval Law,* (Selden Society, Vols 32 and 40)

Fluss, V. 'Feuerpost im Altertum', *Wien. Blätt. für Freunde der Antike* 9 (1933), 77

Forbes, Robert James. *Bibliographia Antiqua,* Vol X and Supp, (Leiden, 1950-2)

———. 'Bibliography of Road Building, AD 300-1840', *Roads and Road Construction,* (1938), 189-96

———. and Dijksterhus, E. J. *A History of Science and Technology,* Vol I, *Ancient Times to the Seventeenth Century,* (Baltimore, 1963)

———. 'Land transport and road-building (1000-1900)', *Janus,* Leiden, XLVI, (1957) 104-40, 201-23

———. *Man the Maker: A History of Technology and Engineering,* (New York, 1958)

———. *Notes on the History of Ancient Roads and their Construction,* Allard Pierson Stichting, Universiteit van Amsterdam, Archaeologisch-Historische Bijdragen III, (Amsterdam, 1934)

————. *Studies in Ancient Technology*, II, (Leiden, 1955)

Hᴀᴛᴛᴏʀ, ᴍ. Lᴇs ᴄʜᴀʀs ᴄᴜʟᴛᴜʀᴇʟs prᴇʜɪstᴏrɪquᴇs ᴇt lᴇurs surᴠɪᴠances aux époques historiques', *Préhistoire*, I, (1932) 19-123

Forward, E. A. *Catalogue of the Collections in the Science Museum, South Kensington*, (Land Transport I, Road Transport, (London, 1926)

Fox, Sir Cyril. 'Sleds, Carts, and Waggons', *Antiquity*, V, (June 1931) 184ff

Frank, Tenney. *Economic survey of Ancient Rome*, (Baltimore, 1933-40)

Fraser, A. B. 'The Greek Cart Horse', *Classical Journal*, Vol 31 (1935/6), 445ff

Fraser, A. D. 'Recent light on the Roman Horseshoe', *Classical Journal*, Vol 29, (1933-4) 689-91

Friedländer, Ludwig. *Roman Life and Manners under the Early Empire*, trans Leonard A. Magnus from seventh enlarged and revised edition of the Sittengeschichte Roms, (London, 1913)

Gasiorowski, Zygmunt J. *The System of Transportation in Poland: its Historical Evolution*, PhD Dissertation, University of California, (Berkeley, 1950)

Gay, Laverne. *Wine of Satan* (novel) (New York, 1949)

Geering, Traugott. *Handel und Industrie der Stadt Basel*, (Basle, 1886)

Gest, Alexander P. *Our Debt to Greece and Rome: Engineering*, (New York, 1963)

Gilbey, Sir Walter. *Early Carriages and Roads*, (London, 1903)

Gille, Bertrand. 'Les Developpements technologiques en Europe de 1100 à 1400', *Cahiers d'histoire mondiale*, III, (1956)

Gilliard, E. 'Problèmes d'histoire routière: l'ouverture du Gothard', *Annales d'Histoire Economique et Sociale*, Vol I, (1929) 177

Gilmore, Harlan W. *Transportation and the Growth of Cities,* (Glencoe, Illinois, 1953)

Ginzrot (Günzrot), Johann Christian. *Die Wagen und Fahrwerke der Griechen und Römer und anderer alten Völker; nebst der Bespannung, Zäumung und Verzierung ihrer Zug- Reit- und Last-Thiere,* (Munich, 1817)

―――. *Die Wagen und Fahrwerke der verschiedenen Völker des Mittelalters und der Kutschenbau neuester Zeiten,* (Munich, 1830)

Goitein, S. D. *A Mediterranean Society.* The Jewish Communities of the Arab World as Portrayed in the Documents of the Cairo Geniza. Vol I, *Economic Foundations,* (Berkeley, 1967)

Goodwin, Astley John Hilary. *Communication has been Established,* (London, 1937)

Gorce, Denys. *Les voyages, l'hospitalité, et le port des lettres dans le monde Chrétien des IVᵉ et Vᵉ siècles* (Thesis: University of Poitiers), (Paris, 1925)

Gordon, C. D. *The Age of Attila,* (Ann Arbor, Michigan, 1960)

Görich, Willi. 'Ortesweg, Antsanvia und Fulda in neuer Sicht', *Germania,* Vol 33, (1955) 68-88

Gouron, Marcel. 'Note sur l'ancienne navigation dans la Petite Camargue', *Bulletin de la Societé d'Histoire et Archéologie de Nîmes et du Gard* (1938-9)

Gowers, W. 'African Elephants and Ancient Authors', *African Affairs,* (July 1948) 173-9

Grand, Roger. *La force motrice animale à travers les âges et son influence sur l'évolution sociale,* (Extr de La Science sociale). (Paris, 1926)

―――. 'L'histoire des transports explique l'évolution sociale', *Les Études sociales,* (1937) 217-54

―――. 'Utilisation de la force animale. Vues sur les origines de l'attelage moderne', *Bulletin de l'académie d'agriculture de France,* Vol 33, (1947) 702-10

―――. and Delatouche, Raymond. *L'agriculture au moyen âge, de la fin de l'empire romain au XVIᵉ siècle* (L'agriculture à travers les âges, collection fondée par Émile Savoy), Vol 3, (Paris, 1950)

Graser, Elsa Rose. 'The Significance of Two New Fragments of the Edict of Diocletian', *Transactions and Proceedings of the American Philological Society,* LXXI (1940), 166

Gregory, John Walter. *The Story of the Road,* (New York, 1932)

Grellet-Balguerie, L. C. 'Note sur les chemins gaulois et sur les voies romaines du Perigord', *Bulletin de la Societé archéologique et historique du Perigord,* (1894) 55-80 and 117-34

Grenier, Albert. *Manuel d'archéologie gallo-romaine,* Vol II, *Les routes,* (Paris, 1931)

Grierson, Philip. 'The Relations between England and Flanders before the Norman Conquest', *Transactions of the Royal Historical Society,* 4th Ser, XXIII, (1941)

Gromodka, Oscar and Müller, Rudolf. 'Über Wagen und Wagenbau', *Technikgeschichte* 23, (1934) p 70

Guey, J. 'Note sur le limes romain de Numidie et le Sahara au IVe siècle', *Mélanges Archéol. hist. École franc.,* (Rome, 1939)

Guilford, Everard Leaver. *Travellers and Travelling in the Middle Ages,* (1924)

Hadas, Moses. *Imperial Rome* (Great Ages of Man), (New York, 1965)

Hagen, Victor W. von. *The Roads that led to Rome,* (Cleveland and New York, 1967)

Hampe, Theodor. *Die fahrenden Leute in der deutschen Vergangenheit* (Monographien zur deutschen Kulturgeschichte, hrsg v Georg Steinhausen), Vol 10, (Leipzig, 1902)

Hancar, Franz. *Das Pferd in prähistorischer und früher historischer Zeit* (Wiener Beiträge zur Kulturgeschichte und Linguistik, Vol XI), (Munich, 1955)

Harlow, A. F. *Old post bags, the story of the sending of a letter in ancient and modern times,* (London, 1928)

Harrison, Herbert Spencer. *A handbook to the cases illustrating simple means of travel and transport by land and water,* Horniman Museum, (London, 1925)

Hartmann, Cyril Hughes. *The Story of the Roads,* (London, 1927)

Haskins, Charles Homer. *The Renaissance of the 12th Century,* (Cambridge, 1927)

————. 'The Spread of Ideas in the Middle Ages', *Speculum,* I, (1926) 19-30

Haudricourt, André G. 'Contribution à la Géographie et à l'Ethnologie de la voiture', *La Revue de Géographie humaine et d'Ethnologie,* Vol 1, no 1, (Jan-Mar, 1948), 54-64

————. 'De l'origine de l'Attelage Moderne', *Annales,* 42, VIII, (1936) 512-22

————. 'Origine de la Duga', *Ann Hist Soc,* II, (1939) 34

————. 'Les Moteurs animes en Agriculture', *Revue de Botanique appliquée,* nos 230-1, (1940)

————. 'Lumières sur l'Attelage Moderne', *Ann d'Hist Soc,* VIII, (1945) 117-19

————, and M. J. B. Delamarre. *L'Homme et la Charrrue à travers le monde,* (Paris, 1955)

Hawkes, C. F. C., and Hull, M. R. *Camulodunum,* (1947)

Hawks, Ellison. *The Romance of Transport,* (New York, 1931)

Heath, Sidney. *Pilgrim Life in the Middle Ages,* (1911)

Hehn, Victor. *Kulturpflanzen und Haustiere,* 8th ed, (Berlin, 1911)

Heichelheim, Fritz M. *Wirtschaftsgeschichte des Alterums,* (Leiden, 1938) 2 vols, (also English translation)

Heizer, Robert F. 'Ancient Heavy Transport, Methods and Achievements', *Science,* CLIII, (19 Aug, 1966) 821-30

Held-Brüschwien. *Rhein-Main Donau. Die Geschichte einer Wasser-strasse,* (Regensburg, 1929)

Hell, M. 'Weitere keltische Hufeisen aus Salzburg und Umgebung', *Archaeologica austriaca,* XII (1953), 44-9

Henne am Rhein, Otto. *Kulturgeschichte des deutschen Volkes,* (Berlin, 1886)

Herman, Zvi. *Peoples, Seas, and Ships,* (London, 1966)

Hill, Mary E. *The King's Messengers, 1199-1377,* (London, 1961)

Hilzheimer, Max. 'The Evolution of the Domestic Horse', *Antiquity,* IX, no 34, (1935)

Histoire Générale des Techniques, ed Maurice Daumas, Vol 1, *Les Origines de la Civilisation Technique,* (Paris, 1962)

Holland, Leicester Bodine. *Traffic Ways about France in the Dark Ages* (500-1100) (PhD Dissertation: Univ of Pennsylvania), (Allentown, Pa, 1919)

Holmberg, Erik John. *Zur Geschichte des Cursus Publicus,* (Uppsala, 1933)

Holmquist, W. 'Germanic art during the first millennium AD', *Kungl. Vitterhets, Historie och Antikvitets Akademiens Handlingar,* XC, (1955)

Hooper, W. *The Pilgrim's Way and Supposed Pilgrim use,* Surrey Archaeological Collection, Vol 44, (1936) 47-83

Hornell, James. *Water Transport: Origin and Early Evolution,* (Cambridge, 1946)

Horwitz, Hugo T. 'Aus der Literatur Zur Geschichte des Verkehrswesens', *Beiträge zur Geschichte der Technik,* XXIII, (1934) 131

————. 'Die Drehbewegungen in ihrer Bedeutung für die Entwicklung der materiellen Kultur', *Anthropos,* 28, 721-57

Hourani, George Fadlo. *Arab Seafaring,* (Princeton, 1951)

Hoyt, Robert S. *Life and Thought in the Early Middle Ages,* (Minneapolis, 1967)

Huntington, Ellsworth. *Mainsprings of Civilisation,* (New York, 1945)

Hutchinson, R. W. *Prehistoric Crete,* (Harmondsworth, 1968)

Hyde, W. W. *Roman Alpine Routes,* (Memoirs of the American Philosophical Society II, 1935)

Imberdis, F. 'Les routes mediévales', *Annales d'Histoire Sociale,* Vol 1, (1939) 411-16 (Postscript by Marc Bloch)

Jackman, William T. *The Development of Transportation in Modern England,* (London, 1916)

Jacobi, H. 'Hatten die Römer Steigbügel'? *Germania*, Vol 6, (1922) 88-93.

Johnson, Irving and Electa. 'Yankee Sails Turkey's History-Haunted Coast', *National Geographic Magazine*, Vol 136, No 6, pp 840-3

Jones, A. H. M. *The Later Roman Empire*, 2 vols, (Norman, Okla, 1964)

Jordan, Karl. *Friedrich Barbarossa*, Persönlichkeit und Geschichte, Vol 13, (Göttingen, 1959)

Joyce, Patrick Weston. *Social History of Ireland*, (London, 1903)

Jullian, Camille. *Histoire de la Gaule*, (Paris, 1908-26)

Jusserand, J. J. *English wayfaring Life in the Middle Ages (XIVth century)*, (London, 1889)

Kaufmann, D. B. 'Horseshoes in Antiquity', *Classical Journal*, Vol 26, (1930-1) 619-20

Kimble, G. H. T. *Geography in the Middle Ages*. (London, 1938)

Klein, J. *The Mesta*: A Study in Spanish Economic History, 1273-1836, Harvard Economic Studies, XXI, (Cambridge, 1920)

Klemm, Friedrich. *A History of Western Technology*, (New York, 1959)

Klettler, P. 'Nordwesteuropas Verkehr, Handel und Gewerbe im frühen Mittelalter', *Deutsche Kultur, Historische Reihe*, ed Alfons Dopsch, (Vienna, 1924)

Klindt-Jensen, Ole. *Denmark before the Vikings*, trans Eva and David Wilson, Ancient Peoples and Places, Vol 4, (London, 1957)

Kötzschke, R. *Allgemeine Wirtschaftsgeschichte des Mittelalters*, 1924

Kranzberg, Melvin, and Pursell, Carroll W. (eds), *Technology in Western Civilization*, 2 vols, (New York, 1967)

Krause, V. 'Geschichte des Instituts der Missi Dominici', *Mitteilungen des Instituts für österreichische Geschichtsforschung*, XI, (1890)

Kreisel, H. *Prunkwagen and Schlitten*, (Leipzig, 1927)

Kulischer, Josef. *Allgemeine Wirtschaftsgeschichte des Mittelalters und der Neuzeit, I*, (Munich and Berlin, 1928)

Labastide, L. de. 'Les voies romaines et merovingiennes dans le département de la Charente', *Bulletins et Mémoires de la Societé archéologique et historique de la Charente*, (1921), 3-81

———. 'La voie romaine de Poitiers à Limoges', Ibid, (1924) 111-32

———. 'Les Voies romaines à La Rochefoucauld'. Ibid, (1930) 121-4

Lächler, Paul, and Wirz, Hans. *Die Schiffe der Völker*, (Freiburg, 1962)

Lacour-Gayet, Jacques. *Histoire du Commerce*, 6 vols, (Paris, 1949-55)

LaFay, Howard. 'The Vikings', *National Geographic Magazine*, Vol 137, No 4 (Apr 1970), pp 492-541

Landström, Björn. *Das Schiff—vom Einbaum zum Atomboot*, (Gütersloh, 1961)

Lane, Frederick C. *Venetian Ships and Shipbuilding in the Renaissance*, (Baltimore, 1934)

Lane, R. H. 'Waggons and their Ancestors', *Antiquity*, IX, (1935) 140ff

Lang, K. 'Über die Enstehung des Wagens', *Völkerkunde*, 6, 58-65

Latouche, Robert. *Les origines de l'économie occidentale*, (Paris, 1956)
(English translation). *The birth of Western economy: economic aspects of the Dark Ages*, trans E. M. Wilkinson, (London, 1961)

Lavergne, Adrien. 'Les chemins de Saint-Jacques en Gascogne', *Revue de Gascogne*, (1879) 363-72; (1886) 485-90; (1887) 5-16

Le Bouteiller, Vicomte. 'Notes sommaires sur quelques voies romaines du pays de Fougères', *Bulletins et mémoirs de la*

Societé archéologique du departement d'Ille-et-Vilaine, (1909-10) 239-51

Ledroit, Joh. 'Die römische Schiffahrt im Stromgebiet des Rheines', *Kulturgeschichtlicher Wegweiser durch das röm.-germ. Zentralmuseum*, no 12, (Mainz, 1930)

Lee, C. E. *The highways of antiquity: a study of the relationship between the development of roads and the rise of the ancient empires*, (London, 1947)

Lee, Norman E. *Travel and Transport through the Ages*, 2nd revised edition (Cambridge, 1955)

Lefebvre des Noëttes, Richard. *De la marine antique à la marine moderne*, (Paris, 1935)

————. *L'Attelage et le cheval de selle à travers les âges*, (Paris, 1931)

————. *La Force motrice animale à travers les âges*, (Paris, 1924)

————. 'La question du fer à cheval', *Bulletin Societé Nationale des Antiquaires de France*, (Paris, 1936) 76-82

————. 'Le système d'attelage du cheval et du boeuf à Byzance et les consequences de son emploi', *Mélanges Charles Diehl*, I, (Paris, 1930) 183-90

Le Grand, Michel. 'L'ancienne navigation de la Midouze et le port de Mont-de-Marsan', *(Bulletin de la Societé de Borda*, (1934) 139-46

Leighton, Albert C. 'A Papal Cipher and the Polish Election of 1573', *Jahrbücher für Geschichte Osteuropas*. Vol 17, No 1, (March 1969), pp 13-28

————. 'The Mule as a Cultural Invention', *Technology and Culture*, Vol 8, No 1 (Jan 1967), pp 45-52

————. 'Secret Communication among the Greeks and Romans', *Technology and Culture*, Vol 10, No 2 (April 1969), pp 139-54

————. 'The Horse and Human History', *Encyclopedia Americana* (1970), Vol 14, pp 390-3

Le Mene, Abbé Joseph-M. 'Voie romaine de Vannes à Locmariaquer. Nouveau trace,' *Bulletin de la Societé polymathique de Morbihan*, 1877, 102-4

Levison, Wilhelm. *England and the Continent in the Eighth Century*, Oxford, 1946

Lewis, Archibald Ross, 'Le Commerce et la navigation sur les côtes atlantiques de la Gaule de V^e au VIIIe siècle. *Moyen Age*, LX (1953) 278-80.

———. *Naval Power and Trade in the Mediterranean*. AD *500-1100*, (Princeton, 1951)

———. *The Northern Seas: Shipping and Commerce in Northern Europe*. AD *300-1100*, (Princeton, 1958)

Ley, W. 'The story of the lodestone', *Natural History, XLII*, (1938) 201-07

Littauer, Mary Aiken. 'Bits and Pieces', *Antiquity*, XLIII, (Dec 1969) No 172, pp 289-300

Lopez, Robert. 'Les Influences Orientales et l'Éveil économique de l'Occident', *Journal of World History*, Vol I. No 3, (Jan 1954), 594-622

———. 'L'evoluzione dei transporti terrestri nel medio evo', *Bollettino Civico Istituto Colombiano*, I. 1953)
(English translation) 'The Evolution of Land Transport in the Middle Ages', *Past and Present*, IX (1956), pp. 17-29 (translated from *Bollettino Civico Istituto Colombiano, I*), (1953)

———. and Raymond, Irving W. *Medieval trade in the Mediterranean world*, (New York, 1955)

Lot, Ferdinand; Pfister, Christian; and Ganshof, François L. *Les Destinées de l'Empire en Occident de 395 à 768* (Histoire du Moyen Age. Histoire Générale), (Paris, 1940-1)

Ludwig, Friedrich Franz Albert. *Untersuchungen über die Reise- und Marschgeschwindigkeit im XII. und XIII. Jahrhundert*, (Berlin, 1897)

Lunn, Arnold. *History of Skiing*, (New York, 1927)

Lydekker, R. *The Horse and its Relations*, (London, 1912)

McClosky, J. M. 'History of military road construction', *Military Engineer*, Washington, Vol 41 (1949), 353-6, Vol 43 (1951), 42-5, 192-5

McCusker, John J., jr. *'The Wine Prise and Medieval Mercantile Shipping'*, *Speculum*, XLI (Apr 1966), pp 279-96

Magoun, Francis P., jr. 'An English Pilgrim-Diary of the Year 990', (Medieval Studies. Pontifical Institute of Medieval Studies) Vol II, (Toronto, 1940) 231-52

Mahr, Otto. 'Zur Geschichte des Wagenrades', *Beiträge zur Geschichte der Technik*, XXIII, (1934) 59

Malm, Gerhard A.; Conser, William R.; and Barnes, Leslie H. *Treasury of Bits*, (Valley Falls, Kansas, 1967)

Mannix, Daniel P. *Those About to Die*, (New York, 1958)

Marcus, Geoffrey Jules. *A naval history of England*, (Boston, 1961)

———. 'The Norse Emigration to the Faeroe Islands', *English Historical Review*, Vol 71 (1956), pp 56-61

———. 'The Navigation of the Norsemen', *Mariner's Mirror*, XXXIX, 112-31

———. 'The Evolution of the Knörr', *Mariner's Mirror*, XLI, 115-22

———. 'The Early Norse Traffic to Iceland', *Mariner's Mirror*, XLVI, 1960

Margary, Ivan D. *Roman Roads in Britain*, 2 vols, London, (1955-7)

Mariage, André. *Les transports à travers les âges* (Conference donnée à la Societé des Ingénieurs civils de France), (January 1935) 7-41

Markland, J. H. 'Early Use of Carriages in England', *Archaeologia*, Vol XX, (London, 1824) 443-77

Marsden, Peter R. V. *A Ship of the Roman Period, from Blackfriars in the City of London*, (London, 1967)

Marsille, L. 'Les voies romaines du Morbihan', *Bulletin de la Societé polymathique du Morbihan*, (1929) 3-58

———. 'Notes sur les voies romaines du département du Morbihan', *Bulletin archéologique de l'Association bretonne*, (1931) 34-44

Marvaud, F. 'Étude sur la voie romaine de Perigueux à Saintes dans la traversée de l'arrondissement de Cognac', *Bulletin de la Societé archéologique et historique de la Charente*, (1863) 271-318

Matschoss, Conrad. *Staat und Technik* (Vortrag 52. Samml. V D I) Breslau 1911)

Meautis, Georges 'Les Romains, connaissaient-ils le fer à cheval?', *Revue des études anciennes*, Vol 36, (1934), 88

Medieval England, ed Austin Lane Poole, (Oxford, 1958)

Megnin, Pierre. *Le Cheval et ses Races*, (Vincennes, 1895)

———. *Historic du Harnachement et de la Ferrure du Cheval*, (Vincennes, 1904)

Merdinger, C. J. 'Roads through the ages', *Military Engineer*, Washington, Vol 44 (1952), 268-73, 340-4

Metraux, Guy, and Crouzet, François (eds). *The Evolution of Science*, (New York, 1963)

Mickwitz, G. *Der Verkehr auf dem westlichen Mittelmeer um 600 n. Chr.* (Festschrift Dopsch), 1938, 74ff

———. 'Un problème d'influence Byzance et l'économie de l'Occident mediéval', *Annales d'Histoire Economique et Sociale*, VIII, (1936)

Mitman, Carl Weaver. 'An outline development of highway travel', *Smithsonian Report for 1934*, (Washington, 1935) 325-45

Mooney, William West. *Travel among the Ancient Romans*, (Boston, 1920)

Moss, Henry St Laurence Beaufort. *The Birth of the Middle Ages*, (Oxford, 1935)

Mötefindt, H. *Geschichtsblätter für Technik und Industrie*, Vol 6, (Berlin, 1919) 30-41

———. 'Der Wagen im nordischen Kulturkreise zur vor- und frühgeschichtlichen Zeit', *Festschift Eduard Hahn*, (1917) 209-40

———. 'Die Entstehung des Wagens und des Wagenrades', *Mannus*, 10, 32-63

———. Articles: 'Kultwagen, Schlitten', in Ebert's *Reallexikon*

———. 'Die Erfindung des Drehschemels an vierrädrigen

Wagen', *Geschichtsblätter für Technik und Industrie*, 6, (1919)

Mumford, Lewis. *Technics and Civilization*, (New York, 1934)

Needham, Joseph. 'Central Asia and the history of science and technology', *Journal of the Royal Central Asian Society*, (1950) 139-41

———. *Science and Civilisation in China*, (Cambridge [In progress])

———, and Lu Gwei-Djen. 'A Further Note on Efficient Equine Harness: the Chinese Inventions', *Physis* 7 (1965), pp 70-4

Neuburger, Albert. *The Technical Arts and Sciences of the Ancients*, (New York, 1930)

Neugebauer, Otto. *The Exact Sciences in Antiquity*, (Providence, RI, 1957)

Newton, Arthur Percival (ed) *Travel and Travellers of the Middle Ages*, (London, 1930)

Oehlmann, Ernst G. 'Die Alpenpässe im Mittelalter', *Jhrb f Schweiz Gesch Zürich*, Vol 3, (1878) and Vol 4, (1879)

Oliver, Jane. *The Ancient Roads of England*, (London, 1936)

O'Lochlainn, Colm. 'Roadway in Ancient Ireland', *Essays and Studies presented to Professor Eoin Mac Neill*, (Dublin, 1940) 465-74

Owen, Wilfred, and Bowen, Ezra. *Wheels*, Life Science Library, (New York, 1967)

Oxenstierna, Eric .*The Norsemen*, trans and ed Catherine Hutter, (New York, 1965)

Pascal, Blaise. 'Pensées', *Oeuvres Complètes*, (Paris, 1954)

Paterson, J. *The history and development of road transport*, Pitman's transport library, (London, 1927)

Patzelt, E. *Karolingische Renaissance*, (Vienna, 1924)

Pflaum, H. G. 'Essai sur le CURSUS PUBLICUS sous le Haut-Empire romain', *Mémoires presentés à l'Academie des In-*

scriptions et Belles-Lettres, XIV, 1, (1940), 189-390

Philipson, John. *Harness: as it has been, as it is, and as it should be*, (London, 1882)

Piggott, Stuart 'The Beginnings of Wheeled Transport,' *Scientific American*, (July 1968)

Pirenne, Henri. *Economic and Social History of Medieval Europe*, (London, 1936)

———. *Medieval Cities. Their Origins and the Revival of Trade*, (Princeton, 1925)

———. *Historie économique de l'Occident mediéval*, (Bruges, 1951)

———.'Un grand commerce d'exportation au moyen âge: les vins de France', *Annales d'histoire économique et sociale*, V (1933), pp 225-33

———, Cohen, G., and Focillon, H. *La Civilisation occidentale au Moyen Age du XIᵉ au milieu du XVᵉ siècle*, (Paris, 1933)

Polge, Henri. 'L'amélioration de l'attelage: a-t-elle réellement fait reculer le servage?', *Journal des savants*, (Jan-March 1967) pp 5-42

Pörtner, Rudolf. *Mit dem Fahrstuhl in die Römerzeit*, (Düsseldorf, 1959)

Potratz, Johannes A. H. *Die Pferdetrensen des alten Orient* (Analecta Orientalla, 41) (Rome: Pontificum Institutum Biblicum, 1966)

Poulson, O. *Skiing*, (New York, 1924)

Pratt, Edwin A. *A History of Inland Transport and Communication in England*, (New York, 1912)

Previté-Orton, C. W. *The Shorter Cambridge Medieval History*, 2 vols, (Cambridge, 1952)

Ramee, D. *La locomotion. Histoire des chars, carosses, omnibus et voitures de tours genres*, (Paris, 1856)

Ramsay, A. M. 'A Roman Postal Service under the Republic'. *Journal of Roman Studies*, 10 (1920) 79ff

———. 'The Speed of the Roman Imperial Post', *Journal of Roman Studies*, 15 (1925), 60ff

Reid, James. 'The evolution of horse-drawn vehicles', *Journal* of the Institute of British Carriage and Auto Manufacturers, XXII (1932), 346

Renard. 'Technique et agriculture en pays trevire et remois', *Latomus*, XVIII, (1959)

Renouard, Y. 'Les Voies de Communication entre Pays de la Mediterranée et Pays de l'Atlantique au Moyen Age', *Mélanges d'Histoire du Moyen Age dediés à la mémoire de L. Halphen*, (Paris, 1951)

Ribton-Turner, Charles James. *A History of Vagrants and Vagrancy*, (London, 1887)

Riepl, Wolfgang. *Das Nachrichtenwesen des Alterums*, (Leipzig and Berlin, 1913)

Roe, Frank G. 'The Wild Animal Path Origin of Ancient Roads', *Antiquity*, III (1929), 299

———. 'The Winding Road', *Antiquity*, XIII (1939), 191-206

Rogers, James Edwin Thorold. *A History of Agriculture and Prices in England*, (Oxford, 1866-1902)

Rogerson, I. (ed). *History of Transport, a Second List* (Bibliographical Series, 10), (Cheltenham-Gloucestershire [Technical Information Service], 1966)

Rose, Albert Chatellier. *Public Roads of the Past: 3500 BC to AD 1800*, American Association of State Highway Officials, (no date)

———. 'Via Appia in the days when all roads led to Rome', *Smithsonian Report for 1934*, (Washington, 1935) 347-70

Rostovtzeff, M. *Social and economic history of the Roman Empire*, (Oxford, 1926)

Rousseau, Pierre. *Histoire des Techniques et des Inventions (Les Grandes Études Historiques)*, (Paris, 1958)

———. *Histoire des Transports (Les Grandes Études Historiques)*, (Paris, 1961)

Roussel, Romain. *Les pèlerinages à travers les Siècles*, (Paris, 1954)

Les routes de France depuis les Origines jusqu' à nos jours (Association pour la Diffusion de la Pensée Française, Colloques. Cahiers de Civilisation), (Paris, 1959)

Runciman, Sir Steven. *A History of the Crusades,* 3 vols (Cambridge, 1951-54)

St Clair, Labert, *Transportation,* (New York, 1933)
Saint-Jours, B. 'La double route romaine de Dax à Bordeaux', *Bulletin de la Societé de Borda,* (1928) 5-22
Salzman, Louis Francis. *English Trade in the Middle Ages,* (Oxford, 1964)
Savit, R. 'Les voies gallo-romaines de la Charente, Études locales', *Bulletin de la Charente,* (1925) 113-18 and 138-43
Savory, Theodore H. 'The Mule', *Scientific American,* Vol 223, No 6 (Dec 1970), 102-9
Sawyer, Peter H. *The Age of the Vikings,* (London, 1962)
Schadendorf, Wulf. *Zu Pferde, im Wagen, zu Fuss. Tausend Jahre Reisen* (Bilder aus deutscher Vergangenheit), (Munich, 1961)
Scheffel, Paul Hugo. *Verkehrsgeschichte der Alpen,* (Berlin, 1908-14)
Scheffer, Johann. *De Re Vehiculari Veterum,* (Frankfurt, 1671)
Schreiber, Hermann. *Merchants, Pilgrims and Highwaymen, A History of Roads Through the Ages,* (New York, 1962)
Sclafert, Th. *L'industrie du fer dans la region d'allevard du Moyen Age,* (Grenoble, 1926)
Semple, Ellen C. *Geography of the Mediterranean Region,* (New York, 1931)
Sewell, Anna. *Black Beauty* (novel)
Sheldon, Gilbert. *From trackway to turnpike,* (Oxford, 1928)
Sickle, Van. 'The repair of the roads in Spain under the Roman Empire', *Classical Philology,* (1929) 77
Simpson, George G. *Horses,* (Oxford, 1951)
Singer, Charles; Holmyard, E. J.; Hall, A. R.; and Williams, Trevor I. *A History of Technology,* Vol II, (Oxford, 1956)
Sion, J. 'Quelques problèmes de transports dans l'antiquité: le point du vue d'un géographe mediterranéen', *Annales d'histoire économique et sociale,* VII, (1935), 628-33

Q

Smolian, Jürgen. 'Zur Frage der Entwicklung der Wagenfederung', *Blätter für Technikgeschichte* No 24, (Vienna,
1962) 148

———. 'Vorgänger und Nachfolger des gefederten Wagens
zur Entwicklungsgeschichte der Kutsche', *Technikgeschichte,*
Vol 34 (1967), No 2, pp 146-63

Southern, R. W. *The Making of the Middle Ages,* (New
Haven, 1952)

Soyer, Jacques Silvain. 'Les voies antiques de l'Orléanais (civi-
tas Aurelianorum)', *Mémoires de la Societé archéologique
et historique de l'Orléanais,* Vol XXXVII, (1936)

Speck, Artur. *Der Kunststrassenbau,* (Berlin, 1950)

Spengler, Oswald. 'Der Streitwagen und seine Bedeutung für
den Gang der Weltgeschichte', *Ostas. Zeitschrift,* 20 (1934),
56ff

Stenton, Sir Frank M. 'The Road System of Medieval England', *The Economic History Review,* Vol 7, no 1 (Nov
1936), 1-21

———. *Anglo-Saxon England,* (Oxford, 1947)

Stephan, Heinrich von. *Das Verkehrsleben im Altertum und im
Mittelalter,* new ed rev by Gottfried North, Goslar, 1966 (1st
pub 1868-9, Raumer's Historisches Taschenbuch)

Stephenson, Carl. 'In Praise of Medieval Tinkers', *The Journal
of Economic History,* 8, No 1, (May, 1948)

Stevenson, D. Alan. *The World's Lighthouses before 1820,*
(London, 1959)

Stewart, Desmond. *Early Islam,* Great Ages of Man, (New
York, 1967)

Stöhr, Kurt. *Das Nachrichten-Wesen des Weströmischen Kul-
turkreises von Völkerwanderung bis zum Tode Karls des
Grossen,* (Jena, Halle, 1933)

Stratton, Ezra M. *The World on Wheels,* (New York,
1878)

Straus, Ralph. *Carriages and Coaches,* (London, 1912)

Stretton, Grace. 'The Travelling Household in the Middle
Ages', *Journal of the British Archaeological Association,*
New Series, XL, (1935), 88

———. 'Some Aspects of Medieval Travel', *Transactions of the Royal Historical Society*, Fourth Series, Vol 7 (1924), 77-97

Strong, L. A. G. *The Rolling Road* (London, 1956)

Strutt, Joseph. *A complete view of the dress and habits of the people of England*, (London, 1796-9)

———. *The sports and pastimes of the people of England*, (London, 1798)

Syme, Ronald. *The Story of Britain's Highways*, (London, 1952)

Tarr, László. *Karren Kutsche Karosse*, (Munich, Basle, Vienna, 1970)

Taylor, E. G. R. *The Haven-Finding Art*, (New York, 1957)

Thompson, James Westfall. *An Economic and Social History of the Middle Ages (300-1300)*, (New York, 1928)

———. 'The Commerce of France in the Ninth Century', *Journal of Political Economy*, XXIII, (1915)

———. *The decline of the missi dominici in Frankish Gaul*, Decennial publications of the University of Chicago, first series, no 4, (Chicago, 1903)

Throckmorton, Peter. 'Ancient Shipwreck Yields New Facts—and a Strange Cargo', *National Geographic Magazine*, Vol 135 (1969), pp 282-300

Thrupp, George Athelstane. *The History of Coaches*, (London, 1877)

Tomkeieff, O. G. *Life in Norman England*, (English Life Series, ed Peter Quennell, (New York, 1967)

Tonning, O. *Commerce and Trade on the North Atlantic AD 850 to AD 1350* (PhD Thesis: Univ of Minnesota, Minneapolis, 1936)

Trassagnac. 'Le reseau d'Agrippa dans le département de la Dordogne', *Bulletin de la Societé historique et archéologique du Périgord*, (1936) 183-90, 245-52, 304-11, 385-92; (1937) 111-20, 181-90, 258-71, 330-48

Treue, Wilhelm. *Achse, Rad und Wagen*, (Munich, 1965)

Trevedy, J. 'Voie romaine d'Yffiniac (fond de la Baie de Saint-Brieuc) à Vannes', *Bulletin archéologique de l'Association bretonne,* (1907) 25-66

Twain, Mark (S. L. Clemens). *Roughing It,* (Hartford, 1872)

Tyler, John Ecclesfield. *The Alpine Passes in the Middle Ages,* AD *962-1250,* (Oxford, 1930)

Usher, Abbott Payson. *A History of Mechanical Invention,* (Cambridge, 1954)

Uzanne, Octave. *La locomotion à travers l'histoire et les moeurs,* (Paris, 1900)

Vaath, J. 'Römische Hufeisen', *Hufschmied,* Vol 52 (1934), 81-4

Vaillé, Eugène. *Histoire générale des Postes françaises,* Vol 1. (Paris, 1947)

Vallois, G. 'Les voies romaines d'Avaricum', *Mémoires de la Societé des Antiquaires du Centre,* (1892-3) 51-85

Vannerus, Jules. 'La Reine Brunehaut dans la Toponymie et dans la Légende', *Academie royale de Belgique, Bulletins de la Classe des Lettres,* 5th series, Vol 24, (1938) 7, 301-420

Vaublanc, de. *La France au Temps des Croisades,* (Paris, 1860)

Vidal de la Blache, Paul Marie Joseph. 'Routes et chemins de l'ancienne France', *Bulletin de géographie descriptive et historique,* (1902) 115-26

Virieux, Edmond. *Aventicum, die Römerstadt* (Schweizer Heimatbücher, 10/10A), German trans (from French) by Dr G. Theodor Schwarz, (Berne, 1961)

Vogel, Walther. 'Ein seefahrender Kaufmann um 1100', *Hansische Geschichtsblätter,* (1912)

———. *Geschichte der deutschen Seeschiffahrt. 1. Von der Urzeit bis zum Ende des XV. Jahrhunderts,* (Berlin, 1915)

Wagner, Eduard. *Medieval Costume, Armour and Weapons,* (London, nd)

Waldis, Alfred. 'La Maison Suisse des Transports et Communication à Lucerne', *Verkehrshaus der Schweiz,* Veröffentlichungen, No 3 (1962)

Walsh, A. *Scandinavian Relations with Ireland during the Viking Period,* (Dublin and London, 1922)

Watney, Marylian. *The Elegant Carriage,* (London, 1961)

Webb, Sidney and Beatrice. *The Story of the King's Highway* (English Local Government), Vol 5

Weber, L. 'Der Schöne Brunnen', *Z. f. Deutsches Altertum,* Vol 63, (1926), 129

Westermann, William Linn. 'On inland transportation and communication in antiquity', *Political Science Quarterly,* XLIII (1928), 364. (Another version in *Classical Journal,* April, 1929, Vol 24, No 7, 483-97)

Wheeler, R. E. M. and T. V. *Verulamium,* Reports of the Research Committee of the Society of Antiquaries of London, No XI, (London, 1936)

White, Lynn, jr. *Medieval Technology and Social Change,* (Oxford, 1962)

————. 'Technology and Invention in the Middle Ages', *Speculum,* XV (1940), pp 141-56

————. 'Eilmer of Malmesbury, an Eleventh-Century Aviator: a Case Study of Technological Innovation, its Context and Tradition', *Technology and Culture,* Vol 2 (1961), pp 97-111

————. 'The Invention of the Parachute', *Technology and Culture,* Vol 9, No 3 (July 1968), 462ff

————. 'The Legacy of the Middle Ages in the American Wild West', *Speculum,* XL, No 2 (Apr 1965), pp 191-202

————. 'The Origins of the Coach', *Proceedings of the American Philosophical Society,* Vol 114, No 6 (Dec 1970), 423-31

Wiesner, Joseph. *Fahren und Reiten in Alteuropa und im Alten Orient* (Der Alte Orient, Vol 38), (Leipzig, 1939)

Wilkinson, C. W. *From Track to By-Pass,* (London, 1934)

Willard, James F. 'Inland transportation in England during the 14th century', *Speculum,* I, (1926), 361-74

————. 'The Use of Carts in the Fourteenth Century', *History,* Vol 17, No 67, (1932)

Wilson, D. M. *The Anglo-Saxons,* (New York, 1960)

Winkelmann, Fr 'Über das Hufeisen', *Germania,* Vol 12, (1928) 135-43

Winter, Dr Heinrich. 'Who invented the compass?' *Mariner's Mirror,* XXIII (1937), 95-102

———. 'Die Nautik der Wikinger', *Hansische Geschichtsblätter,* XLII, (1937), 173-84

Wolff, Theo, *Vom Ochsenwagen zum Automobil. Geschichte bis zu neuester Zeit* (Wissen und Können, Vol 10), (Leipzig, 1909)

Wright, Thomas. *A History of Domestic Manners and Sentiments in England During the Middle Ages,* (London, 1862)

Wright, William Henry Kearley. *Locomotion; Past and Present,* Transactions of the Plymouth Institution and Devon and Cornwall Natural History Society, (1897-8)

Yeo, Cedric A. 'Land and sea transportation in Imperial Italy', *Transactions and Proceedings of the American Philological Society,* LXXVII, (1946), 222

Zeuner, Frederick E. *A History of Domesticated Animals,* (New York, 1963)

Zinnser, Hans. *Rats, Lice and History,* (Boston, 1940)

Index